FOREIGN POLICY AND LEGISLATURES
AN ANALYSIS OF SEVEN PARLIAMENTS

FOREIGN POLICY AND LEGISLATURES
AN ANALYSIS OF SEVEN PARLIAMENTS

Edited by :
MANOHAR L. SONDHI

abhinav publications

First published in India 1988

© Manohar L. Sondhi

All rights reserved. No part of this book may be reproduced or transmitted in any form or by any means, electronic or mechanical, including photocopying, recording or by any information storage and retrieval system, without permission in writing from the publishers.

ISBN 81-7017-233-0

Publishers
Shakti Malik
Abhinav Publications
E-37, Hauz Khas
New Delhi-110016

Printers
Patel Enterprises
at Sunil Printers
C.B. 1067, 75/1 Ajay Palace, Naraina,
New Delhi-110028

Contents

Acknowledgements	vii
Introduction	ix
1. Parliament and Foreign Policy in Britain —*James Callaghan*	1
2. The Influence of the British Parliament on Foreign Policy —*Cliff Grantham & Bruce George*	8
3. The Japanese Diet and Foreign Policy —*Saburo Okita & Akio Watanabe*	34
4. The Knesset and Israel's Foreign Relations —*Netanel Lorch*	56
5. Israel's Experience with Legislative-Executive Relations in the Field of Foreign Relations —*Hemda Golan*	75
6. The Sri Lanka Parliament and Foreign Policy —*Shelton U. Kodikara*	95
7. The European Parliament and Foreign Policy —*Juliet Lodge*	113
8. The New Zealand Parliament and Foreign Policy —*Ramesh Thakur & Antony Wood*	134
9. Coping with Super Power Pressures on Indian Foreign Policy: An Assessment of the Indian Parliament's Performance —*Manohar L. Sondhi*	162
10. Parliament and Foreign Policy: A Study of the Parliamentary Discussion on the 1974 Nuclear Implosion —*Srikant Paranjpe*	185
11. The Foreign Policy Debate in Canada's Parliament —*Joe Clark*	200
Bibliography	208
Contributors	218
Index	225

Acknowledgements

I am grateful for the goodwill of all the contributors to this volume, who endorsed the need for bringing together studies analysing the current state of legislative-executive relations in the field of foreign policy. The support of Ms. Flora MacDonald, Minister of Employment and Immigration, Canada, and Mr. Reuven Dafni, Vice Chairman of Yad Vashem (The Holocaust Martyrs' and Heroes' Remembrance Authority), Jerusalem, helped in securing contributions from Canada and Israel.

4th Feb, 1988　　　　　　　　　　　　　　MANOHAR L. SONDHI

Introduction

In recent years there has developed an interest in analysing the wide variety of contextual factors shaping parliamentary efforts to influence foreign policy. The authors of the essays dealing with seven different parliaments take into account the specific variables in the domestic and international environments. Although the particular problems of each parliament have only limited aspects in common with each other, valuable comparative generalisations can be made which throw considerable light on the relationship between the executive and legislative branches in the domain of foreign policy.

At the time when Hans J. Morgenthau made his major contribution to the realist theory of international relations, it was generally believed that the cultural and political environment in which foreign policy was produced need not be considered holistically in order to apply realism's concepts of "power" and "interest". In recent years both scholars and policy-makers have become aware of the need for profound and drastic change in the theoretical perspectives in the study of foreign policy. The exploration of the relationship between national politics and foreign policy has addressed itself to some of the omissions of the narrow conceptualisation of foreign policy provided by the realist definition of international politics. Among the more important elements in the relevant context are foreign policy interest groups, political parties, institution-building processes and public opinion. The elements which make for the cohesion and fragmentation of the policy-making process must be taken into account.

The aim of this study is to place the reader—both scholar and policy-maker—in a position to judge the prospects and problems of legislative roles in foreign policy and to show how legislative options have been enlarged to cope with the complexity that characterises contemporary international relations.

Each of the parliaments has unique features and a distinctive political setting, but divergent legislative experiences can properly be the subject of comparative study since flexibility of political processes are evident across the world.

We begin with Britain, a country whose experience is inextricably linked to the two-party system. Writing from his experience as Prime Minister, James Callaghan points out the new dimensions of the British system in an era in which the division between foreign and domestic policy is now an artificial one. He describes how the floor of the House of Commons has been the setting for policy modification, and concludes with his assessment of future developments.

Cliff Grantham and Bruce George, the latter with his experience in the House of Commons, trace the changes that have occurred in the legislative overseeing of foreign affairs in Britain. They point to the shift which is visible since 1979 with the establishment of the Foreign Affairs Committee, and reflect on its organisational potential for making Parliament a more effective policy-influencing body in foreign affairs.

Saburo Okita, with his experience as foreign minister, and Akio Watanabe point to the basic features "cooperation-cum-competition" characterising the Japanese political system and describe the role of the Bureaucratic-LDP complex in determining the policy influence of the Diet in foreign affairs. The authors also reflect on the Diet's involvement in the treaty process, its role in maintaining Japan's image as a peace-loving country and its institutional practice in the formulation of external economic policy.

Netanel Lorch traces the modalities of the relationship between the Knesset and the Israeli executive adapting over time to the external pressures on the country.

Hemda Golan points out the structural aspects of the legislative-executive relationship in Israel and outlines the impact of these on the policy-making framework.

Shelton Kodikara traces the parliamentary dimensions of the conflict between the UNP and the SLFP in Sri Lanka, and poses questions of bipartisan support on the major foreign policy crisis facing the country. This essay was written before the India—Sri Lanka agreement leading to the induction of the Indian Peace keeping Force into Sri Lanka.

Introduction

Juliet Lodge analyses the historic tensions in the European parliament, and reveals both the sources of strength and the limitations of the institution in contributing to the development of an independent European foreign policy. She takes account of the changes following the EEC's adoption of the Single European Act.

Ramesh Thakur and Antony Wood discuss the changing patterns of legislative influence in New Zealand, a country where a lively debate on foreign policy issues and anti-nuclear legislation have cast a shadow on the ANZUS security relationship.

Manohar L. Sondhi discusses how legislative influence in India varies across policy areas in national and cross-national perspectives and is compatible with an effective foreign policy towards the two Super Powers.

Srikant Paranjpe analyses a single legislative case, the parliamentary discussion on the 1974 nuclear test and analyses the balance of influence on policy articulation in the Indian parliament.

As Foreign Minister of Canada, Joe Clark considers the foreign policy performance of his own country and assesses the role of legislative activism in Canada.

All the essays in this volume represent a wide range of perspectives and approaches, and offer new insights into the growing field of inter-parliamentary studies. They show that the study of parliamentary politics is essential for understanding foreign policy-making and the underlying forces of stability and change. Each author has either participated in or closely studied the legislative exercise of foreign policy responsibilities. Their insights are specific to each parliament, but raise issues of process and policy which should be of interest to students of comparative foreign policy.

The Indian experience with parliamentary democracy clearly constitutes a valuable body of material for the study of legislative-executive interaction in a developing country. Although many countries in Eastern Europe, Latin America and Africa claim to be democracies, their political life is organised in a way which leads to general cynicism about democratic politics. In Asia, which includes West Asia, India alongwith Israel, Sri Lanka and Japan, have all generated genuine democratic models. Other states will find it instructive to look at India's parliamentary history and examine the political context of Indian foreign policy. It has become increasingly clear that the processes of peace and development are extremely complex and there are hardly any self-contained normative political models which can be recommended for solving long-term domestic and foreign policy problems. The similarity in social and cultural background between the Indian elite and those in the other South Asian countries which are now members of SAARC can help to create new institutions, roles and identifications which can strengthen constitutional governments and lead to a more just regional society in the future.

In turn, India should develop a greater receptivity to parliamentary ideas and forms which have worked elsewhere to consolidate political support and legislative effectiveness. India has in the past adapted and modified British parliamentary ideas to fit particular needs and circumstances of both domestic politics and foreign policy. The assessment in the two essays on Britain in this volume encourages the conclusion that some of the new innovations and prescriptions from Westminster can be adapted to Indian problems. The main characteristics of the legislative styles of Japan and Israel derive from the situation in Japanese and Israeli domestic politics, and the efforts to cope with economic and strategic vulnerabilities, respectively. The study of these two countries may help Indian scholars to re-examine the policy-making framework and analyse alternative political options open to India in deciding on the future of the international economy and security choices.

The adversarial nature of Sri Lanka's politics, and the development of parliamentary party policies on the ethnic question can help to contrast the adaptive and opportunistic ways in which legislatures can exercise their power and responsibility in foreign affairs.

The holding of direct elections to the European Parliament and the new strands of policy which can be detected in the policy pronouncements at Strasbourg are generalisations from European experience which might be applicable to the future perspective of SAARC nations, as distrust and discord are replaced by a new collective self-image of political cooperation.

Finally mutual reinforcement could be the outcome

Introduction

of consultations on parliamentary matters between India and other Commonwealth countries, like New Zealand and Canada, since they follow the same model of parliamentary democracy. Both the permanent officials and the parliamentarians of these countries should have a strong incentive for bilateral and multilateral cooperation, to promote the comparative discussion of common political and administrative problems.

It is hoped that this volume will produce an increased understanding of the parliamentary process, promote meaningful dialogue among legislators and policy-makers, and indicate the areas which need further research in the parliamentary role in foreign policy.

Parliament and Foreign Policy in Britain

JAMES CALLAGHAN

From the outset it should be stated that foreign policy in Britain continues to remain an area of legislation and concern, somehow set apart from the mainstream of public interest. Though in many ways we live in a world of far greater interdependence, foreign policy, save at times of national crisis or external threat, remains of less immediate concern to the electorate. Voting studies have shown that foreign policy issues come fairly low on a list of voting priorities.

To some extent this is a measure of Britain's reduced world status, to some extent a result of the fact that though foreign policy may exist in the form of an overall Government approach it may not be encapsulated into specific legislation. It is also, however, a result of the continued separation of policy into home and foreign affairs and the association which the word 'foreign' carries in the minds of a domestic populace more concerned with policies which may affect their immediate lifestyles. In many senses, however, this division between foreign and domestic policy is now an artificial one. In most cases foreign policy will be bound up with issues of economic policy, trade, defence, agriculture, industry and Government action across the domestic board. This interdependence between foreign and domestic policy has accelerated with Britain's membership of the European Community; it has nevertheless been a process whose beginnings long predate that event.

To some extent, therefore, the erosion of a clear cut distinction between domestic and foreign affairs has opened up the foreign policy-making process. The Foreign and Commonwealth Office now shares responsibility for foreign policy with a whole collection of other departments — the Treasury, the Board of Trade, the Department of Agriculture and Fisheries, the Ministry of Defence and so on. Moreover, there are a host of committees at all levels of Government — ministerial, official and mixed—which draw their membership from a range of departments. More important issues of policy will reach the Cabinet, but lesser issues may be dealt with at lower committee level. Policy as a whole may emerge from an accumulation of recommendations and decisions by both Ministers and civil servants arrived at through a process of discussion, negotiation and compromise between the various departments.

This is not to underestimate, however, the personal weight of Ministers or of individual departments at various times. Ernest Bevin, one of our greatest foreign secretaries undoubtedly benefited in Cabinet from the close personal friendship and the support of the Prime Minister, Clement Attlee. Similarly, at other times the Foreign Secretary and the Foreign Office have successfully defended a corner or argued a new line. The Foreign Secretary may also be given prime responsibility for the conduct of overseas negotiations. This was certainly my own experience as Foreign Secretary during our re-negotiation of British membership of the European Community. It is also a fact that at times of international crisis the Foreign Office and the Foreign Secretary play a major role.

But the nature of the involvement in foreign policy issues of a multiplicity of departments who represent different interests acts as an important factor in circumscribing foreign policy choices. Given that the total sum of possible Government expenditure is finite, this may mean effectively that a system of checks already exists within the Executive. Overseas aid is one example of an issue where demands on resources from other Ministries may determine the final sum as a result of a process of debate and negotiation in Cabinet.

Outside the Executive there exist other checks—pressure groups, the media and of course Parliament.

The British system of Parliamentary sovereignty means that

the Executive is drawn from the Legislature and is constitutionally responsible to it. The Government derives its authority to govern by initially securing and subsequently retaining the confidence of a sufficient number of elected Members of Parliament—usually a majority—to whom members of the Government are individually and collectively accountable for their powers. Constitutionally, therefore, the Legislature or Parliament may prevail upon the Government to change its policies or even to bring about a change of Government itself. In this sense Parliamentary Government is constitutionally described as responsible Government in the sense that the interests of the governed are represented through the Legislature, rather than directly through such devices as the referendum, although as I shall discuss later, referenda have been used.

The rise of the political party in Britain has had far reaching implications for parliamentary checks on the Executive. In the nineteenth century the increase in the size of the electorate precipitated by the series of Reform Acts, meant that organising electoral support could no longer be left to ad hoc means. Party organisation became necessary to gather the vote and this developed as a means not only of securing support outside Parliament but of ensuring Party discipline within it. Parliament was transformed from an elective chamber in which shifting combinations of MPs, often acting as individuals, formed and sustained a Ministry, into a forum in which competing parties struggled to win power as disciplined and cohesive groupings. In 1867 Walter Bagehot, the great Victorian political economist, had described the British political system as superior to the American separation of powers precisely because Cabinet Government was composed of a group of men drawn from Parliament and constitutionally accountable to it. This is what is meant by the sovereignty of Parliament.

In practice, however, there is an important shading in this description. The electorate has often shown its distaste for a divided party. It wants a clear message put before it simply and unitedly. The need for unity requires strong internal party discipline which must be exercised by the party leaders and this has led to the Cabinet acquiring unrivalled power. Thus although one hundred years ago Britain experienced a twenty-two year period in which no single party was able to secure a majority, since 1945 party discipline has been much tighter. Revolts on the floor of the Chamber with some Government members voting with the Opposition do occur—the most notable was in 1940 when a combination of Labour and dissenting Conservative Members removed Neville Chamberlain as Prime Minister and installed Winston Churchill in his place. But nowadays, given the existence of party whips, the most effective revolts that succeed in changing Government policy take place away from the Chamber in crowded party meetings of the Government's own Members of Parliament.

The system of party whips means that, given a majority, the Government of the day can command the support of its own backbenchers for Government legislation, thus ensuring its successful passage through Parliament. In this sense Parliamentary checks on the Executive are weakened. There remain, however, a series of channels through which influence may be exerted on the Government. Prime Minister's Question Time, twice weekly, and the written and oral questions put to individual Ministers provide opportunities for both an attack and a defence of Government policy; the regular meetings of the full Parliamentary Party, whether Labour or Conservative, allow backbenchers a forum for expressing their views on current or forthcoming legislation. Moreover, the smoking rooms, the tea rooms and the bars in the House of Commons are often useful venues for bending a Minister's ear. If sufficient numbers of Government backbenchers express their concern, and the concern of their constituents, in this manner, a Government may be pressurised into altering policy. There exist means, therefore, for backbenchers to circumvent a whipping system which applies only when votes are held, and to apply pressure before legislation comes to a vote.

The floor of the House may also be the setting for policy modification. In May 1980 the Government was forced by such protests to renege on an agreement between the Foreign Ministers of the European Community to make trade sanctions against Iran retroactive to November 1979. Persistent questioning may also bring subjects to debate. In 1984 the Government was pressurised by a series of questions on the sinking of the *General Belgrano* during the course of the conflict with Argentina, to present and defend its case in Parliament. There are of course also the Opposition Day debates when matters of foreign policy will be raised.

Since 1979 there have also existed departmental-related select commitees composed of eleven members drawn from all the political parties, charged by the House with examining the "expenditure, administration and policy" of the government departments to which they correspond. These committees exercise their scrutiny by seeking evidence, both written and oral on their subject of enquiry. Over the last few years the Foreign Affairs Select Committee has looked into a variety of subjects—United Kingdom membership of UNESCO; the abuse of diplomatic immunities; the economic and political security of small states; and the events surrounding the weekend of 1st-2nd May 1982, relating to the conflict with Argentina over the Falkland Islands.

In carrying out these inquiries, the Committee will send for written evidence from the Government department and from other bodies involved in the formulation and execution of policy, and from pressure groups and outside bodies. Once this written evidence has been digested, the Committee will call for witnesses for examination at an oral session. Once the Committee has gathered its evidence it will report to the House. The report itself will usually contain comments and recommendations and may gain widespread publicity. There is no provision, however, for automatic debate in the House although the Government has agreed to reply to all such select committee reports. Their work can, however, have considerable impact; in the last Parliament, committees' recommendations on a wide range of matters, from the Canadian Constitution to the efficacy of the civil service, 'mis-information' in the Falklands campaign and Concorde, made a considerable impact on Government policy. Generally their effectiveness varies from Committee to Committee depending upon the ability of the Chairman and also the Clerk of the Committee.

The existence of Select Committees has also had important indirect effects relating to the Executive. Their powers of scrutiny have made Ministers and civil servants prepare policy more rigorously, have persuaded Whitehall of the need to publish more material about policy and policy judgements, and have made the exposure of weak policy much more likely.

Moreover, by forcing Government to explain its policy in detail, the Select Committee can generate informed public debate and discussion which lies at the root of democracy.

As legislation passes through Parliament there also exist opportunities for detailed scrutiny and discussion, not only on the floor of the House but in standing Committees where Ministers will be called to make detailed explanations and where the intricate details and workings of legislation will be analysed. Moreover, the last few years have seen the House of Lords assert greater authority over the passage of legislation, through its powers of delay as a second chamber.

The existence of pressure groups and the growing power of the media may also act as checks on Government by limiting freedom of action or setting limits within which policy may be framed in accordance with the current climate of opinion. But this is a feature of our society rather than an element of our Parliamentary system and, though marked, cannot be regarded as either an infallible or a dependable check. Moreover, in practice both pressure groups and the media may act to reinforce rather than scrutinise Government policy.

Referenda have been employed in the past, most notably in 1975 over Britain's continued membership of the European Community, but this is an exception rather than a norm in a system which relies on delegated responsibility rather than direct participation in the Parliamentary process. But delegation need not mean abrogation of interest or influence; the strength of democracy lies in the psychological investment which the electorate makes in its worth, in its efficacy and in its relevance to everyday life. Hitherto, foreign policy has not claimed public interest on the same scale as domestic policy save at times of national crisis or over specialised issues. Paradoxically, however, our growing interdependence as nations and the growing interdependence between foreign and domestic policy have largely nullified the distinction between the two. One obvious check on the Executive is the climate of opinion which prevails and, related to this, the ever present prospect of the next election. Should foreign policy be placed on the national agenda, should foreign affairs develop a national constituency, the checks on a government's freedom of action would be greater.

Parliament and Foreign Policy in Britain 7

Parliament has a particularly important role to play in encouraging this development. As a sounding board for national debate it should be used to encourage popular consciousness of the importance of foreign policy in a domestic not simply an international context; as a responsiblity which no nation can ignore in an interdependent world, as an issue, moreover, which should not simply be left to the 'experts'.

The Influence of the British Parliament on Foreign Policy

CLIFF GRANTHAM and BRUCE GEORGE

In seeking to assess the influence of the British Parliament in the sector of foreign affairs, it is necessary first to have some understanding of the British legislature's role within the general policy making process. Philip Norton's classification of legislatures based on policy-making is probably the most useful in this respect. The classification distinguishes between policy-making legislatures, policy-influencing legislatures and legislatures with little or no policy impact.

Policy-making legislatures, such as the US Congress, are in a position not only to amend or reject government proposals, but also to substitute proposals of their own. In other words, they can — and frequently do — play an active part in the initiation and formulation of policy.

Policy-influencing legislatures, on the other hand, are restricted to amending or rejecting government measures with which they disagree—they have no capacity to substitute policies of their own.

Those legislatures with little or no policy impact, self evidently, can neither modify (let alone reject) proposals nor put forward any of their own.

Like most other democratic Commonwealth legislatures, the British Parliament falls within the second category, i.e., as a policy-influencing body. Historically, this has been the position since the passage of the 1867 Reform Act. Prior to that, the

British Parliament enjoyed—albeit for a short period — a role akin to that of a policy-maker, for while it did not itself govern (it never has), it did act as a powerful check as well as an important initiator in the decision-making process; its relationship with Government was one based on mutual dependence.

The nature of that relationship was to change—profoundly and permanently—after 1867. Lost were any claims Parliament may have had to being an important actor in the policy-making process. The so-called "golden age" of Parliament was over.

The Reform Act of 1867—reinforced by the Representation of the People Act of 1884—extended the franchise to encompass the majority of working men. This major enlargement of the electorate meant that voters were now too numerous to be contacted other than through mass, organised political parties. Individual Members of Parliament could no longer keep in touch with—let alone bribe—their electors. The result, as Richard Crossman noted, was that "organised corruption was replaced by party organisation."

The growth of a mass electorate and the ensuing growth of mass membership of organised political parties, combined with various institutional, environmental and internal party pressures, resulted in Members of Parliament being dependent upon a party label for election *to* Westminster and deferring to party leaders *at* Westminster. The House of Commons became a party-dominated institution, heavily dependent upon Government for information and the generation of public policy. By the twentieth century, the House of Commons was a marginal actor in the making of public policy. The relationship between the two was almost one of master (the Government) and servant (the House of Commons). Parliament had lost the two major functions ascribed to it by the noted constitutional historian of the nineteenth century, Walter Bagehot in "The English Constitution" (1867). These functions—the elective (choosing the Government) and legislative (making policy) — passed to the electorate and to the Government respectively. Parliament's role became a reactive one, subjecting Government measures to scrutiny and influence. But even here, its capacity as a policy influencer became increasingly ineffective as the twentieth century wore on. As Government grew and became more specialised, Parliament lacked both the will and the resources to subject the executive to effective scrutiny, and nowhere was this more apparent than in the area of foreign affairs. Indeed, one may be excused for relegating the role of Parliament in foreign affairs to the third category, such was its impact. The Government for its part came to rely increasingly on outside bodies for advice and assistance in the formulation of policy. Parliament found itself dealing with twentieth century Government using nineteenth century procedures.

In the context of foreign affairs, the widely held view of a relative, if not absolute, Parliamentary impotence in an area traditionally regarded as being a matter of Executive prerogative, has been supported by the historical tendency towards an ad hoc Parliamentary approach in such matters.

Thus, since at least the sixteenth century, Select Committees have considered issues such as overseas trade, treaties, diplomatic relations, human rights, inquests into military failure, colonial government and legal systems, and the grievances of British subjects abroad, but rarely in a systematic manner. By the late nineteenth century, the frequency and importance of such committees had diminished, and their role declined to one of deliberation. In this century, first the Estimates Committee and then the Public Accounts Committee have covered foreign affairs in a somewhat tangential manner, whereas the more recent Defence and External Affairs Sub-Committee of the Expenditure Committee sought to have more direct relevance. However, in terms of an examination of policy, this body leaned heavily towards the defence sphere and, with a few exceptions, confined its foreign affairs analysis to the functioning of embassies and British representation abroad. The diminishing role of Parliament in foreign affairs exercised pressure groups outside Westminster, who were to find a natural ally in the Labour Party. Ideologically, the elitism and secrecy inherent in foreign policy-making offended that Party, which, as early as 1921, recommended the establishment of a Foreign Affairs Committee.

In the contemporary period Parliament's limited role in this sector has been variously acknowledged, including by a current Cabinet Minister, the Home Secretary Douglas Hurd—himself a former Foreign Office official and later a Foreign Office Minister. Addressing a conference of political scientists in 1981, he told the audience that the role of Parliament in the formation of foreign policy was deserving of particular study. "Past procedures" he admitted, "have not really allowed for much effective Parliamentary influence."

Our intention in this examination is to assess the relationship between the British Parliament and the sector of foreign affairs, charging Parliament's declining capacity over the last century to exert scrutiny of Government in the conduct of foreign affairs, and to assess the extent to which that decline has been halted or partially reversed as a result of developments since 1979, namely the establishment of a permanent body of scrutiny.

Foreign Affairs*

The last century then has witnessed a decline in the role of Parliament to that of a limited policy influencer, and within that context, the nation's external relations, that is foreign affairs, has been one in which parliamentary influence has been most limited. Why should this be so? The explanation can be found in a number of factors, peculiar to foreign affairs, each requiring some consideration. The first, and most distinctive factor, is that the conduct of foreign affairs is largely a Crown prerogative. "No person or body save the Queen, by her accredited representatives, can deal with a foreign state so as to acquire rights or incur liabilities on behalf of the community at large." The Crown's function in this regard is now exercised on its behalf by the Government. The powers vested in the Crown are carried out, therefore, unilaterally by the Government; these include the declaring of war and making of peace,

---

*Providing a satisfactory definition of foreign affairs is not an easy task. In particular, the dividing line between what constitutes foreign affairs and what constitutes defence is often a fine one. This problem can be overcome by using the term 'security', though this tends to veer more towards defence than foreign affairs. For the purpose of this chapter, the term foreign affairs is used to encompass relations with foreign governments (including member States of the European Community) and the views of Her Majesty's Government on events taking place outside the confines of the United Kingdom.

the acquiring and ceding of territory, according recognition to foreign States and Governments, the sending for and receiving of Ambassadors and the appointment of British consular officers to name but some of the more important.

Although in principle powers in respect of foreign affairs belong exclusively to the Crown and by inference to the Government, Parliament is frequently consulted, particularly with regard to the declaring of war and making of treaties, and if any measure calls for an appropriation of public money or for a change in domestic law, then legislation must be introduced and Parliament's formal assent sought. However, legislation in the area of foreign affairs is, as a consequence of the prerogative, rare and in any case, as Peter Richards has noted in *Parliament and Foreign Affairs*, "... in normal circumstances British Ministers can negotiate secure in the knowledge that their actions will obtain parliamentary approval."

Because foreign policy matters rarely require legislation, there is little reason for detailed discussion on proposals. Parliament may scrutinise the Government's foreign policy through general debate, but it is rarely called upon to provide formal, definitive assent to it. Motions approving or expressing opinions are declaratory only. "The result is" Philip Norton observes, "that the Government has a much freer hand, formally and to some extent in practice, in the conduct of foreign affairs than it has in areas in which legislation or definitive authorisation by the Commons is required."

The second factor concerns the extent to which foreign affairs attracts cross-party agreement. Although political parties may disagree on emphasis, broadly speaking a consensus develops on the thrust of foreign policy. "Not infrequently" therefore, James Barber notes in *Who Makes British Foreign Policy?* "party differences give way to an overall national view."

There are several reasons for this bipartisan approach. The major Opposition party, seeing itself as a future Government, will not want to create a rod for its own back for when it returns to office. Electorally, Opposition leaders will see the merit of being seen to support the Government when it is acting in Britain's interests abroad. This, however, is not always the case. The Government's decision in 1956 to commit troops to the Suez Canal and, more recently, to allow American F. 111

bomber aircraft to take off from British bases before the raid on Libya, and to refrain from imposing strict sanctions on South Africa, for example, came in for sustained criticism from all quarters of the House.

The most likely reason, however, for the measure of all-party agreement, is that Members on both sides of the House will not wish to allow inter party squabbles to threaten perceived national interests or security. The effect of this is well summarised by William Wallace in *The Foreign Policy Process in Britain*:

> Where the front benches are united, as they most often are, the tradition of bipartisanship in foreign policy serves to damp down debate, to lend the respectability of national interest to the accepted consensus and to label criticism as somehow extreme, if not also disloyal.

However, the adage 'politics ceases at the water's edge' has been under considerable strain, particularly since the late 1970s, and especially in the sphere of security policy, where the postwar consensus has been seriously eroded.

A third major obstacle to the influence of Parliament in foreign affairs is what Wallace describes as "the peculiar secrecy in which foreign policy matters are discussed and decided in Britain." In seeking to suppress the dissemination of information and the raising and airing of contentious issues, the Government will often fall back on the claim of secrecy, arguing that to reveal too much would be to act contrary to the national interest. It is a claim often disputed but one rarely overcome.

The fourth factor is the lack of political saliency attached to foreign affairs. Even though more Members of Parliament list foreign affairs as one of their primary interests than any other sector of policy—193 in total (Trade and Industry is second with 135), the fact is that the area of foreign affairs is so vast and Members' time and commitments so pressing, that the parliamentary attention paid to it—other than in times of crises—is in reality fractional. A demonstrated interest in, and desire to help solve, the complexities of the Middle East or the famines of Africa, is probably not going to get a Member re-elected; a proven concern for the issues directly affecting his constituents just might. As we shall see also, the time devoted on the floor of the House to discussing foreign affairs is restricted. It is unlikely, therefore, to be an area in which a Member can carve out a name for himself. Hence, despite the interest expressed in foreign affairs, the involvement of most Members will at best be cursory. It is far more likely that their time will be spent on constituency problems or mastering the complexities of economic, social welfare and a host of other domestic policies.

These then are the factors peculiar to foreign affairs, a combination of which, Norton concludes, "has meant that the ability of the House to engage in the scrutiny and influence of foreign policy has been severely limited. It is one of the few sectors in which its limited role is both formal and real." This limited capacity—almost incapacity—of Parliament to exert influence over foreign policy is further in evidence when examining the methods and procedures that have hitherto been employed.

Traditional Methods of Scrutiny and Influence

The traditional methods of scrutiny and influence open to Parliament in foreign affairs—as in all other areas—can be divided between those activities that take place on the floor of the House of Commons and those that take place away from the chamber. The position in the House of Lords is considered separately below. Questions to Foreign Office Ministers, debates on foreign affairs and statements by Government spokesmen constitute those opportunities available on the floor of the House.

Each Foreign Office Minister (there are six in total, including in the one House of Lords) has responsibility for a particular sphere of foreign policy, the Secretary of State assuming overall responsibility for the workings of Foreign and Commonwealth Office (FCO). Together they appear before the House of Commons every fourth Wednesday to answer questions from Members on both sides of the House. (In the 1976/77 session, the FCO moved from a three-weekly to a four-weekly cycle for answering questions). Questions are tabled in advance and appear on the House of Commons Order Paper. Question Time occupies the 55 minutes immediately prior to the main business of the day, 20 minutes being devoted to European Community matters and upto 35 minutes to the rest of the world. On average, that allows for 7 questions on European issues and 13 on the rest of the world.

The Minister is usually well prepared—his task often being to simply reiterate Government policy, and that from a civil service brief before him—and even though supplementary questions can be more searching, the Minister will normally have been well briefed on all eventualities.

During the 1985/86 session, 681 questions were asked on foreign affairs, though these included Private Notice Questions (questions asked at a short notice with the Speaker's permission on urgent matters) and their supplementaries. The provision for oral questions on foreign affairs has declined considerably over the years, and the feeling among many within the House is that the existing arrangements are inadequate. Statistics from the Table Office, for example, show that the amount of hours per year for oral questions in this area has dropped from 19 hours per session in 1959/60 to 7½ hours per session by 1977/78, the number of days on which they are held dropping from 30 days to 16 during the same period. In addition, a special slot of ten minutes every fourth Monday is allotted to questions addressed on foreign aid to the Overseas Development Administration wing of the FCO.

Although Question Time provides a useful device for extracting information and sometimes provides for stimulating exchanges, it cannot be said to be an effective means of exerting parliamentary scrutiny or influence.

The same can be said of foreign affairs debates on the floor of the House. Debates on foreign affairs are infrequent and of those that are held, few take place on substantive motions; as we have seen, the House is rarely called upon to give definitive assent to policy in this sector. Most debates take place on 'take notice' motions or on motions for adjournment (or their equivalent). Because the debates are not on substantive issues, they tend often to be disparate and unstructured. Indeed, as Douglas Hurd observed during his days as a Foreign Office Minister:

Foreign affairs debates on the floor of the House are not on the whole sparkling occasions. The front-bench speakers normally undertake a tour of the horizon, dealing summarily with a wide range of complicated issues. The attendance is usually thin. Backbench speakers tend to concentrate on a particular subject on which they are expert and enthusiastic. The debate thus jumps from one subject to another. There is a lack of focus and thus of impact.

Statements by Foreign Office Ministers provide the final means available to Parliament to question the Government's foreign policy on the floor of the House. The nature of ministerial statements varies considerably; on some occasions they will be used to report on meetings of such bodies as the European Communities Foreign Affairs Council and on other occasions, the Minister will appear before the House at short notice to update Members on major world developments. During the 1985/86 session, 20 statements were made to the House, including one on the evacuation of British subjects following the accident at Chernobyl in the USSR and another on South African incursions into Botswana, Zambia and Zimbabwe. After the statement has been delivered, there is an opportunity for Members to question the Minister on any matters arising from it. The length of the ensuing debate and the number of Members who may take part is at the discretion of the speaker; the more important the topic, the longer the debate.

Of the means of scrutiny off the floor of the House, the most regularly employed is that of written questions. These are questions tabled for answer in writing. They allow Members to obtain statements and information for which there is not time on the floor of the House or which (particularly those involving much factual data) do not lend themselves to oral answer. In the 1985/86 session, 2274 written questions were answered by Foreign Office Ministers. MPs also often supplement formal questions by writing letters to Ministers—about 10,000 such letters are written each month. However, most are written in pursuit of constituency concerns and few constituency matters impinge upon the responsibility of the Foreign Office. Hence, as one observer noted in a study of the subject: "The major department which attracts the least parliamentary mail is the Foreign Office. Its Ministers are little burdened with having to reply to MPs' letters." The remaining official avenue available to Members is that of the Parliamentary Commissioner for Administration (the Ombudsman), an official appointed to investigate cases of maladministration within Government Departments. However, he has no authority to consider policy, relatively few cases are referred to him for investigation, and of those that are not many concern the Foreign Office.

Three other means of scrutiny are worthy of consideration: two are unofficial, the other is down the corridor from the House of Commons. The first unofficial means is that of party committees. Both the Labour and Conservative parties in Parliament have their own foreign affairs committees, the Conservative committee dating back to 1924, the Labour committee to 1945. These meet regularly (usually weekly) to discuss issues of current concern, to discuss forthcoming parliamentary business in their area of interest and to listen to invited speakers. They provide a useful channel for making the views of interested Members known to their party leaders and provide a useful informing function; but they are not strictly speaking parliamentary bodies and recently have been overshadowed by the new Select Committees.

The second unofficial means of scrutiny is provided by all-party groups. These encompass subject groups and country groups. Subject groups provide an opportunity for Members from both sides of the House to discuss topics of interest to them. There are approximately 100 such groups, several of which impinge on the sector of foreign affairs, including an Overseas Development Group, a European-Atlantic Group and a group which campaigns for the Release of Soviet Jewry. Membership of such groups varies considerably as does their activity. Some groups meet regularly and, on occasion, lobby : others exist in name only. The more active groups also provide a forum for outside bodies to brief members, often in the form of a presentation to the group.

The country groups are similar except that each is concerned with Britain's relations with a particular country. Thus, for example, among over 100 such groups, there is an Anglo-Albanian Group, a British-Australia Group and an Indo-British

Group. Most operate under the auspices of the Commonwealth Parliamentary Association or the Inter Parliamentary Union.

Like party committees, all-party groups are essentially information-gathering rather than policy-influencing bodies, though they lack the regular proximity to party or Government leaders, which gives the party Committees a measure of influence. The scrutinising body down the corridor from the Commons is the House of Lords. This provides a useful supplement to the scrutiny undertaken by the House of Commons. Though lacking the political impact of the elected lower House, it has greater opportunity for general debate—the timetable is less crowded than in the Commons—and can call upon considerable expertise when debating foreign affairs; it includes among its members several former ambassadors, diplomats and Foreign Office officials and Ministers. Its influence has been enhanced on those rare occasions, when the Foreign Secretary has sat in their House, the most recent being Lord Carrington. Normally, though, ministerial representation is not so elevated and the House has to do with one Foreign Office Minister of State. It also lacks any committee for the scrutiny of foreign affairs, though it has achieved a well-deserved reputation for the scrutiny of draft European Communities legislation undertaken by its European Communities Select Committee.

All the official and unofficial devices are supplemented by resources available to individual Members of the two Houses. Thus the House of Commons' Library for example, employs three professional researchers specialising in foreign affairs. Members may also call upon the research bodies of their respective party headquarters, the Conservative party providing the most extensive service through its Research Department. Material supplied by the House of Commons' Library and the party headquarters tends to take the form of information summaries. Members also have a research allowance which permits them now to hire a research assistant, but few utilise assistants with a specialist knowledge of a particular policy sector. Hardly any, for example, would be expected to have a detailed knowledge of foreign affairs. These research allowances and facilities should not be overstated and in many cases Britain falls a long way behind its competitors in this respect.

In combination, then, the devices traditionally available to

Parliament for scrutiny of foreign affairs are varied. Most, though, have failed to keep abreast of developments within Government and none has overcome the limiting factors peculiar to foreign affairs.

Legislative Scrutiny

Given that foreign affairs has always been one of the concerns of government (unlike many sectors which have only been acquired over the last 100 years), there is a substantial volume of legislation on the statute book dealing with the nation's external relations. Taking foreign affairs in its broadest definition, one of the most substantial additions took place in 1972 with the passage of the European Communities Act. However, as noted earlier, foreign affairs by its very nature does not inspire many Bills per session; Bills sponsored by the Foreign and Commonwealth Office in session 1985/86 are listed in the table at the end of this Chapter.

However, parliamentary scrutiny of legislation in this sector is limited not only by the small number of measures introduced, but also by the nature of the legislative process. After being given a Second Reading in plenary session, Bills are referred to Standing Committees. Despite their name, these are ad hoc bodies, a committee being constituted afresh for each Bill. Unlike Select Committees (set up to advise and report), Standing Committees have no power to examine witnesses or receive evidence from outside bodies. Membership reflects party strength in the full House proportionately, and proceedings take place— as on the floor of the House — on a partisan basis. The task of the committee is to examine the Bill clause by clause. In practice, most time is taken up discussing early contentious clauses with little time given to detailed scrutiny of the remainder of the Bill. Generally, debates follow typical party lines and in the event of a vote a majority for the Government is normally assured. Serving on a Standing Committee is therefore one of the least rewarding aspects of parliamentary life and legislative scrutiny—albeit one of the most time-consuming elements—is regarded by many authorities as the least effective scrutiny undertaken by the House. On occasion the the House will exert itself, as for example on the Iran (Temporary Provisions) Bill in 1980 which was withdrawn under pressure from Government backbenchers. However, that pressure was exerted on the floor of the House—not in the Standing Committee—and was very much the exception, not the rule.

Given the nature of foreign affairs as a Crown prerogative, the opportunities for MPs or Peers to introduce legislation are rare. Bills affecting foreign affairs have been introduced under the Private Members Bill procedure, but in common with most measures introduced in this way, very few ever find their way on to the statute book. Thus during the 1985/86 session, the South Africa (Sanctions Proposed) Bill was introduced in the Commons by the Labour MP, Richard Caborn, and the United Nations (Namibia) Bill in the Lords by Lord Hatch of Lusby. Neither got beyond their preliminary stages.

Financial Scrutiny

Just as it generates little legislation, foreign affairs (unlike defence) does not make great demands on the public purse. The Foreign and Commonwealth Office ranks among the lower half of Government Departments in terms of expenditure. Nonetheless, the conduct of foreign affairs—in particular, the maintenance of British embassies and consulates around the globe—is not cost free and such expenditure falls within the purview of Parliament's traditional task of financial scrutiny.

Prior to 1979, such scrutiny was undertaken principally by Public Accounts Committee (the PAC, concerned with *post hoc* scrutiny of expenditure), from 1912 to 1971, the Estimates Committees and, from 1971 to 1979, the Defence and External Affairs Sub-Committee of its successor body, the Expenditure Committee. The problems of *post hoc* scrutiny by the PAC were reflected in Vilma Flegmann's study of the Committee's investigation of overseas services, when she concluded: "The Overseas Services have not been one of the major dispensers of public funds during the last 12 years, though they have earned the doubtful distinction of having provided one of the best known examples of mismanagement of public funds during this period."

The study of the financial aspects of foreign affairs comprised but one part of the Estimates Committee and the Defence and External Affairs Sub-Committee's work, with the Sub-Committee relegating foreign affairs to a poor second place after defence. What investigation it did undertake was confined usually to manpower and expenditure on embassies, though occasionally entering into more contentious areas.

Scrutiny of expenditure in foreign affairs was—as in other sectors of government responsibility—largely deemed by most authorities to be inadequate. Scrutiny on the floor of the House was gradually reduced, through procedural changes, to constitute a formal part of the activities of the House and scrutiny by committee was disparate and lacking in depth. One of the most important and longstanding tasks of Parliament had become one of its least well fulfilled.

Reversing the Trend

By 1970, observers could be forgiven for regarding Parliament as a peripheral and largely irrelevant body in the policy cycle. Within the institution itself, a sense of frustration was apparent; MPs were increasingly aware of their inability to subject Government to effective scrutiny and influence. A limited attempt to exert greater scrutiny through the use of investigative Select Committees was attempted in the late 1960s—with the creation initially of two committees, on Agriculture and on Science and Technology—but the experiment failed to live up to the optimistic expectations of its proponents (the Agriculture Committee, for example, was wound up in 1969 after coming into conflict with the Ministry of Agriculture and the Foreign Office) and the Government remained adamantly opposed to any committee on foreign affairs.

Frustration with Parliament's marginalised role had two significant consequences in the 1970s. Outside the House, pressure built up for major constitutional reform. Within the House, Members—goaded by the authoritarian leadership style of Prime Minister Edward Heath—began to indulge in a degree of voting independence not previously witnessed; the Heath Government actually suffered six defeats as a result of Conservative backbenchers voting with the Labour Opposition. In the subsequent period of Labour Government (1974-79), Labour MPs made use of this new found freedom, imposing a variety of defeats on their leaders, including on major issues. This behavioural change also led to an attitudinal change on the part of MPs. Recognising what they could achieve by using their power of the vote, many began to adopt what Samuel Beer has characterised as a participant attitude toward Government, displacing their old deferential attitude. They now wanted to be more involved in the policy cycle—to serve as policy-influencers—and were prepared to utilise their new political clout to achieve that goal. This sea change within Parliament was to find tangible manifestation in major structural reform in 1979.

Recognising the incapacity of the House to undertake sustained and effective scrutiny of Government, the Select Committee on Procedure recommended the creation of a series of investigative Select Committees in 1978, covering the principal Government Departments. Within the House, pressure built up for the committee's recommendations to be implemented and in 1979—in conjunction with a reform-minded Leader of the House, Norman St. John-Stevas—MPs voted overwhelmingly for the creation of the committees. They were approved despite, rather than because of, the Cabinet. Few Cabinet Ministers were well disposed towards them—Prime Minister Margaret Thatcher was among the opponents—but they were not prepared to go against the strength of feeling within the House itself. Hence, the House acquired fourteen investigative Select Committees. They differed from their sporadic predecessors in two major respects: Firstly, they were the creatures of the House, the result of pressure from backbenchers rather than the consequence of Government initiative and, secondly, they were comprehensive in scope, covering virtually all Government Departments. (The exception was the Law Officers' Department.) For the first time, the House had a Select Committee devoted exclusively to the investigation of foreign affairs.

The Foreign Affairs Committee—like its fellow committees—was established in November 1979. In common with the other committees, it had eleven members, but was one of only three committees permitted to appoint a sub-committee. (The sub-committee appointed was given the task of studying overseas development.) The remit of the Committee was broad, its powers narrow. Standing orders provided common terms of reference: "to examine the expenditure, administration and policy of the principal Government Departments ... and associated public bodies." In the case of the Foreign Affairs Committee (the FAC) the principal Government Department was the Foreign and Commonwealth Office (FCO), encompassing also the Overseas Development Administration (ODA): the associated public bodies included the British Council, the Commonwealth Development Corporation, the Crown Agents and the External Services of the British Broadcasting Corporation (the BBC). The powers of the Committee were those traditionally vested in Select Committees: to send for persons, papers and records; to sit notwithstanding adjournments of the House; to adjourn from place to place; to report from time to time; and to appoint specialist advisers. The powers were useful—and have been variously employed—but could hardly be described as extensive. No formal decision-making capacity, and no powers of sanction, were conferred. The bifurcation between Select and Standing Committees was maintained. Legislative oversight remained divorced from the operation of the new committees.

By agreement between the two main parties in the House, the chairmanship of the new committees was divided between the parties (seven Conservative and seven Labour in the 1979-83 Parliament. nine Conservative and five Labour in the present Parliament). The chairmanship of the FAC went to a Conservative, Sir Anthony Kershaw, who has remained in the chair since. Committee membership reflects party strength in the House, and so the Committee has enjoyed a Conservative majority since its inception. Of the current (1987) members, seven are Conservative and four are Labour. Conservative members have comprised a mix of ex-Ministers (four in the present Committee, including two ex-Cabinet Ministers), 'new boys' returned for the first time in the 1979 or 1983 general elections (two) and what might be termed established backbenchers (one). Some members have an established interest in foreign affairs—Sir Anthony Kershaw, for example, is a former junior Foreign Office Minister—but several, about half the members, do not. The Commitee is serviced by two clerks and one committee assistant. In addition, the committee may call upon the services of specialist advisers. Advisers are generally appointed for a particular inquiry, though the duration of the appointment is not usually specified. The majority of those who have advised the committee have been academics, drawn from the universities and research bodies, others have been retired Foreign Office officials and retired service personnel. During the period 1979-83, the committee (and its sub-committee) utilised 30 advisers; it is significant that between 1983 and 1986 the number fell to seven, four being appointed to assist in UK-Soviet relations.

How then has the Committee operated? And with what effect? In common with the other committees, it has been active and well supported by its members. Attendance at the Committee in the 1979-83 Parliament was high (78%) though relative to other committees so too was the turnover of members— only four members served for the full life of the Parliament. In that Parliament, the Committee held a total of 135 meetings, 71 of them evidence-taking sessions; the sub-committee met 114 times, fifty of these to take evidence. Among witnesses appearing before the Committee were eighteen Ministers and 136 civil servants. In pursuit of its enquiries, the Committee made fifteen visits abroad. In terms of the number of reports it issued, it was the second most prolific committee of the Parliament; it issued twenty-one, compared with twenty-four issued by the Treasury and Civil Service Select Committee. In the first two sessions of the present Parliament, the Committee issued ten reports and made four visits abroad.

In line with its terms of reference, the Committee's reports have encompassed the expenditure, administration and policy of the FCO and associated public bodies. In the last Parliament, three separate reports were devoted to the estimates; in the present Parliament, three have similarly been concerned with the estimates, a fourth has been issued on overseas programme expenditure. The second enquiry undertaken by the Committee after it was established in 1979 was on the actual organisation of the FCO, an enquiry undertaken principally in order that the committee members themselves could be better informed about its workings; the report itself embodied no recommendations and required no Government response. Most reports, though, have been concerned with significant issues of foreign policy. In the first session of its existence, for example, it issued reports on the 1980 Olympic Games and the consequence for British policy of the Soviet invasion of Afghanistan.

In subsequent sessions, it issued reports on the patriation of the Canadian Constitution, on Anglo-Soviet relations, the Falkland Islands, Grenada, the events surrounding the sinking of the Argentine battleship *Belgrano* during the Falklands war, famine in Africa, and the UK membership of UNESCO. Other reports were less grand in their coverage. Thus, for instance, in 1983 the Committee issued a report on the Wiston House International Conference Centre and another on ODA's scientific and special units.

The reports, though, do not reflect the full extent of the Committee's activity. It has taken evidence on a number of issues on which it has not issued formal reports, including Poland, arms sales, Namibia, the British Council, the situation in South Africa and UK-Soviet relations. It has also held general evidence-taking sessions with successive Foreign Secretaries. Over and above this, it has used the opportunity of its overseas visits to build informal links with parliamentarians in other legislatures and has held meetings in Britain with visiting politicians and delegations. It also now holds off-the-record meetings with returning British Heads of Mission.

In combination, then, these constitute an impressive array of activities undertaken by a small body of already busy politicians. Energy, though, cannot necessarily be equated with effect. To what extent has the Committee furthered the capacity of the House to subject Government to scrutiny and influence in the sector of foreign affairs? The answer is a multi-faceted one given the diverse range of Committee activity.

On the negative side, the Committee labours under a number of disadvantages common to all Select Committees. It has no decision-making powers. It can only advise the House. Hence, to influence the House and, directly or through the House, the Government, it has to rely upon the persuasiveness of argument and, wherever possible, the unanimity of its members. It is generally agreed by MPs that a unanimous—thus bipartisan—report carries greater influence than one where members are divided along partisan lines. Despite the bipartisan reputation of foreign affairs, the FAC has not been division-free. In the 1979-83 Parliament, in the course of agreeing reports there were ninety-four votes taken in Committee, though almost half of these took place during consideration of one particular report (on the Carribean and Central America); a further ninety-four divisions took place on a partial draft report on the Falkland Islands, though sixty of these involved MPs voting against their own side. Ten reports were agreed without a division.

If the Government chooses to ignore a committee report—and several, as on Afghanistan and the Falkland Islands, have deviated from official Government thinking—there is little the Committee can do. The Government is committed wherever possible to respond to committee reports within two months, but there is no commitment to take any action. Furthermore, the Committee itself could do little should a Minister or official refuse to appear before it in the course of an enquiry. The House refused to confer a power to compel Ministers' attendance in 1979. Neither limitation should be exaggerated: often a Committee in issuing a report is not seeking solely to influence a change in Government policy (indeed, it may be addressed to a different audience) and no Minister or official has failed to appear when requested to do so. Nonetheless, many Members are critical of the absence of powers to compel attendance should that prove necessary. And once before Committee, no Minister can be forced to answer—though that is a problem that is hardly peculiar to Committees of the British House of Commons.

The Committee, as with all committees, also suffers from constraints of time. This dictates extreme selectivity in the choice of topics. This is apparent in the field of expenditure scrutiny. Though the Committee's record is better than most in terms of the number of reports it has issued on the estimates, it is unable to subject the estimates of the FCO to regular and sustained scrutiny. Indeed, the broad rubric of the Committee gives it less of a formal incentive to investigate expenditure than was the case with the Estimates Committee and the Sub-Committee of the Expenditure Committee.

Arguably a more significant limitation is the absence of any formal link between Committee deliberations and proceedings on the floor of the House. There is no established procedure under which a Committee can ensure that a report it issues—on however significant an issue is debated by the House. However, the link between the two is not non-existent. Where Committee reports are relevant to a particular debate, the reports are listed—'tagged'—on the Commons Order Paper. Among FAC reports 'tagged' have been those on the Canadian Constitution, the Overseas Aid Budget, Grenada, and the Falkland Islands. More significantly, the House now has three Estimates Days a session on which specific estimates may be debated. The estimates for debate are chosen by the Liaison Select Committee, a body comprising primarily the chairmen of Select Committees and one independent of Government. The Liaison Committee has taken to choosing for debate estimates on which Select Committees have issued reports; hence, Estimates Days have become in effect days for debate of particular Committee reports, and to date three of the debates have been on reports from the FAC—on the Turks and Caicos Islands in 1983, on Grenada in 1984 and on overseas aid in 1985. Debates are short and no divisions have been held. Members participating are usually members of the relevant Select Comitee. Nonetheless, the new procedure helps develop linkages between the Committee and the floor of the House and forces the Government to respond in plenary session to reports which it may not necessarily wish to see debated.

These limitations are general to Select Committee. The FAC has also had to labour under two which are particular to it. Firstly, it has had to contend with a Department which has a reputation for secrecy and for being disdainful of Parliament. Historically, it has been opposed to the creation of a Foreign Affairs Committee. Secondly, the FAC has had to contend, at least in the first Parliament of its existence, with the political problem of its own sub-committee. The first problem has not been as significant as might have been expected. Despite continued disdain for any form of parliamentary scrutiny by many middle-ranking FCO officials, the FCO has been one of the few Departments to appoint parliamentary liaison officers and has generally co-operated with the Committee in its enquiries. In the last Parliament, it submitted a total of 202 memoranda to the Committee, the largest number submitted by any Government Department to a Select Committee. In its enquiry into the organisation of the FCO, the Committee interviewed a wide range of officials within the Department, from the Permanent Secretary down, and in its report expressed its gratitude for the cooperation which it had received. The second problem has been of a somewhat different order.

When it was appointed in 1979, the FAC decided unusually to appoint a sub-committee comprising ten members, i.e. all the members of the main Committee minus the Chairman. This produced a sub-committee of five Conservative and five Labour members. To further complicate matters, one of the Conservatives was regarded suspiciously by his colleagues (he later became the only Conservative MP to defect to join the Social Democratic Party) and an ally of the Labour members. The result was a majority of members critical of Government policy on overseas development. This situation did not commend itself to the Government supporters on the sub-committee who started to boycott its proceedings. Instead of constituting an asset, the sub-committee became something of an embarrassment to the FAC and at the beginning of the 1983 Parliament it decided not to re-appoint it. Overseas Development thus came within the remit of the whole Committee, a move favoured by a majority of Members on both sides of the Committee.

The limitations, though in some cases significant, have not proved as limiting as critics anticipated (or supporters feared). Against these must also be set the strengths of the Committee in adding to the policy-influencing capacity of the House. These strengths have taken different forms and may be listed as follows.

Firstly, there are those strengths which are common to the Select Committees. Among these is an important agenda-setting role. The Government (and, on Opposition Days, opposition parties) control the timetable on the floor of the House. Select Committees determine their own agenda. Though normally determined after discussion with the relevant Department, a Committee agenda may cover issues that the Government would prefer not to be the subject of enquiry. Hence, the Committees have a power—as agencies of the House—to ensure that particular issues either remain or come onto the agenda of political debate. The FAC in particular has not avoided issues which the Government would prefer not to have investigated. Among these were the events surrounding the sinking of the *Belgrano* during the Falklands war. Indeed, the Committee set a precedent by being the first to allow the live radio broadcasting of its proceedings when it questioned former Defence Ministers Michael Heseltine and John Nott in late 1984.

A further advantage accruing to Committees from their own agenda is the capacity to respond flexibly as new issues arise. This is especially relevant in the context of the FAC which may wish to take evidence quickly in the wake of one of crises that are endemic to foreign affairs. In mid-1986, for example, the Committee responded to events in South Africa by escalating its study of the subject to encompass twice-weekly meetings with a range of spokesmen from South Africa. Such flexibility stands in sharp contrast to the the position in the chamber where interruptions to existing business are not encouraged and emergency debates rarely granted.

The committees have served also to enhance the scrutinising capacity of the House through providing, for the first time, a degree of institutional specialisation. Before 1979, the only means available to MPs to develop specialist knowledge was through the unofficial party committees or, briefly, the sub-committees of the short-lived Expenditure Committee. The existing means of parliamentary scrutiny detailed in the preceding section provided no significant scope for developing specialist knowledge. Now, the Select Committees allow for specialisation within the House on a continuous basis. Increasingly, the House has at its disposal a body of expertise on each particular sector of Government responsibility. That expertise adds not only to the authority of the committees but also to their capacity to ask relevant questions. This body of expertise is reinforced by the ability of committees not only to question but also to travel. This has been particularly important in the case of the FAC, which has extensively used the opportunity to acquire first-hand knowledge of what is happening in various parts of the world. In 1985, in pursuit of its enquiry into famine in Africa, it travelled to Sudan, Ethiopia, Mali and Senegal. In 1986 it undertook an enquiry into the Far East and travelled to all the countries round the Pacific Basin; in the Phillipines it held a meeting with President Aquino. Such a capacity to acquire first-hand knowledge is, of course, one denied to the House as a whole.

Specialisation has helped produce more knowledgeable Committee members. Through their activities, these informed members are able to ensure a better-informed House. This is achieved primarily through their reports to the House and through their evidence-taking sessions. Reports can summarise information obtained by Committees and highlight the saliency of particular points. In this context, Committees can perform a useful function without making any recommendations. The FAC report on the organisation of the FCO sought no change in policy or organisation but provided a valuable guide—not previously available—on how the ministry actually worked. Its 282 page report on "Famine in Africa" contained a great deal of data and analysis, much of it contained in submissions from a wide range of authoritative bodies, including the Red Cross, the UN Food and Agriculture Organisation, the World Food Programme, the UN High Commissioner for Refugees, the British Embassy in Khartoum, Christian Aid and the Catholic Fund for Overseas Development.

Not all enquiries result in the publication of reports. Some sessions are held in order to allow information to be gathered through general question-and-answer sessions. These allow a range of views to be expressed that parliamentarians otherwise might not hear. Thus, the FAC in its enquiry on South Africa interviewed not only the South African Ambassador but also the President of the African National Congress, Oliver Tambo. In its enquiry on UK-Soviet relations, the Soviet Ambassador volunteered to give evidence and brought with him an arms negotiator; between them, they gave evidence for over two hours. By such activity, the Select Committees provide the House with much new information and also with alternative views and opinions to those provided by Government. Hence, they have done much to reduce the monopoly previously enjoyed by Government over information, especially in the secrecy-prone sector of foreign affairs.

Secondly, there are factors peculiar to the FAC which strengthen its role. One derives from the interest expressed in the subject by Members and by its wider political significance. More MPs, as we have seen, have declared an interest in foreign affairs than in any other single subject. This makes the FAC a popular one with Members, thus enhancing its standing within the House. Its choice of topics for enquiry have also given it a higher public visibility than many other committees. As we have mentioned, the questioning of Michael Heseltine and John Nott on the sinking of the *Belgrano* was broadcast live on radio; its report on the subject was reported extensively in the national media. The significance of the Committee is enhanced also by the limited opportunities available to the House to scrutinise foreign affairs; as we have seen, it is a sector in which the House's scrutinising capacity is particularly deficient. The relevance of the FAC was also marked during the period that the Foreign Secretary was in the House of Lords (Lord Carrington, 1979-82) and hence not available to be questioned in the House of Commons; the Committee provided the only authoritative source before which he could be questioned by MPs.

In combination, then, these attributes have more than justified the existence of the FAC. But what impact has it had on public policy? The question is not one amenable to empirical answer. Some reports clearly appear to have had an impact upon Government thinking, most notably (and frequently cited) is its report on the Canadian constitution which influenced official thinking not only in London but also in Ottawa. As Bruce George and Michael Woodward conclude in their study of the case:

> One cannot with any precision say what would have happened to patriation had not the First FAC Report come out as it did. It legitimised opposition and magnified it, provoking greater interest among MPs and more pressure on Ministers. It assisted the opposition in Canada and supported the FAO and Canadian High Commission who must have been warning the Canadian Government of the unease in the British Parliament; had there not been the 'November accords', the Bill would undoubtedly have had a rough passage, and may have faced defeat. The care and thoroughness with which the Report was prepared, and the bipartisan support for its conclusions within the Committee, allied to the timing of its deliberations, meant that Parliament had to consider the issue, however much the Governments of both Britain and Canada denounced the relevance of its findings.

The impact of the rest of its activity, though, is less observable. By its evidence-taking and its reports it has helped produce a better informed House of Commons and ensured that the Government has been more open and more prepared to justify its policies; and, on the basis of this, one can make a plausible case for the Committee having had an important 'ripple' effect on Government and on informed opinion. But its influence is amenable to no empirical test; judgement has to be intuitive rather than born of hard data. The general assessment of Members of Parliament, and of academic observers, is that the Committee has provided a valuable adjunct to the House in seeking to exert scrutiny and influence of Government, arguably the most important advance in this sector in the twentieth century.

Conclusion

Since the nineteenth century, Parliament has been—and remains—a limited actor in the policy cycle in Britain. Factors peculiar to foreign affairs have made it especially marginal in that sector of Government responsibility. It has lacked the political will and the institutional capacity to overcome the Government's entrenched position. Recently, some change has been witnessed : a greater willingness to indulge in the influencing of policy developed in the 1970s and, as a result of that, a new institutional capacity—in the form of the Select Committee on Foreign Affairs—has been introduced. The change has been welcome but modest. Relative to the position in a policy-making legislature such as the US Congress, it may even appear irrelevant. However, compared with the position pertaining to Britain in 1979 it is a significant advance. It has not served to move Parliament more in the direction of a policy-making body, but what it has done is to make it a somewhat effective policy-influencing body. Clearly, much more could be achieved, but Parliament has at least made a tentative step in the right direction.

Table X

Bills sponsored by the Foreign and Commonwealth Office during the 1985/86 Parliamentary Session :

— Australia Bill.
— British Council and Commonwealth Institute Superannuation Bill.
— Commonwealth Development Corporation Bill.
— Crown Agents (Amendment) Bill.
— European Communities (Amendment) Bill.
— European Communities (Spanish and Portugese Accession) Bill.

References

Parliament and foreign affairs :

James Barber, *Who Makes British Foreign Policy?* (The Open University Press, 1976).

Peter Richards, *Parliament and Foreign Affairs* (George Allen and Unwin, 1967).

William Wallace, *The Foreign Policy Process in Britain* (Royal Institute of International Affairs/Allen and Unwin, 1977).

David Vital, *The Making of British Foreign Policy* (Allen and Unwin 1968).

Select Committees :

Gavin Drewry (ed), *The New Select Committees* (Clarendon Press : Oxford, 1985).

Dermot Englefield (ed), *Commons Select Committees : Catalysts for Progress?* (Longman : London, 1984).

A case study :

Bruce George MP and Michael Woodward, 'The Foreign Affairs Committee and the Patriation of the Canadian Constitution' in Dilys Hill (ed.) *Parliamentary Select Committees in Action* (Strathclyde Papers on Government and Politics, 1984).

General :

Philip Norton (ed), *Parliament in the 1980s* (Basil Blackwell : Oxford, 1985).

The Japanese Diet and Foreign Policy

SABURO OKITA and AKIO WATANABE

The Japanese political system today is fundamentally governed by the post-war Constitution of Japan that came into force forty years ago (3 May 1947). Drafted and adopted during the brief post-war period when a defeated Japan was administered by the victorious Allied (primarily American) military authorities, this Constitution was obviously influenced by the United States Constitution in some places, yet it is basically patterned after the parliamentary democracies of the United Kingdom and Europe, and its political arrangements are clearly different from the United States' presidential system with its tripartite division of powers and its checks and balances. As such, the post-war Constitution of Japan continued the tradition of parliamentary government that was begun with the adoption of the Meiji Constitution in 1889.

Just as in other countries where the majority party forms a Cabinet that then takes the helm of the ship of state, in Japan the Diet serves primarily to endorse domestic and foreign policy initiatives taken by the Cabinet, and the Diet rarely if ever initiates policies on its own that are distinct from or in conflict with those of the Cabinet. In this, the Japanese system differs from the American system of government in which President and Congress, both elected to represent the will of the people, are equal partners in government, each with its own powers. Consequently, any analysis and assessment of the role of the

Japanese Diet in the present system of government is better made in comparison with the British and other parliamentary forms of government than with the American system.

In these parliamentary countries, the cabinet, deriving its legitimacy from the will of the majority (as expressed by the majority party in the parliament), works through the bureaucracy to formulate and execute the total range of domestic and foreign policies. In that the executive functions under the cabinet, this system may also be termed cabinet government. In the Japanese Constitution of 1889, the Diet had relatively little authority and the Cabinet was conspicuously independent of the Diet as part of the long historical legacy in which the bureaucrats wielded power in the emperor's name. This influence is part of today's modern tradition.

Yet there is one other feature characteristic of the modern Japanese system of government—the very strong influence of the ruling Liberal Democratic Party (LDP)—which appears, at first blush, to contradict the explanation given above. Unlike in the other industrial democracies, Japan has seen the evolution of a party system in which one strong party maintains continuity in power without transition to other parties, and this continuity of power has in turn contributed to making the ruling party (the LDP) a very strong policy force. Except for a brief period of about one and a half years (from May 1947 to October 1948) in which the Japan Socialist Party and the Democratic Party formed coalition governments, the conservative parties have maintained their hold on the reins of government throughout the post-war period, this trend reinforced with the merger of the two conservative parties in 1955 to form today's LDP. This single party has remained in power for over 30 years.

One of the consequences of this situation has been that ruling-party politicians have developed an improved grasp—relative to the bureaucracy—on the information and skills needed for policy formulation and execution. The LDP currently holds over 300 seats in the 512-seat House of Representatives, houses its party offices in a large building near the Diet Building itself, and maintains its Policy Affairs Research Council (about which more later) as a highly developed policy deliberation body. All the legislation and treaties that the Cabinet submits to the Diet for deliberation and approval must be previously cleared by the ruling party's deliberative process, and conversely it may be said that any legislation or treaty that clears this hurdle is virtually assured of passage in the Diet, given that the ruling party has a clear majority and that the strict party discipline that exists all but rules out the possibility of dissident Diet members' voting in defiance of instructions. Seen in this light, Japan's current political system might best be termed one of party government.

This is not, however, to imply that the ruling-party politicians completely dominate the bureaucracy. While the elected officials do have more authority by virtue of their popular election, the bureaucracy of non-elected officials (given the bureaucracy's entrenched position and vast size, and despite the recent efforts of politicians) still has a better grasp of the information and administrative machinery. Thus the relationship between politicians from the ruling party and the civil service officials overall is one of cooperative co-existence, albeit underlain by a subtle tug-of-war for power.

The question of what functions the Diet fulfils in the formulation and implemention of foreign policy must, therefore, be examined in the context of these basic features characterizing the Japanese system of government. In so doing, it would be wrong to limit our assessment to the Diet system *per se*, and the issue cannot be fully understood without also looking at the activities of the ruling party—an institution that some people have termed an extra-parliamentary parliament and others "the third house of the Diet" in reference to the fact that Japan's Diet is bicameral—and individual Diet members.

2

Because the Diet's most visible involvement in the making of Japanese foreign policy is in the deliberation on and approval of treaties, this is a fitting place to begin this study. Article 73 of the Constitution gives the Cabinet the authority to conclude treaties, yet contains the proviso that "it shall obtain prior or, depending on circumstances, subsequent approval of the Diet."

While it is theoretically possible to conceive of different

meanings for the Constitution's "prior" approval, this is generally taken to mean not prior to the Cabinet's signing the treaty but prior to its ratification. In effect, the Japanese practice is that treaties and other international agreements signed by the Cabinet do not formally come into force until the exchange of the instruments of ratification following approval by the Diet. (Not all international agreements require ratification, and those agreements that go into effect without ratification do not require Diet approval.)

This said, it should be noted that Japan's post-war parliamentary history contains no instances in which a treaty or other international agreement submitted to the Diet for its approval had to be amended or rejected because it failed to win approval. On the issue of amendment, the accepted political interpretation is that the Diet is asked to decide not on the text of the treaty but only on whether or not to approve the treaty.* As a result, it is inconceivable that the Diet should amend a treaty signed by the Cabinet. Even on the issue of approval or non-approval, the Japanese system of parliamentary government ensures that approval will be forthcoming except in those exceptional cases when there are sharp differences of opinion within the ruling party.

In the two score years from the First Session of the Diet convened in 1947 through to the 107th Session of the Diet adjourned in late 1986, a total of 615 treaties have been submitted to the Diet for approval. All of them have been approved.

Of course, not all treaties sail effortlessly through the Diet. In the 91st Session of the Diet (21 December 1979 to 19 May 1980), held when the co-author of this Chapter, Okita was Minister for Foreign Affairs, 42 treaties were submitted to the Diet for approval and all were approved within that Session. This set a new record for the greatest number of treaties submitted and approved in any one Session of the Diet, yet the reason for this heavy concentration of treaty deliberations and approvals in this particular session was that Diet deliberations got sidetracked in several earlier sessions and most of the treaties were held over until this 91st session. Yet even these delays in the Diet

---
*The actual text of the treaty is studied by the Cabinet Legislation Bureau before the Cabinet signs the treaty, and the Diet takes no part in this process.

were not so much because the treaties themselves were controversial but rather because the balance of power between the Cabinet and the Diet was very evenly balanced and it was difficult to obtain Diet cooperation for government policies. At the time, the executive (Cabinet) experienced considerable difficulties in managing its relations with the Diet, both because the government and opposition parties held roughly the same number of seats in the Diet and because there were a number of political groups within the ruling party that were not favourably disposed to Prime Minister Ohira. Indicative of the relationship between the Diet and the Cabinet as it then existed is the fact that the budget proposal submitted by the Cabinet was rejected by the House of Representatives Standing Committee on the Budget (a very rare occurrence, and the only time this had happened since the Standing Committee on the Budget rejected the fiscal 1948 budget proposal submitted by the Socialist and Democratic coalition Cabinet) and only just barely passed by the full session of the House.

It does occasionally happen that the opposition parties refuse to deliberate or withhold their approval of a treaty, in effect holding the treaty hostage, as a means of frustrating and obstructing the government's other policies. However, not all delays are of this nature, and it also sometimes happens that approval is delayed or difficult to obtain because the text of the treaty is controversial. The best-known example in this category is the 1960 revision of the Security Treaty between Japan and the United States. In this instance, the opposition parties, egged on by the daily demonstrations massed outside the Diet Building and encouraged by the mass media's coverage, used all the means at their disposal to try to block the treaty's approval. The government party finally approved the treaty at a special session of the House of Representatives Special Committee on the United States-Japan Treaty of Mutual Security and Cooperation at which the opposition parties were not present and this was subsequently approved by the House of Representatives again in the opposition parties' absence. It proved impossible, however, to convene the House of Councillors, and the decision of the House of Representatives stood as the decision of the Diet in accordance with Article 61 of the Constitution. Under this provision, failure of the House of Councillors to take action within 30 days of receipt of the treaty from the House of Representatives results in the decision of the House of Representatives' being the decision of the Diet. There have been a few other cases, both before and after 1960, in which this provision was invoked and treaties approved with the approval of only the House of Representatives. Examples include the 1958 Agreement Between the Government of Japan and the Government of the United Kingdom of Great Britain and Northern Ireland for Cooperation in the Peaceful Uses of Atomic Energy, the 1958 Agreement for Cooperation Between the Government of Japan and the Government of the United States of America Concerning Civil Uses of Atomic Energy, and the 1974 Agreement Between Japan and the Republic of Korea Concerning the Establishment of Boundary in the Northern Part of the Continental Shelf Adjacent to the Two Countries. This last is the outstanding example of a treaty that provoked a storm of political debate, and it took six sessions of the Diet spread over a three-year period to get it approved.

As noted above, the conclusion of treaties is a power accruing to the Cabinet, and as such treaties differ from other legislation in that there can be no treaties submitted by individual Diet members for approval. In that sense, the Diet inevitably has to respond to Cabinet initiatives, but this passivity is somewhat mitigated and the Diet's role somewhat more active in the case of multilateral treaties. This is especially so when Diet members press the government to have Japan accede to multilateral treaties to the drafting of which Japan was not a party. Typical here are the ILO conventions. The issue of Japan's becoming a party to ILO Convention 87 guaranteeing freedom of association, for example, was submitted to the Diet in 1960 yet not passed until 1965. This issue was first championed by the labour unions, and it was union pressure that led the government finally to submit this Convention to the Diet for approval. Following that, it took another five years and shepherding by three different Cabinets before the Convention was approved, mainly because there was determined opposition within the LDP to any concessions to the labour unions or to the labour-supporting Socialist Party and the government had to be very wary of this opposition within the government party so as not to endanger the Cabinet's survival.

Even today, Japan is still not a party to many of the ILO conventions, and there are nearly 40 unapproved agreements just among those that the government is considering ratifying. One of these that has been prominently discussed recently is Convention 156 providing for sexual equality in employment opportunities.* In addition, the Convention Relating to the Status of Refugees, the International Convention on the Elimination of All Forms of Racial Discrimination, and other multilateral treaties drafted and signed under the pressure of international public opinion are exposed to a greater or lesser degree of public scrutiny before being submitted to the Diet for approval. Although the Convention Relating to the Status of Refugees did receive Diet approval and Japanese ratification in 1981, the International Convention on the Elimination of All Forms of Racial Discrimination has yet to be ratified.

While all the above multilateral treaties were drafted without the participation of the Japanese government, there are also a number of multilateral treaties that the Japanese government had a hand in drafting yet which remain unratified. Including those that date back to pre-war years, they number approximately 20, although there are only half a dozen such major post-war treaties in this category. Among others, these include the Convention for the Protection of Cultural Property in the Event of Armed Conflict, signed by Japan and 49 other countries at the Hague in 1954, and the International Convention Against the Taking of Hostages.

There are a number of reasons why the government would sign a treaty yet not submit it to the Diet for approval, from technical reasons such as the need to coordinate domestic laws and regulations for consistency with the treaty's provisions to political reasons. The Treaty on the Non-proliferation of Nuclear Weapons approved by the Diet in 1976 is an example of a treaty whose submission for Diet approval was delayed

---

* According to the 24 December, 1986, *Nihon Keizai Shinbun*, the four major Japanese labour organizations have recently pressed the Minister of Labour to work positively for ratification of this and other ILO conventions. Noting that Japan has ratified only 32 of the total 162 ILO conventions, and only 9 of the 17 conventions designated by the ILO as basic conventions, the labour organizations contend that this is hardly a record befitting a leading industrial country.

for political reasons. While the government finally signed this treaty in 1970 after long and involved domestic political debate, Prime Minister Sato, who had signed the treaty, was unable to submit it to the Diet for approval.

In the case of the Treaty on the Non-proliferation of Nuclear Weapons, there was a broad stratum of opposition to ratification, cutting across party lines, in both the government party and the opposition parties. Generally, the government and government party tend to be less enthusiastic about promoting multilateral treaties, especially those proclaiming such general ideals as human rights, freedom, peace and natural conservation, than they are about promoting treaties involving economic issues or other issues having a practical impact upon vested interests, and the pattern is generally one of the opposition parties' pressing for these multilateral treaties' approval by the Diet.

Even so, once the Cabinet has signed a treaty and submitted to the Diet for approval prior to ratification, Diet approval can invariably be obtained unless there are extraordinary extenuating political circumstances. The Diet is unable to touch the actual text of the treaty, and in most cases the treaty passes even without any exhaustive deliberation on its implications. The exceptions are cases when the government and opposition parties are of nearly equal strength and the Cabinet is not absolutely sure that it has the majority to ensure Diet approval or when there are sharp divisions within the government party or the Cabinet itself. Yet the possibility exists that Diet members themselves can take the initiative for the approval of multilateral treaties when the Cabinet or executive is not actively pushing for their approval.

3

From the government's perspective, it is most efficient to minimize Diet involvement in all stages of the treaty process. Yet from the perspective of maintaining parliamentary government principles, the Diet's power to deliberate treaties should be respected to the maximum possible extent. This issue of how to balance these conflicting positions is a question common to the role of the Diet in foreign policy everywhere.

In Japan's case, the government's formal position was stated on 20 February 1974, in the House of Representatives Foreign Affairs Committee by the then Minister for Foreign Affairs Ohira, who said, in response to questioning, that whether or not a treaty requires Diet approval is based upon three criteria: (1) whether or not the treaty requires the enactment of new legislation or the amendment of existing legislation, in which case Diet approval is obviously required from the perspective of not infringing upon the Diet's authority to enact legislation, this category is generally agreed to include treaties impinging on territorial issues or other issues of national sovereignty; (2) whether or not the treaty entails fiscal or financial disbursement, with the understanding that Diet approval is needed for the conclusion of any international treaty that entails disbursements above and beyond the normal budget as already approved by the Diet or by law, this also being in obvious deference to the Diet's power to pass on the government budget; and (3) whether or not the treaty is an international agreement that requires ratification before it comes into force, which treaties generally require not simply the signatory procedure but the weightier ratification procedure because of their involving important political issues.

While international commitments can go by many names, including treaties, administrative agreements, exchanges of notes, protocols, and others, the above three criteria apply to all international commitments regardless of name. Conversely, it may be said that the executive is able to conclude any international commitment that does not fall under one of the above criteria without Diet approval, even if the agreement is formally called a treaty. Thus the executive is able to act on its own to enter into international agreements when they are administrative agreements to a treaty that has already received Diet approval, and are in accordance with legislation already on the books and within the budgetary provisions already enacted.

The incident that directly caused the government to formulate this official position was the Diet deliberations on the protocol revising the Agreement for Cooperation Between the Government of Japan and the Government of the United States of America Concerning Civil Uses of Atomic Energy in 1973. Because it was anticipated that there would later be an exchanges of notes adjusting the maximum amount of enriched uranium supplied to Japan under Article 9 of this Agreement, the question arose as to whether or not this exchange of notes could take place without any Diet approval or role. While such an administrative agreement would not itself require Diet approval under the criteria enumerated above, the government agreed that it would "submit information" to the Diet (specifically to the Foreign Affairs Committee) in the case of an administrative agreement subsequently altering the implementation and execution of a treaty even if that treaty had already been approved by the Diet.

Administrative agreements are thus a grey zone, and the government resorted to administrative agreements in the early years of Japan's post-war parliamentary history to get around long drawn-out deliberations that were anticipated in some instances. The most glaring example of this is the Status of Forces Agreement that was signed as an administrative protocol to the Security Treaty Between Japan and the United States of America concluded at the time of the San Francisco Peace Treaty of 1951 and which was treated as not requiring Diet deliberations and approval despite the issue's political importance. In 1960, when the Treaty was revised and the Treaty of Mutual Security and Cooperation Between Japan and the United States of America was signed, both the Treaty and its accompanying agreement regarding facilities and areas and the status of United States armed forces in Japan were submitted to the Diet.

The government's position as elucidated in February 1974 provided a tentative end to the prolonged dispute between the Cabinet and the Diet over the extent of the Diet's treaty deliberation powers. At present, there are no direct challenges to this authority. However, the question of how much Diet involvement there should be in economic cooperation and other international commitments has the potential for becoming the focus of new controversy.

Because international commitments for economic cooperation and assistance entail fiscal disbursements, it may be logically argued that they should obviously be subject to Diet deliberation and approval in keeping with the second criterion in the government's position. However, such is not the case.

Rather, funding for this overseas assistance is included along with funding for other purposes in the total funding for the ministries and agencies having jurisdiction over such overseas assistance—the Ministry of Foreign Affairs, Ministry of Finance, Ministry of International Trade and Industry, and Economic Planning Agency, among others—as drawn up by these ministries and agencies in their budget requests and subsequently whittled down and totalled up by the Ministry of Finance for submission to the Diet by the Cabinet as the national budget bill for the fiscal year. Thus the only opportunity the Diet has to debate the overseas assistance budget is when it debates the total budget bill. Once the budget has been passed by the Diet, budgetary disbursements are executed by the executive and the specific programmes for assistance to specific countries are not submitted for Diet deliberation. (Of course, Diet approval would be needed were the executive to want to enter into a commitment for overseas assistance outside the scope provided for in the budget as passed, but this is a purely hypothetical and theoretical construct).

Because the government's budget bill is completed and finanalized before it is submitted to the Diet, so that there is no leeway for amendment or revision in the Diet's deliberative process except in the most extraordinary circumstances, the question thus boils down to one of how much, if any, input individual Diet members can have prior to the bill's submission to the Diet. Both government and opposition Diet members attempt to lobby the various ministries and agencies in concert with groups of petitioners from their constituencies on most issues, but any attempt to exercise such pressure regarding the budget for overseas assistance would be very unusual in that overseas assistance does not work to any particular election district's advantage and no district has a special vested interest in its budget provisions.

More important here is the role of the LDP's policy-making machinery. The LDP Policy Affairs Research Council is divided into a number of divisions corresponding to the areas of interest of the various ministries and agencies. For example, the Foreign Affairs Division corresponds to the Ministry of Foreign Affairs, the Commerce and Industry Division to the Ministry of International Trade and Industry, and the Educational Affairs Division to the Ministry of Education. These divisions and their counterpart ministries and agencies then join together in the budget formulation process to ensure funding for their programmes. For example, the Ministry of Foreign Affairs' budget requests are taken before the LDP Policy Affairs Research Council Foreign Affairs Division—frequently with joint participation by the Special Committee on External Economic Cooperation and a few other related groups—and discussed there. However, this discussion by LDP Diet members is not so much to conduct a rigorous examination of the Ministry's budgetary requests as it is to support the Ministry in its subsequent negotiations with the budget-controlling Ministry of Finance.

Responsibility for overseas economic assistance is shared by a total of eleven ministries and agencies including the Ministry of Foreign Affairs, the Ministry of International Trade and Industry, and the Economic Planning Agency, and the economic assistance budget is thus doled out among these ministries and agencies, being included, as noted earlier, in the total budgetary request for each ministry and agency. After being pared down in negotiations with the Ministry of Finance, this total request is then put together with the pared requests from other ministries and agencies and the draft national budget for the national government as a whole is again reviewed by the top executive leaders leading LDP officials, and the Ministry of Finance leadership before emerging as the government-LDP budget proposal for submission to the Diet.

This government budget proposal is virtually a finished product by the time it is submitted to the Diet for approval, and it would be very rare for the Diet to revise the budget bill. (In fact, the Diet has revised the budget bill only three times in post-war Japanese history.) The budget bill is submitted to the Standing Committee on the Budget in both the House of Representatives and the House of Councillors, but Diet members tend to use the debate on this bill not so much to discuss specific points of the budget *per se* but rather as a center-stage opportunity to state their positions on the whole range of political issues and to question the government on these issues. Even in the Diet's Foreign Affairs Committee and other committees (here too, there are committees corresponding to the executive's organizational structure), the tradition is not one of examining and debating specific budget items. In addition to these institutional factors, debate on specific budget items is inhibited by the fact that the budget proposals submitted for deliberation include only the grand total and the category sub-totals (e.g., the budgets for the Overseas Economic Cooperation Fund and other executive bodies), and there is no information available on how much is to be disbursed to any specific country or for any specific project.

For all of these reasons, the Diet's role in formulating policy on overseas economic assistance is very marginal, and not even the ruling party's policy-making machinery plays much of a role, being only appendages to the responsible ministries and agencies. While there are some people who argue that the system needs to be changed to require Diet approval of the specific economic assistance agreements as one way of rectifying this view does not have wide support at present.

Yet this not to say that the Diet is totally uninterested in economic assistance issues. Albeit after the fact, the Diet does question the government in considerable detail on how effectively Japanese assistance is being used, so meticulously in fact that one Ministry of Foreign Affairs official has speculated that Japanese assistance is probably the more economically effective for it.

Until recently, econonomic effectiveness—meaning not whether or not the aid will work to Japan's benefit and the benefit of specific Japanese companies but rather whether the aid will be effective from the point of view of promoting economic development in the recipient country or whether it will go to waste—was the basic criterion for Japanese economic assistance. Yet in recent years, there has been increasing pressure on Japan to extend foreign assistance as a means of providing relief (i.e., for humanitarian considerations), for political and cultural reasons, and for other ends that do not have strictly economic justifications. However, public opinion in Japan, including the Diet, has not been very favourably disposed to such forms of assistance, since they are often seen as a waste of money in strictly economic terms.

So far, public opinion has been supportive of increases in the budget for economic assistance, and economic assistance has been among the few items that have consistently achieved considerable increases even as the total level of government expenditures was being held to zero or near-zero increases. However, as the total spent on economic assistance has grown, and as this assistance has become increasingly involved in non-economic realms, it may be expected that Diet supervision will become stricter in the years ahead. Whatever the ultimate outcome, it is clear that public opinion, reflected both within the Diet and at large, is a major albeit invisible factor affecting the formulation of foreign assistance policy.

4

Japan does not have tradition of the Diet's enacting legislation to guide government policy formulation. In the United States, Congress tries to influence the exective's foreign policy by enacting laws such as the Taiwan Relations Act or to limit the President's foreign policy negotiating leeway by enacting laws such as the Trade Expansion Act, but such things do not happen in Japan.

Even so, it frequently happens that the Diet passes resolutions designed to nudge the government in the direction of certain foreign policy positions or to serve notice that certain positions are unacceptable. A few examples should suffice to make this point.

The restoration of territorial sovereignty is the most common subject of such Diet resolutions. When the Ryukyus were under American military jurisdiction, there were repeated Diet resolutions calling for their restoration to Japan, a goal that was finally achieved when residual sovereignty became reversion in 1971. While there is no telling how much these resolutions did to buttress the government's negotiating position, they were dramatic expressions of a consistently strong public opinion in favour of reversion. Likewise, the Diet has passed repeated resolutions calling for the return of the small Northern Territories off Hokkaido that are now an issue of contention between Japan and the Soviet Union, For the Japanese government to faithfully observe the letter of these resolutions in its negotiations with the Soviet Union would commit the government to this position and limit its flexibility (in that the resolutions demand the return of all four islands and island groups and do not permit any concessions on this demand). Since, of course, no resolution could win Diet approval that did not first have the approval of the majority party, it may be said that the territorial position expressed in these resolutions is also the position of the government itself. As such, the other side in such negotiations may reasonably be expected to assume from these repeated resolutions that there has been no change in the Japanese government's position.

The most sensitive issue for Japanese public opinion is that of possible involvement in overseas military conflicts, because it has a direct bearing on the question of how to maintain Japan's reputation as a peace-loving country. The Diet has frequently passed resolutions condemning nuclear testing by India and other powers and calling for a comprehensive nuclear test ban. Referring to Japan itself, the House of Representatives adopted the three non-nuclear principles of non-possession, non-manufacture, and non-introduction in November 1967. Other well-known resolutions in this area are the House of Councillors' June 1954 resolution against sending Self-Defence Forces personnel overseas and the House of Representatives' March 1981 resolution against weapons exports. This last is especially interesting in that it was a multi-stage progress. Under questioning in the House Standing Committee on the Budget, Prime Minister Sato stated on 21 April 1967, that Japan would not export weapons to any communist country, to any country subject to a United Nations resolution embargoing weapons exports to that country (e.g., the Republic of South Africa), or to any country which is or is feared likely to become a party to an international conflict. Some years later, under Prime Minister Takeo Miki, the Cabinet formally approved a policy statement on weapons exports that included the three provisions set forth by Prime Minster Sato plus a statement that Japan would be most reluctant, in keeping with its peace Constitution and the provisions of the Foreign Exchange and Foreign Trade Control Law, to export weapons to any country at all, and it was this 21 February 1976, Cabinet policy statement that was the basis for the 1981 House resolution against weapons exports.

There is, however, some question as to how binding these Diet resolutions are. In the strict legal sense, it may be said that they are not binding, Nevertheless, it would be difficult for the government to act in flagrant violation of the expressed will of the Diet as "the highest organ of state power" (Article 41 of the Constitution). In that sense, it may be said that Diet resolutions are politically binding. This is especially so in that the resolutions are often adopted by unanimous acclamation (or at times with only the Communist Party in opposition or abstention), meaning that it would be very difficult to pass a new resolution amending a resolution once it is passed.

In fact, however, many of these Diet resolutions originated in government policy declarations to the Diet. The three principles restricting weapons exports, for example, were adopted by the government on its own initiative to provide guidelines for the application of the Export Trade Control Order to control the export of weapons. They were later extended to a Diet resolution when the question arose in the Diet as to whether or not a particular private-sector company's exports fell into the weapons category and the resolution was passed by way of pressing for the rigorous application of these principles by the government.

The three non-nuclear principles are a somewhat similar case. These three principles were originally adopted by the government as internal policy guidelines, and they were passed as a Diet resolution only later, as a concession to the opposition parties (which had been pressing for the passage of such a resolution) in order to win these parties' support for the agreement with the United States governing the reversion of the Ryukyus when that agreement was submitted for Diet approval.

As seen in these two examples, the politics of passing Diet resolutions is typical of the post-war Diet deliberations over Japanese foreign policy. While Diet debate takes place both in standing and special committees and in the full session, the Foreign Affairs Committee, for example, meets only twice a week, once to discuss treaty approvals and once to question the government about its positions on foreign policy issues of general interest. In addition, foreign policy issues are frequently taken up in the Standing Committee on the Budget. Question time in each House is allotted to each party in proportion to the number of seats it has in that House, such that most of this question time is allocated to the ruling party by virtue of its majority. However, LDP Diet members do not have to ask questions in the Diet, since they have ample opportunity to ask questions and to get explanations from the government in the party's own policy-making bodies and elsewhere, which forums often yield more candid exchanges of views than those in the Diet. For ruling-party Diet members, the Diet is thus not so much an opportunity to criticize the government and expose policy fallacies as it is one to elaborate on these policies. Thus the debate in the Diet—be it in committee sessions or in plenary sessions—is primarily that between the government and the opposition. In the light of this, current practice in the House of Representatives Foreign Affairs Committee is for ruling-party Diet members to yield some of their allotted time to opposition Diet members, probably in the hope that giving these people disproportionate time to ask questions will, if not satisfy them, at least mitigate their dissatisfaction.

There is one very distinct pattern that emerges from this Diet debate between the government and the opposition parties: that of the opposition's pressing the government and questioning minutely as to whether or not a policy statement or policy action might not be inconsistent with a previous government policy statement or stated legal or treaty interpretation. Thus Cabinet Ministers find themselves under constant scrutiny as to whether or not their current statements are consistent with statements made in the Diet by previous Cabinet Ministers many years earlier. It may seem odd that the current Cabinet and current ministers are constrained by statements made by previous Cabinets and previous ministers, but this is an accepted part of modern Japanese politics in that the same party has held the reins of power for an extended period and that the government is thus expected to exhibit policy continuity despite changes in the composition of its Cabinets. This expectation of policy continuity, changes in cabinet line-ups notwithstanding, is further buttressed by the traditionally strong policy-role played by the standing bureaucracy.

Even if a Cabinet or a Cabinet Minister has a specific policy or legal interpretation, it is to the government's advantage to avoid having this policy or interpretation embedded in a Diet resolution and to leave as much manoeuverability as possible for responding to new situations and circumstances as they arise. The Diet resolution on the three non-nuclear principles is the prime example here. At the time, Prime Minister Eisaku Sato and his Cabinet came down heavily against the passage of a Diet resolution embodying these principles even though the opposition had proposed such a resolution many times. However, the Cabinet later withdrew its opposition and agreed to the passage of a Diet resolution on the three non-nuclear principles in order to win opposition cooperation and to get the agreement with the United States on the Ryukyus reversion approved by the Diet on schedule.

Because Diet resolutions are the product of political dealing between the LDP and the opposition parties, even though they often originate in government policy positions, they are also in part "won" by the opposition from the government and LDP. So long as the government is unable to ignore these political dynamics within the Diet, it is possible for the Diet to influence government policy formulation through subtle means.

5

Given this situation, what are we to make of the role of the Diet in Japanese government foreign policy formation?

Setting aside political systems such as that in the United States for the time being, the general practice in countries with parliamentary forms of government is for the parliament (the Diet in Japan's case) to be the final endorser of policies formulated and adopted by the Cabinet. Very seldom does the parliament itself initiate policy formation, be it concerning domestic policies or foreign policies. While provision does exist for individual Diet members to submit legislation concerning domestic political issues, by far the majority of all bills originate with the government. On foreign policy, given that the executive is invested with the authority to conclude international agreements (treaties), it is logical that all these bills and other initiatives should originate with the Cabinet.

In addition to the fact that the Diet itself cannot sign an international agreement, it has also been pointed out that the fact that foreign policy does not directly impinge upon the vested interests of any major constituencies or constituents means that this is not a prime subject of interest for Diet members, and this is another factor tending to make the Diet more passive about foreign policy issues. The third reason for this relative lack of Diet involvement in foreign policy is that foreign policy, in so far as it concerns national security and the ultimate national interest, lends itself to supra-partisan consensus and hence is not seen as a fit subject for Diet debate.

Most people—Diet members included—would respond negatively or only vaguely if asked about their perceptions of the Diet's role in the formation of Japanese foreign policy. As if to demonstrate this, people who leave the Ministry of Foreign Affairs to go into politics have less chance of being elected than candidates with professional backgrounds in the other ministries and agencies. And once elected, Diet members compete for assignment if not to the prestigious Standing Committee on tha budget, then at least to Finance, Commerce and Industry, Agriculture, Forestry and Fishery, and other standing committees with strong ties to domestic special interest groups, and assignment to the Foreign Affairs Committee is not a particularly coveted post.

As such, it may be felt that the Diet's role is insignificant, at least in so far as it concerns the making and execution of Japanese foreign policy. However, the authors feel that the Diet is both potentially and actually a more significant factor in the formulation of Japanese foreign policy than most people realize.

The first reason for this is that, even though it is difficult for the Diet to take the initiative in the conclusion of International agreements and other treaties, it is possible for Diet members to make their views known to treaty negotiators not only in the obvious post-signatory process of deliberations relevant to treaty approval but also in the pre-signatory negotiating stage through their questions and comments in the Diet. At the very least, the Diet is fully able to highlight the issues involved. Moreover, even after the treaty is signed and ratified, it still has to be put into effect and there is considerable room for Diet deliberations to affect the way the treaty is executed and enforced. Specific examples here include the question of how "Far East" is to be defined in Article VI setting forth the scope of the United States-Japan Treaty of Mutual Security and Cooperation and the interpretation of which matters regarding the American military's use of facilities in Japan shall be subject to prior consultation under the Exchange of Notes pursuant to the same Article VI. Until recently, these were among the opposition parties' favourite topics of discussion in the Diet.

The second reason is that, as clearly demonstrated by the ILO conventions, it is possible for the Diet rather than the government to take the initiative in pressing for the ratification of multilateral treaties and other international agreements. In this way, domestic public opinion, backed by the force of international public opinion, is able to push the government to take certain actions and move in certain ways. While this is not foreign policy in the traditional sense of the term, the increasing interdependence among nations means that there is an increasing tendency for people to focus on whether or not domestic practices and activities are compatible with internationally accepted practices and ideals. Likewise, the tendency is also for increasing attention to be paid to the shared assets of all mankind (such as peace-keeping, disarmament, human rights, natural conservation, the preservation of cultural assets, and other concerns transcending national borders), which tendency may well work to enhance the Diet's role in this aspect of foreign policy.

The third reason is that foreign assistance, in so far as it entails considerable fiscal disbursements, can reasonably be expected to be a subject of some interest to the Diet. So far, the Diet has not demonstrated any great interest in this issue, but this is probably because the scale of foreign assistance disbursements was relatively small (and was distributed among the budgetary requests of a number of different ministries and agencies such that it was not seen as a single lump sum) and because there has been a broad public consensus that it is dangerous to increase defence spending but desirable to step up economic assistance to the developing countries, However, there is a very real possibility that foreign assistance may increasingly be a focus of serious Diet debate, both because it is questionable whether or not the system can tolerate continuing increases in foreign assistance within a general context of budgetary austerity and because the actual forms this policy takes are gradually moving from the less controversial emphasis on economic devements to non-economic realms.

Finally, the authors would like to say a word or two about some of the issues in external economic policy, an area which it has been impossible to treat at any satisfactory length in this paper. There is a crying need to have serious treatment and discussion of the role that individual Diet members and the Diet as a whole play or potentially play in the area of economic friction. Here, however, the authors will only deal very briefly with a few of the main features. While there is increasing pressure for Japan to further open its markets, there is in Japan, as in any other country, opposition to this from constituencies or other vested interest groups that would be adversely affected by market opening. While a broad consensus is finally emerging on both the need and the desirability of further opening the Japanese market, there is still strong opposition and resistance on specific policies to implement that opening, and it is unlikely that there will be any sudden, wholesale shift to market-opening. As in any country, it is the Diet members who depend upon particular vested interest groups or constituencies for their voter and financial support, who are the mainstay of the protectionist forces. Unlike in the United States Congress, however, Diet members are very unlikely to propose, much less pass, protectionist legislation or resolutions directly embodying the positions of these special interest groups.* For better or worse, the pattern

---

* According to the *Asahi Shimbun* (30 December 1986), four opposition parties (the Socialist, Komei, Democratic Socialist, and Communist parties) recently submitted a joint bill for the protection of the Japanese fishery industry. Declaring that the United States, the Soviet Union, and other countries have unjustly restricted Japanese international fishing activities, this bill calls for retaliatory limitations on or an embargo against imports of fishery products from these countries. The LDP also considered submitting a similar bill at one time, but decided against it. Although there is no chance of this opposition bill being enacted so long as the LDP holds a majority in the Diet, it is nonetheless a symbolic expression of opinion. While this does not represent the sort of protectionist legislation opposing market opening that is discussed in this paragraph, it is clearly an attempt to protect and promote fisheries interests in a climate of increasing harsh international competition. This bill may also signify a new trend in the Diet in that the opposition took up a protectionist cause and that the Communist party was among its co-sponsors.

in the Japanese system of interest aggregation and interest articulation is for these various special interest groups to be represented within the different stages of the ruling party's policy-making machinery and then homogenized with other interests for inclusion in government policy. Given this, the determining factor in the formulation of Japanese external economic policy is that of how well the ruling LDP's policy-making machinery can control the interplay of policies advocated by specific special interest groups (such as rice farmers or the agricultural cooperative) and their specific advocacy ministries and agencies (in this case the Ministry of Agriculture, Foresty, and Fisheries) and coordinate these special interests and the accompanying bureaucratic clash in the interests of the whole. It is, in effect, a question of political leadership.

The Knesset and Israel's Foreign Relations

NETANEL LORCH

Introduction

In order to understand the complex, sometimes ambivalent relationship which exists between the Knesset and the Government of Israel in the field of foreign relations, it is vital to take into account a number of basic political and constitutional facts.

First, Israel is a parliamentary democracy, modelled—consciously—after those of Western Europe. It's President, indirectly elected as Head of State, is basically a symbol, a figurehead; executive power is vested in the Government which—as long as it enjoys the confidence of the majority of the 120 members of the Knesset, and its actions are in conformity with the law of the land — has ample authority to take decisions, without prior consultation with the Knesset or any of its constituent bodies.

Second, throughout its history Israel has been in a state of war. At first, beginning with the Arab invasion on the morrow of its establishment, with all of its neighbours; and later, following the Peace Treaty of 1978 with Egypt, with some of them. This is not just a formal, juridical fact; it is part of a deplorable reality. There has hardly been a month without some casualty as a result of terrorist action, aided and abetted by one or more of Israel's neighbours, or military action undertaken directly by a State's armed force. As a result, Israel's Foreign Relations are closely linked with its defence, more closely even than in the case of other 'normal' countries. One of the Parliamentary corollaries is that the same Knesset Committee deals with Foreign Affairs and Defence, and that, dealing with the subject of this paper, inevitably means dealing, at least to to a certain extent, with matters of Defence also.

Thirdly, Israel is a non-aligned country, in the strict sense of the word. It does not belong to any block, or treaty organization. Whereas its way of life and form of governance is obviously in the Western, democratic, liberal tradition, and it sets great store by the support of certain Western nations, above all the U.S., its policies are strictly its own, and it has no formal treaty obligations to consult or coordinate with anyone, on the executive or the Parliamentary level.

The Knesset and Treaty-Making Power

When Israel's Basic Laws—which ultimately constitute its Constitution—were framed, it was envisaged that whilst the Government of the day would be free to negotiate and to sign International Treaties, Conventions and Agreements, the Knesset would retain the power to ratify; so much so, that the Basic Law concerning the President states that "Agreements ratified by the Knesset will be signed by the President." However, the Government has been empowered both to sign and ratify International Instruments, so that the Knesset has never ratified, and—except on ceremonial occasions and for ceremonial purposes—the President has never signed an International Agreement. This state of affairs has been criticized intermittently, but consistently, by the opposition of the day, and frequently also by members of coalition parties, while it has equally consistently been adhered to by the Government of the day, for which evidently the status quo has been convenient. However, in the course of one of the recurrent debates about the subject, held in 1963, the then Minister of Justice, on behalf of the Government, gave a solemn undertaking to enable the Knesset to debate major international instruments prior to final signature or ratification. The practice enunciated at that time, which is akin to the Ponsonby Rule adopted by the House of

Commons, has in fact been followed ever since. This leaves the Knesset formally without any authority—beyond that of a vote of no-confidence, which would bring down the government but would not affect the validity of the Treaty which occasioned the no-confidence vote; in practical, political terms, however, it is inconceivable that a government would proceed with the signing and ratification of a Treaty which has been rejected by a majority of the Knesset. In view of its fundamental importance, some extracts from the 1963 Motion for the Agenda, may be of interest.

The author of the motion was a member of a leftwing opposition party, but—as may be seen from several interjections—he had the support of the leader of the major opposition party on the center right, Menachem Begin.

J. RIFTIN (Mapam):
...It seems to me that the time has come to reinforce the moral validity of the agreements signed in Israel's name by according them the appropriate parliamentary ratification. My proposal is a modest one. It does not say that everything has to be brought before the Knesset plenum; it is enough to bring most agreements before the Foreign Affairs and Defence Committee or any other appropriate Committee...unless some of the Knesset members, say, a third of the members of the Committee, demand that the convention be brought before the Knesset plenum.

Volume 12 of Conventions, for example...covers a variety of topics. An agreement which was signed in 1952 was published in 1961. It is true that this is not aesthetic, and even disrespectful, not only towards the Knesset. It refers to a mutual aid agreement in matters of defence with a tiny country—the U.S. I think that when that agreement was signed...it would have been nice if those Knesset Members who get enthusiastic about agreements of this kind could have raised their hands and voted for it, while those—like myself—who believe that it is against the country's best interests could have voted against it. Then everyone would have known that this was no conspiratorial document which was concealed between 1952 and 1961...Respect for international relations demands an arrangement of this kind.

There is another category which may have been published

at the right time, in 1961 or 1962, but should have been debated in the Knesset. If there were arrangements concerning atomic energy...the Foreign Affairs and Defence Committee (or the Economics Committee if peaceful uses were concerned) should have been involved.

There are also a great many arrangements which should possibly have been given more formal validity. Many friendly agreements have been signed with Asian and African countries. I think it would have brought them honour if the Knesset had ratified them.

We have heard people say that they feel sorry for the Knesset, that they do not want to burden it with additional work. But there are two kinds of agreements. There are those which can be ratified virtually automatically. For example, on the basis of a Section in the Entry Into Israel Law, the Minister of the Interior asks the Internal Affairs Committee to approve certain reciprocal arrangements concerning waiving entry permits on service and diplomatic passports. Every member of the Internal Affairs Committee can tell you that when the Government submits proposals of that kind there is a short lesson in geography in the Committee, people find out where the country is, people would like to visit those distant lands, and fifteen minutes later the resolution is passed unanimously. I think that there are a great many arrangements of that kind which can be ratified almost automatically during the course of the Knesset's regular work.

But it is inconceivable that problematic, controversial issues of foreign relations, which really require consideration not only by the Government but also by the parliament, should be ignored by the Knesset....

Since the issue is a very weighty one, I hope that the committee which will deal with this bill requiring that appropriate ways be found of obtaining parliament's ratification of international arrangements, will study the matter thoroughly... It may amend and improve the proposal. There is no doubt that the representatives of the Government, inculding the Foreign Ministry, will make an important contribution to the debate in the Committee, and when the proposal returns to the plenum for debate it will already have been through a collective discussion with the cooperation of the Government's representatives in the appropriate committee.

The Minister of Justice, D. JOSEPH: Distinguished Speaker and Knesset, MK Riftin's proposal raises an important constitutional point, but the Government thinks that this does not conform with the division of labour between the various organs of the State, and could also place an unnecessary and unjustified burden on the proper administration of the country's affairs and its relations with other countries.

...In accordance with the prevailing law...the Government has the authority to sign international conventions, including international contracts and treaties. In this respect it makes no difference if the convention is bilateral or multilateral. The Government may bestow that or any other authority on one or more of its Ministers.

On 8 March 1951 the Government decided to empower the Foreign Minister or anyone appointed by him to sign international agreements and conventions on behalf of the Government. On 31 May 1951 the Government decided that all international conventions should be brought before the Government for ratification after they have been signed.

M. BEGIN (Herut): According to international law, ratification is usually the job of parliament.

The Minister of Justice, D. JOSEPH: That is not so... This situation holds in Israel and many other countries.

This decision applies solely to conventions which, in accordance with their provisions or international public law... must be ratified in addition to being signed in order to be binding. Whether a given convention needs to be ratified or not is a legal question which depends on the interpretation of each individual convention.

Conventions which have to be ratified by the Government in accordance with the aforementioned decision of 31 May 1951 are brought before the Government by the Ministries concerned. When the Government has decided to ratify a convention it authorizes the Foreign Minister to implement that decision. When the implementation of a convention requires a change in the law it is customary and desirable to delay ratifying the convention until the appropriate legislative procedures have been completed in the Knesset.

The Government may also bring a certain convention before the Knesset if it sees fit to do so because of its political or economic importance. This may be done through a statement to the Knesset before the ratification of the convention by the Government, or [by proposing that the Knesset ratify it. If the Knesset has ratified a convention in accordance with a proposal, it requires the signature of the President, though this does not apply to conventions which have been ratified by the Government, even if a statement regarding them has been made to the Knesset.

In April 1949 the Government decided that "The Minister who shall sign conventions with foreign countries which have been ratified by the Knesset and signed by the President of the State is the Foreign Minister."

That sums up the situation to date. Thus, the authority to sign international conventions and agreements is totally in the hands of the Government. If it so desires, it may bring a convention before the Knesset and ask for its approval. Only then will the convention be signed...by the President of the State. But the Government does not have to take that course. It is entitled to sign any international convention on its own, and this is as binding on the State as any other executive action undertaken by the Government. The Knesset's supervision of the Government's action is no different with regard to international conventions than to any other action undertaken by the Government...

Only in one instance is the Government unable to act independently and requires the Knesset's cooperation, i.e., when the implementation of an international convention requires legislation in order to make it the binding law of the country. This does not restrict the Government's excutive powers in any way, however, in those cases, too, it is the Government alone which signs international conventions, but in this case the legislature, i.e. the Knesset, must act in addition to the executive, since it alone is authorized to enact the laws of the land.

MK Riftin proposes that we change that arrangement,

and that the Knesset become a partner, whether through the plenum or a committee, in the process of signing conventions. In other words, he seeks to obscure the dividing line between executive and legislative activities. Instead of leaving the full parliamentary responsibility for signing conventions with the Government, he wants the Knesset committees, or the entire Knesset, to take the decisions and accept the responsibility for signing contracts, agreements or conventions with foreign countries.

This confusion of spheres and transfer of responsibility from one authority to another does not appeal to me. In my view, the existing situation is preferable to the arrangement MK Riftin proposes. Clear parliamentary responsibility by the Government is necessary and desirable in this area of Government, as it is in others. The concentration of authority in the Government's hands assures quick and efficient treatment which cannot be obtained within the framework of the proposed arrangement, especially in matters of urgency, such as when the President or Minister of a foreign country is visiting Israel for a few days and it is desirable and useful to sign international agreements with them immediately and on the spot, as has often happened recently.

It is true that there are countries where an arrangement similar to the one proposed by MK Riftin obtains. But I have two answers to that. First of all, one must examine whether the overall structure of the central powers in those countries is similar to ours... Secondly, our system is the same as that of many other countries which we regard as an example of good government... such as England and the British Commonwealth countries... Thus, our conclusion is that there is no need to introduce the basic changes proposed by MK Riftin, and I, therefore, suggest that his proposal be removed from the agenda, and I see that I have surprised you.

Nevertheless, the Government thinks that there is a possibility of apprising the Knesset Members of international conventions at earlier stages than is currently the case. I would like to stress that I am referring to the dissemination of information and giving Knesset Members the chance to study the agreement. Even in accordance with what I am about to say, the authority and responsibility for signing conventions will be in the Government's hands in future too. But the Government agrees to bring the texts of conventions signed on behalf of the State before the Knesset—in addition to the conventions which are brought before the Knesset in any case because of the need to discuss the laws required for their implementation—if they deviate from routine agreements which have little or no special significance. The Government will usually do this before the formal ratification of those conventions.

This procedure ... will apprise the Knesset Members of the conventions soon after they are signed, and generally before they are made binding by being ratified. In cases of agreements which do not require ratification but become binding upon being signed, the information will be given soon after the convention has been signed. A similar procedure will be instituted as regards international conventions involving several countries which Israel has joined or is about to join. I think that this plan will contribute to strengthening the Knesset's position in the sphere of international relations without disturbing the Government's work or obscuring its responsibility.

...I disagree with MK Riftin's claim that his proposal would reinforce the moral validity of conventions... I do not think that it can be said that a convention has no moral validity after the Government of Israel has agreed upon it. He can say that it is desirable that it should be discussed in a wider forum, but there is no need to say that it will grant moral validity which supposedly does not exist, or not to a sufficient extent, when the Government of Israel decides to sign an agreement or convention with another government.

Nor do I think that there is any justification for saying that "the honour of international agreements requires an arrangement." International agreements are accorded every honour by the existing system which, as I said, exists in many enlightened countries, and we have never heard complaints or accusations to the effect that this system, either here or elsewhere, does not accord sufficient honour to international agreements.

Formality is all well and good, but efficiency is more important. In my view, efficiency will be achieved if we continue with the current system... I, therefore, repeat my suggestion that we reject MK Riftin's proposal...

J. RIFTIN (Mapam): Mr. Speaker, distinguished Knesset, I really must praise the Minister of Justice. He can surprise us. I never imagined that the inertia of removing something from the agenda would be so powerful with regard to a proposal which is undoubtedly modest. It gives extensive powers to the Government or the coalitionary majority within it; it empowers the Foreign Affairs and Defence Committee primarily; it does not automatically transfer everything to the Knesset plenum. And I permit myself to say... that I think that when a proposal of this kind is brought before Israel's parliament...this may be of interest both locally and abroad, because this is customary in most countries.

...I would like to read out the concluding sentence of a study on this subject published by a Jerusalem university publishing house and based on an analysis of the situation in dozens of countries by Ms. Lapidoth. It reads: "Our conclusion is that while the practice in Israel regarding international conventions does not negate international public law, it contains some deviation from the course accepted today in most countries, as well as contradicting Israel's Transition Law. The Knesset should be on its guard lest it lose its authority in the sphere of making agreements; it must demand that Section 6 of the Transition Law be implemented so that it does not become a dead letter, as is the case in most countries."

I would like to ask the Minister of Justice whether...he does not think the subject at least worthy of study? Perhaps the information you have been given is wrong. Other experts on international law should be consulted...

M. BEGIN (Herut): Did you mention what is contained in the Transition Law and was ratified by the Knesset?

J. RIFTIN (Mapam): I did, MK Begin, at the beginning of my speech. When he mentioned separation here, the Minister of Justice thought that he was fighting for separation between the legislature and the executive. Sir, if everyone were to follow your example, the Minister of Finance might well claim that the Knesset should not be burdened with approving taxes and customs impositions, and that we should trust the Treasury...The Transition Law specifically mentions "Conventions with other countries which have been ratified by the Knesset." What conventions have you brought before the Knesset for ratification? It does no honour to either the Transition Law or the international practice of most countries.

Forgive me, but it is strange to say that only matters which directly concern Israel's internal affairs should be brought before the Knesset. I told the Knesset about an agreement regarding entry permits. If someone should be allowed to enter Israel, that has to be approved in Israel. But if there is a military agreement which at a given moment can oblige the citizens of Israel to join some military escapade or war doesn't that directly concern Israel's internal affairs? Don't international labour contracts directly affect Israel's labour laws?

M. BEGIN (Herut): Or extradition agreements.

J. RIFTIN (Mapam): we have experts on extradition even when there is no extradition agreement. That may not directly affect Israel's internal affairs. That is an exception, and that is why I refrained from mentioning it.

Be that as it may, to say that a subject which has been raised by members of all the party groups over the years should be removed from the agenda...exceeds all bounds, with all due respect for the present Government's democratic tendencies. The proposal to prevent its being reviewed by any of the Knesset's committees...does not bring honour to the State of Israel, the Knesset or Israel's relations with other countries. I suggest that the Minister of Justice refrain from hastening along the path which is that of a light-headed administration which dismisses the superme authority of the nation—the Knesset...

The Speaker, I. YESHAYAHU-SHARABI : We will now take the vote.

The Vote

Those in favour of MK Riftin's proposal   26

Those against 42
The proposal is not adopted.

(Translated from *Divre Haknesset*, 204th Sitting of the Fifth Knesset, of January 1963 (13 Teveth 5723).

Whereas the Armistice Agreements signed in 1949 were not brought before the Knesset either before or after being signed, after 1963 all major international agreements were indeed brought to the Knesset. This was the case with the Separation of Forces Agreements with Egypt and with Syria, 1974, and—again—with the Camp David Accord with Egypt, and the Peace Treaty with that country. The debate concerning the latter stands out in the annals of the Knesset: it was one of the longest debates in its history, with more participants than any other—118 out of 120 MKs took part, and it was one of only two debates (not counting ceremonial occasions)—up to the time of writing—which were televised live *in toto*; moreover, it was the only debate on record in which the major opposition party, Labour obliged its members to vote in favour of the Treaty proposed by the Government, whereas the major coalition party granted its members freedom of choice. Although the original commitment of the Government was to inform MKs soon after signing in fact in the important cases mentioned above—the Knesset was informed and was able to debate the issue before the actual signing took place. The procedure followed by successive Governments in the course of the last two decades, involving Prime Ministers from different parties, has been to bring the document before the Knesset after its text has been finalized and initialled. This has sometimes—notably in the case of the Camp David Accords—resulted in almost indecent haste; in that case both PM Begin and President Sadat delayed their departure from Washington to await the outcome of the Knesset vote.

Although this procedure has enabled the Knesset to have its say, the proposal to change the law and to give the Knesset a formal role in Treaty-making has been repeated, over the years, but always rejected.

Political Debates

Paradoxically, although the Knesset's powers in the field of foreign relations are more limited than is the case with most other Parliaments, the Knesset has devoted about 30 per cent of its total debating time to political debates, percentagewise more than any other Parliament. This can be explained not only by the paramount importance of the subject for a country in Israel's position, but also by the widespread interest amongst the public at large, and consequently by the publicity and political benefits which can be derived from participation in such debates. The most memorable debates in the Knesset, and some of the most dramatic ones, were devoted to foreign policy; first and foremost amongst them was probably the one about German Reparations, in January 1952. The arguments for and against the agreement with the Federal Republic of Germany perforce entailed a stock taking of Jewish history, and an evaluation of the holocaust and its corollaries. On both sides of the house similar sentiments were expressed, with opposing conclusions. The Holocaust was cited by one side as forbidding any contact between Israel and Germany or Germans, and by the other as serving notice that the surviving Jews, in their renewed sovereignty, were obliged to use each and every avenue open to them to strengthen their land, economically and in all other ways. The Reparations debate was the only one during which demonstrators outside the Knesset physically assaulted the Knesset building, by hurling stones through its windows; it was the occasion for the first instance of the expulsion of an MK from a number of sittings, because of misconduct.

The subject of relations with Germany was to predominate in Knesset debates for a considerable number of years thereafter; in the context of arms sales to, and purchases from, Germany; the activity of German scientists assisting Egypt's military research, development and manufacture of weapons, and ultimately the establishment of diplomatic relations between the two countries. In a way it curious to note that whilst Israel's existential, perennial problem is obviously its relationship with its Arab neighbours—the dramatic tension in discussing issues connected with that problem has been far less than the tension generated by the above debate, possibly due to its far-reaching consensus concerning Israel-Arab issues. The Israel-Arab issues have a pragmatic day-to-day character (as opposed to the issue of long-term solutions) among the major parties, except for certain periods, notably during the War in Lebanon from 1982 to 1985.

This does not mean that Israel-Arab relations were neglected; on the contrary. When agreements were discussed, as mentioned above, or Sadat was received, as will be mentioned later, the issue of Israel's policies vis-a-vis the Arab World, including the future of the Administered Territories after 1967, has occupied a major share of debating time, whenever a newly constituted Government asked for a vote of confidence, or a general political debate was held, on the initiative of Government or parts of the Knesset.

Beyond these areas of major interest, the Knesset Plenary has been siezed with Foreign Policy issues—not only in full-dress debates, but also in Motions for the Agenda (roughly comparable to the Adjournment debate in the House of Commons and other legislatures of the Westminster model). In a typical Session, twenty years ago, one would have found motions concerning the reported sale of Israeli arms to Portugal, to be used in its colonial wars (vehemently denied by the Government); Israel's vote on South Africa—condemning apartheid but rejecting breaking of diplomatic relations, etc.

Matters of specific interest would be raised in parliamentary questions; thus, for instance, a few weeks before the abduction of Adolf Eichmann from Argentina, a Minister replying to a question blandly stated that he could not confirm reports that Eichmann was, at the time, in Kuwait...

Addresses by Heads of State

Quite early, the Knesset adopted a rule that visiting Heads of State—Emperors, Kings and Presidents, would be invited to address the House, from its rostrum, in solemn session. Subsequently, the Presidents of the General Assembly of the United Nations, the European Parliament, the Parliamentary Assembly of the Council of Europe, and the Interparliamentary Union were added to the list. Whilst these addresses normally constitute ceremonial occasions, in a few more memorable instances they became political events of national and international importance. This was the case when President Carter addressed the House at the time of a critical impasse in the peace negotiations with Egypt, when President Carter utilized the opportunity to present specific proposals for solving the impasse; his speech was listened to in silence, but the following speech by Prime Minister Begin was interrupted several times so that the Speaker found himself compelled to expel an MK from the sitting. The entire sitting was broadcast live, and the expelled MK gained instant international fame, notoriety or—in any case—recognizability.

Probably more than any other Knesset Sitting, the one which will be remembered is that of 21 November 1977—when President Sadat, at his specific request, addressed the Knesset. After five wars between Egypt and Israel, the Head of State of the most populous and internationally important Arab country came to the Chamber symbolizing Israel's sovereignty, to declare, "In the name of Allah the merciful" that there would be "no more war". From hereon Egypt was willing to recognize Israel and maintain good neighbourly relations with it. The conditions enumerated in that speech, both in bilateral Egypt-Israel context and concerning the Palestinian question were onerous, for Israel. However, it was the dramatic, symbolical gesture of Sadat's visit and speech, as well as the subsequent separate meetings in the Knesset with all political party groups, which caught the imagination. For the present writer, at the time Secretary-General of the Knesset the moment when Sadat, President of Egypt, laid a wreath near the monument and eternal flame, just outside the Knesset, commemorating all Israeli soldiers who died in the course of Arab-Israel wars, most of them fighting against Egypt—was amongst the most profoundly moving experiences of a not uneventful life.

It may be assumed that the fact that the Hebrew word "Knesset" has been incorporated in the international vocabulary and no longer requires translation, is due to a large extent to these addresses and their widespread coverage.

Supervision

The function of supervising and controlling the Executive,

in the realm of foreign relations, is carried out primarily by the Foreign Affairs and Defence Committee, one of the ten permanent ("Select"—in Westminster parlance) committees of the Knesset. In a way, this Committee serves regularly as a mini-Knesset, both initiating debates on its own and continuing political debates which started in the Plenary. The statutory powers of this Committee are strictly limited—it hardly ever votes and the number of bills tranferred to it after the first reading is small, unlike the Finance, and Law and Constitution Committees. Its prestige, however, is considerable and membership on the Committee is sought after by many, on all sides of the House. As a result of pressures from members, the membership of the Committee has, at the time of writing, reached the number 25, well over one fifth of the members of the House. It is distributed between the various Knesset factions in proportion to their numerical strength; so far an ad hoc formula has always been found which would exclude the Communist party, or the list of which it is a component (normally between 4 and 5 MKs), from membership. Smaller coalition partners have frequently been allotted seats on the Committee by their larger, "richer" (in seats) partners. Even when their party participated in the coalition, the leaders of some parties, notably Mapam, preferred membership on the Committee to membership in the Government, where they could not expect more than a Ministry of secondary importance. Leaders of the main opposition parties, former Prime Ministers, Foreign Ministers and Ministers of Defence would normally be allotted seats on the Committee by their respective parties. At the time of writing, its Chairman is Mr. Abba Eban, a former Ambassador, Minister of Foreign Affairs and Deputy Prime Minister. Amongst its members are four more ex-Ministers and General Rafael Eitan, a former Chief of General Staff. The Committee has regular meetings with the Prime Minister and Foreign Minister of the day (and with officials responsible for Defence—which do not concern us here), about once a month while the Knesset is in session. In addition they have ad hoc meetings devoted to specific subjects, and meetings with senior officials, with the consent of the respective Minister. Without the strict time limits and other procedural constraints prevailing in the Plenary, the conduct of foreign policy, from its broad outlines down to minute details of implementation, is brought up at the Committee for discussion and criticism. All the Committee's meetings are closed to the public, and to the media; all its members are required to sign a specific undertaking to refrain from divulging any information from the Committee's proceedings to unauthorized persons. All the same, leaks do frequently occur, to the point where certain Ministers have declared publicly that they would not present secret information to the Committee. A major part of the Committee's work is carried out by small, compact specialized sub-committees. Whilst these are concerned primarily with defence-related subjects, they also deal with areas of both political and military significance, such as arms procurement and sales and the control of the Intelligence Establishment. It should be noted that leaks from these sub-committees are practically unknown. Although—as a veteran journalist has stated—most members of the Foreign Affairs and Defence Committee "never, or very rarely" leak the proceedings (Asher Walfish, *Jerusalem Post* 22 May 1986) and those who do can be counted on the fingers of one hand, in the judgement of several observers, the very fact of leaks has seriously undermined the Committee's standing by diminishing the willingness of Government officials to give it full, including secret, information. In fact, the same journalist states, "A Cabinet Minister will always be more forthcoming with a trustworthy reporter than he is with the Knesset's most prestigious Committee. The same reporter also has an advantage over the Committee mentioned because he can cross-check with more than one Cabinet Minister, whereas the Committee hears only one Minister at a session.

In reply, the Chairman of the Committee has vigorously defended its record. He has claimed that those members who felt the Committee was not getting more information from the Ministers than they could glean from the media were being unfair. "Three people at least," he stated, speaking primarily of Defence issues," the Prime Minister, the Defence Minister and the Chief of the General Staff give us full and interesting briefings. The fear of leaks perhaps deters them from naming sources or adding colourful details which could propel material inevitably into the arms of the media. They do not seek sensations...We have more information but less power of decision than the Cabinet. They wield the power of decision without being informed...Ministers and Generals have admitted to us that the very exercise of coming to the Committee to explain themselves forces them to think in a manner which they would not otherwise do. Without us, they would live from day to day. Because of us, they sharpen their faculties." The sharpening of executive faculties is not normally included in the enumeration of Parliamentary functions, and yet it may in the end be the Committee's most important contribution.

War and Peace

Some of the most important foreign policy decisions in Israel's situation are obviously related with problems of war and peace, specifically the question, whether under given circumstances force should be employed, and if so, its precise objectives and targets, means and methods. In many cases prior public debate of such a potential operation is liable to cause delays, to alert the adversary and thus to abort it *ab initio*, or seriously diminish its chances of success. On the other hand, any normal parliamentary proceeding, even if it is restricted to discussion in Committee, by its very nature, requires time and may not be immune to leaks. The procedure adopted by successive Israeli governments, in order to bridge the inevitable gap between the military necessity of speed and secrecy, and the parliamentary need for time and openness, has been to inform the Chairman of the Foreign Affairs and Defence Committee and the Leaders of the Opposition, who—as a rule—would be senior members of that Committee, of a forthcoming operation, shortly before zero hour, but with sufficient time to cancel the operation if that is found advisable, following the discussion. The emphasis in the above is on "inform" not "consult"; consultation would normally require a widening of the circle and lengthening of time allotted, and would blur the distinction between the power of the executive to execute, and of the Parliament to control and supervise, *ex post factum*. The procedure described above was followed by Prime Minister Rabin just prior to the Entebbe Operation, when Menahem Begin and Dr. Rimalt were the leaders of Gachal, the major opposition faction; they agreed, at the time, to support the operation, implying that in the case of failure they would refrain from attacking the

Government for the decision. Subsequently, immediately before Operation Peace for Galilee in 1982, Prime Minister Begin reciprocated by informing Mr. Peres and some other senior leaders of the Labour Opposition, of the impending operation designed to eradicate bases in the South of Lebanon from which attacks against Israel had been undertaken.

Knesset as Foreign Policy Instrument

The Knesset maintains relations with other Parliaments both within the framework of inter-parliamentary bodies and on a bilateral level. Some of these are institutionalized and structured : the Knesset is a member of the Inter-parliamentary Union and regularly sends delegations to its bi-annual meetings; it has observer status with the Parliamentary Assembly of the Council of Europe, at Strasbourg, and a delegation of from two to four members, from coalition and opposition, would normally attend the Plenary meetings of the Assembly, as well as certain committee and political group meetings. Committees of the Assembly -- usually one per annum — are invited to hold regular meetings in Jerusalem, on Knesset premises. As of 1978, the Knesset—on the basis of a memorandum signed by the present writer in his former capacity as Secretary-General of the Knesset and by the then Secretary-General of the European Parliament, Hans Nord—holds annual meetings with the European Parliament, alternately in Europe and in Israel, in order to discuss problems arising between the EEC and Israel, the situation in the Middle East. One specific subject is usually agreed upon in advance of each meeting. Parliamentary delegations have been exchanged with many countries, including Egypt soon after the signature of the Peace Treaty between both countries. The Speaker of the House has on several occasions been invited by his colleagues, or—in turn—has hosted many of them, specifically on the occasion of the inauguration of the new Knesset building, in 1966. None of these contacts between MKs and their counterparts from other Parliaments are diplomatic, in the narrow sense of the term; they do not involve negotiations or signing of agreements. Even when they terminate in resolutions or in joint communiques, these are in the nature of recommendations or opinion. However, in the age of mass media, they may on occasion be of importance for the creation of a favourable climate, in itself one of the main objectives of modern diplomacy.

Conclusion

The Power of the Sword used to pertain to the kings; the Power of the Purse to Parliament. In a way, that distinction has been preserved in Israel, with the important qualification that the Knesset can at any time vote the King's successor, the Government, out of office. In a strictly formal sense the Knesset has, by law, delegated all the major functions of shaping and implementing Foreign and Defence Policy, including that of signing and ratifying international agreements, to the Government. Indeed, a step by step analysis of all the major foreign policy decisions adopted in Israel's turbulent history will show few instances of a direct, demonstrable input of the Knesset, or its Committees. However, the inordinate percentage of the Knesset's time devoted to foreign policy debates has not been wasted, nor is the prestige of the Foreign Affairs Committee unwarranted. As a forum for discussion, as a platform from which both Government and opposition can clarify their positions, as a venue for occasions of symbolic value, as an organ for *ex post facto* supervision and control, as a contributor, for better or worse, to the creation of an international climate, of an environment, it has played, and continues to play, a major role.

Israel's Experience with Legislative-Executive Relations in the Field of Foreign Relations

HEMDA GOLAN

The Knesset and its Powers

The State of Israel is a representative parliamentary democracy wherein the Government is subordinated to the Knesset—Israel's parliament—which, unlike other parliaments, was elected to be both the legislative body and the constituent assembly of Israel.

For a variety of reasons, historical and other, Israel—like Great Britain which administered the mandate of Palestine from 1920 to 1948—as yet has no comprehensive written constitution. The decision in this respect was taken by the first Knesset in 1950, shortly after the establishment of the State. The Resolution, known as the Harari Resolution, was a compromise between opposing views concerning the need for a written constitution. It stated that:

(1) A written constitution would not be immediately adopted by the Knesset and,
(2) The Constitutional, Legislative, and Judicial Committee of the Knesset would prepare a series of "Basic Laws" which, after being adopted by the Knesset, would form the Constitution of the state (5 *Divre HaKnesset* pp. 1721-2, 1743).

Since that Resolution, eight Basic Laws have been adopted by the Knesset, namely:

Basic Law: The Knesset (1958),
Basic Law: Israel Lands (1960),
Basic Law: The President of the State (1964),
Basic Law: The Government (1968),
Basic Law: The State Economy (1975),
Basic Law: The Army (1976),
Basic Law: Jerusalem, Capital of Israel (1980), and
Basic Law: The Judiciary (1984).

(An authorized English translation of the above-mentioned laws can be found in the appropriate volumes of the annual government publication: *Laws of the State of Israel*.)

Two more Basic Laws have been prepared by the Constitutional, Legislative, and Judicial Committee of the Knesset, namely "Basic Law: The Bill of Rights", and "Basic Law: The Legislation". However, they have not as yet been adopted by the Knesset. None of these Basic Laws deal explicitly with the division of roles between the executive and legislative branches in the field of foreign policy.

The status of the Basic Laws, as distinguished from other laws, is not clear and there exist different views on this subject among legal authorities. Some claim the absolute supremacy of all clauses of the Basic Laws over all other laws so as to invalidate those clauses in regular laws which contradict any clause in a Basic Law. Others hold the view that no supremacy exists at all and that only the importance of the matters dealt with by such laws entitled them to be called "Basic Laws", so that a Basic Law can be amended or repealed by a later law of the Knesset, whether entitled a "Basic Law" or not. The prevailing opinion, however, is that only those provisions of the Basic Laws that are entrenched are supreme to other laws and that any law in contradiction thereof is therefore void. A decision to this effect was given by the Supreme Court sitting as a High Court of Justice in Bergman *vs.* The Minister of Finance [23 *Judgements of the Supreme Court* (I), 1969), p. 693]. The proposed "Basic Law: The Legislation" states the rule of supremacy of the entrenched clauses of the Basic Laws and provides for a procedure before a special Constitutional Court which can declare any law which contradicts an entrenched provision of a Basic Law void, if not enacted in all stages of its enactment by a special majority of the Knesset, required for the amendment of the entrenched provisions. Article 5 of this bill also requires a majority of two thirds of the members of the Knesset for the adoption of a Basic Law or for its amendment.

Besides being the consitutent assembly and the legislative body, the Knesset is also the body which has the duty "to bring forth" an effective government—the executive—and to control it. Before the enactment of "Basic Law :The Government" the Knesset-Government relationship was governed by the Transition Law 5709-1949 (*Laws of the State of Israel*, vol. 3, p. 3) as amended during subsequent years.

The main means by which the Knesset controls the Government is via the Government's need to receive the confidence of the Knesset, to which it is collectively responsible. Accordingly, when a Government is formed it must present itself to the Knesset, announce the basic lines of its policy, and ask for an expression of confidence. The Government is then constituted only after and only for as long as the Knesset has expressed confidence in it. In the case of non-confidence, the Government shall be deemed to have resigned (Articles 3, 4, 16 and 24 of "Basic Law : The Government," *Laws of the State of Israel*, vol. 22, p. 257). It should be noted, however, that a Knesset which brings about the resignation of one Government and does not bring forth another in its place that enjoys the confidence of the Knesset must enact to dissolve itself (Article 34 of "Basic Law : The Knesset", *Laws of the State of Israel*, vol. 12, p. 85). The dependence thus created between the legislative and executive bodies establishes a balance of power between them which insures their proper functioning.

Needless to say, a Government which wants to stay in power will seek to get the support or the control of the majority of the members of the Knesset.

In addition to the need of the Government to seek the confidence of the Knesset, the Prime Minister and each of the other Ministers of the Government have to make a declaration of allegiance to the State of Israel and its laws, and pledge to carry out their functions and comply with the decisions of the Knesset

(Article 16 of "Basic Law : The Government"). The exact meaning and constitutional significance of this declaration, which obviously refers also to the relationship between the Knesset and the Government, apparently giving supremacy to the decisions of the Knesset, was debated in the Knesset as early as 1951, and has not yet been resolved. On 21 May 1951, six separate motions were presented to the Knesset, each of which purported *inter alia* to direct the then Interim Government to release certain persons interned by executive order on suspicion of forming part of an ultra-religious underground movement, and to bring them to a speedy trial. The Speaker, doubting whether the Knesset could debate "an order" to the Government, referred this procedural question first to the Knesset Committee and eventually to the Knesset itself. During the debate which followed, the supporters of the respective motions advanced a threefold argument : that the Knesset is sovereign and, therefore, may adopt any resolution which it deems proper; that there is no constitutional doctrine of separation of powers and therefore the Knesset may give Ministers administrative directions; and that if the motions were passed then the Ministers must, pursuant to their declaration, put them into effect. The opponents, while admitting that there was no formal constitutional separation of powers in the laws, argued that "informal" constitutional boundaries existed separating the legislative from the executive functions which ought never to be violated by the Knesset, for otherwise it would be usurping the powers of the Government and upsetting the established constitutional balance. A Minister, so it was asserted, is not bound by law or conscience to carry out resolutions which the Knesset "constitutionally" ought not to adopt, especially where the resolutions are in conflict with the discretion vested by law in him. A resolution directing the Government to perform, or refrain from performing, an administrativ eact pursuant to its legal powers is not a "constitutionally" binding resolution (9 *Divre HaKnesset* p. 1802 and seq.). The view that the Knesset "ought" not give the Government administrative directions in an area delegated by law to the latter may be sound. It is nevertheless assumed from this debate that if the Knesset chooses to give such directions, they must be obeyed : an established Government cannot disregard them without resigning. In the actual case under consideration a compromise solution was eventually worked out—the Knesset decided to avoid the constitutional issue and voted on the motions themselves (9 *Divre HaKnesset*, p. 1922 and seq.).

The question of the legal validity of the basic lines of policy laid down by a government while seeking the confidence of the Knesset was raised in 1971 when the Government agreed after discussions with the Government of the United States of America to enter into political negotiations which could lead to a partial arrangement in the Suez Canal area. Knesset Member Menahem Begin argued that such negotiations were in contradiction to the basic lines of the Government which were approved by the Knesset on 15 December 1969, according to which "without a peace treaty, Israel would maintain in full the situation as it was at the time of the cease fire." (Statement to the Knesset by Prime Minister Meir, reproduced in its English version in *Israel's Foreign Relations, Selected Documents*, vol. II, p. 883). The issue was referred to the Attorney General of the Government who ruled that the basic lines are not laws and not even a decision of the Knesset. They are a summary of the programme operation of the Government and not normative rules. Such programmes may be changed in case of changes in circumstances. He ruled, however, that it would be proper for the Government to bring to the knowledge of the Knesset a material change in its basic lines in order to keep the confidence of the Knesset (Directives of the Attorney General, no. 21.410 of 1.1.72). The Attorney General also ruled that the Government is not legally bound to cease operating in a matter which is under debate in the Knesset so long as the matter has not been embodied in a law (Directives of the Attorney General no. 21.460 of 1 May 1970). In this respect, it should be mentioned that on 23 November 1977, Member of the Knesset M. Shahal repeated in a Private Bill a suggestion of Mr. Begin according to which if the Knesset has decided to debate a matter in plenary or to refer it to one of its committees the Government cannot take any action on the matter until the completion of the debate. The Minister of Justice, Mr. S. Tamir, saw in this approach intervention of the legislative authority in the areas of function of the executive authority. The matter was referred to a committee but no further action was ever taken (*Divre HaKnesset*. vol. 81, p. 510).

The constitutional and parliamentary role of the Knesset is also exercised through its Standing Committees, which have a strong impact on the activities of the Government. According to Article 21 of "Basic Law; The Knesset", the Knesset is empowered to elect Standing Committees from among its members and to establish other committees for specific purposes. This article also states that the functions of the committees, their powers, and their procedures will be defined in the Rules of Procedures of the Knesset except when defined by law. Such Rules of Procedure (hereafter, the Rules) were adopted by the Knesset on 26 July 1967 and published (*Reshumot*. Yalkut Hapirsumim no. 1420, p. 590). They have since been amended. The law does not mention the various special committees and leaves them to the Rules: it does, however, sometimes refer to the Standing Committees and specifically names them and their spheres of competence. Thus, for example, the Foreign Affairs and Defence Committee is given the power to approve certain orders of the Minister of Defence with regard to the mobilization of reserve forces for special duties, which is a power of subordinate legislation [Defence Service (Consolidated) Law, 1959, sec. 26(b)]. The membership of the committees is chosen in proportion to the parties' strength in the Knesset, thus safeguarding the rights of minority parties. At present, the Knesset has ten Standing Committees, of which the Foreign Affairs and Defence Committee deals with the foreign relations of the State. These committees are considered to be auxiliary instruments for the greater specialization and efficient dispatch of Knesset business.

Each of the Standing Committees is given an area of governmental activity as its sphere of competence. Within this area the committee is primarily concerned with legislation referred to it for consideration by the Plenary of the Knesset. However, in practice it also deals with other matters sent to it by the Knesset. Under its terms of reference it may also demand "explanations" and "information" from a Minister, who is bound to comply with such requests on any subject to which his responsibility extends [Rule 13(b)]. Although a Standing Committee possesses the power to act, in practice it does not act as a primary instrument of direct control over the Government. However, its recommendations or its views have great weight on the activities of the Ministries. This stems from the very nature of the relationship between the Knesset and the Government, which is founded on mutual trust and cooperation.

To the power of control of the Knesset over the Government one should also add its power to control the State Budget and finance, its responsibility for the institution of the State Comptroller, and its right to ask for information. The control over the budget is through the need of enactment of a law which will annually fix the budget of the State [Article 3(a) (1) of "Basic Law: The State Economy"] and for the need of a law in order to impose taxes. As to the State Comptroller—this institution was established by the State Comptroller Law (Consolidated Version) 5718-1958. In the exercise of his functions, the State Comptroller is responsible only to the Knesset and is independent of the Government. The functions of the State Comptroller are stated generally to be the examination of the finances of the State and their administration of the economic enterprises of the State and its property, and the carrying out of the various other duties specified in the law. As to its power to ask for information, three specified instruments exist. Any member of the Knesset may ask a "notice question" (Rules, 37-44) or for a "motion" [Rule 71]. Also, the Knesset is empowered under Article 22 of "Basic Law: The Knesset" to establish commissions of enquiry—either by empowering one of its Standing Committees or by establishing an ad hoc committee among its members —in order to inquire into matters decided by it. The powers and functions of such committees are fixed by the Knesset and each commission must include representatives of parties who are not members of the Government, according to their party strength in the Knesset. The powers of inquiry of such commissions do not include the power to force witnesses to appear nor the power to force them to testify under oath. Without such powers the practical effectiveness of such commissions is doubtful.

A "notice question" may be asked by any Member of the Knesset on any matter of fact entering into the sphere of functions of the Minister who is called upon to reply. The question is presented to the Speaker of the Knesset who decides on its admissibility. In fact, the Rules put very few restrictions on the contents of such questions. They may deal with any conceivable governmental activity, ranging from matters of grave international importance to those of purely personal and individidual interest. Ministers are questioned in direct proportion to the interest taken by the public in their activities at a given time. As in many other matters, it may be fashionable at times to question particular ministers. The Rules, however, make inadmissible questions which contain irrelevant or defamatory matter or matter injurious to public morals or to the dignity of the Knesset. Hypothetical or abstract legal questions are likewise not allowed. The questioner must be informed of a decision not to admit a question with the reasons thereof. A Minister may decline to answer for any one of a number of reasons: the matter "may not fall within his sphere of functions" (if it falls within that of another minister, the question will then be transmitted through the Prime Minister to the proper Minister), the matter may be wholly outside the "answer authority" of any Member of the Government: or to answer "publicly" may be injurious to the State (Rule 411). In the last case, the question was raised as to whether a Member of the Knesset may ask that the answer be given to him privately. This question was referred to the Attorney General and his answer was negative (Directives of the Attorney General no. 21.417 of 1 July 1974). The High Court of Justice stated in HCJ 37/79 Bogdenovsky *vs.* Minister of Culture [33 *Judgements of the Supreme Court* (2), p. 66] that a Minister does not have the duty to reveal the sources of information on which he bases his answers even if it offends the questioner. The questions must be answered within 21 days and a period of half an hour is devoted twice each week to the answering of questions. Each question is published and tabled, and the Minister— or another Minister representing him or his deputy—reads his answer to the Knesset.

A notice question may be a matter of grave concern to a Minister and his governmental department. The procedure helps to enforce Ministerial responsibility, provides some check on the departments, and is used quite often. During the last session of the Knesset almost a thousand questions were presented, almost 80 per cent of which were answered.

According to Article 31 of the Rules, the daily agenda of the Knesset is fixed by the Speaker of the Knesset upon the "recommendations" of the government. Under Rule 34, the Government is entitled at any time and without prior notice to make a statement to the Knesset, in which case—upon the request of 30 members of the Knesset—a debate may follow 24 hours later. In fact, the Government, if it so wishes, may monopolize the Knesset's agenda and attention. A motion presented by a Member of the Knesset will be included in the agenda unless it implies an insult to a person or a judgement against a person, or concerns a matter which is sub judice (Rule 71d). Any member may also propose a matter to be included in the daily agenda as a matter of urgency. During the last session of the Knesset a total of 443 motions were presented.

A motion of no-confidence may be proposed only by a Knesset party either as a separate item on the agenda or at the close of a debate on any other item. Such a motion takes precedence over any other item on the agenda, but cannot be voted on the day it is proposed. The Government may, however, make any issue a matter of "confidence" and announce in advance that a certain vote will be considered a vote of confidence (*8 Divre Haknesset* 980, 1103, 1109) or subsequently decide that a defeat will entail its resignation. In order to prevent such a situation, Article 5 (b) of "Basic Law: The Government" states that the Prime Minister has to be chosen from among the Members of the Knesset and that the other Ministers may be chosen also from among the Members of the Knesset. In fact, Members of the Government are usually Members of the Knesset, and lead their respective parties in the Knesset. Their presence in the Knesset strengthens their responsibility to it and facilitates the cooperation between them and the legislature. It is through their influence that the Government is able to muster the necessary Knesset support for its programmes and policies. They also insure that members of their parties will be represented on the various committees and that their voice will be heard in the more important Knesset debates in proportion to their relative parliamentary strength.

It should be noted that the Governments of Israel have always been coalitions of two or more parties and, under the existing system of election by proportional representation it is not likely that any party will secure an absolute majority in the Knesset. The power of the parties is accordingly reflected in the work of the Knesset. In addition, the Rules provide that some of the more important debates in the Knesset are to be conducted along party lines. These debates include those on the establishment of a Government and its resignation, motions proposing a vote of no-confidence in the Government, the proposal of the budget, debates on foreign affairs and defence policies, and certain other matters that the Government has informed the Speaker that it will treat as a vote of confidence. Furthermore, any matter that ten Knesset members, or two parties having a total membership of no less than eight, request to be debated along party lines is so debated. The Knesset Committee allots the overall time for such a debate and this is divided among the parliamentary parties according to their relative strength. The Rules provide that a member from the largest opposition party shall open the first round of the debate, to be followed by a member from the largest Government party (Rules 45-47). The system provides the Knesset with inner stability, helps to ensure the maintenance of the rights of minority parties, and provides an effective balance between the Knesset and the Government.

The Government and its General Powers

In spite of its formal subordination to the Knesset, Governments in Israel have also from a parliamentary point of view, distinct areas of action, powers and responsibilities, most of which are not defined by law. The "Basic Law: The Government" does not define the powers of the Government and only states that the Government is the Executive Authority of the State. Under Article 14 of the Law and Administrative Ordinance 5708-1948 (*Laws af the State of Israel*, vol. I), all the powers which were conferred by law upon His Britannic Majesty or one of his Secretaries of State, upon the High Commissioner for Palestine the High Commissioner in Council, or the Government of Palestine were conferred to the Government, except for the power to legislate. Also, under Article 29 of "Basic Law: The Government," the Government possesses the residuary power to perform any action that has not legally been conferred on any other authority. To these powers should be added those few which are specifically conferred by law to the Government. Under Article 31 (a) of "Basic Law: The Government," the Government has the power to divest any Minister of powers directly bestowed upon him by Knesset legislation and assume such powers itself or transfer them to some other Minister. It is generally held that the Government has an inherent power to initiate, formulate, and execute policies which would best serve the interests of the State. It is furthermore presumed to have "implied and resultant powers" to serve such interests.

Ministers charged with carrying out Government policy in their respective departments have the following powers: those directly conferred by an enabling statute on individually-designated Ministries, and those which have been initially vested by Knesset legislation on the Government and which have later been transfered by it to designated Ministries. Such powers include those of the former Mandatory Government vested in the Government by Article 14 (a) of the Law and Administration Ordinance. Each Minister is responsible in his individual capacity before the Knesset for the acts of his department. However, as in England, it is not clear in which cases he should resign from his ministerial office and this may change in each case according to the circumstances. This was the view of the commission which was established by the Government on 18 November 1973 under the Investigation Commission Law 5729-1968, after the Yom Kippur War in order to investigate the events which preceded the war, including the activities of the civil authorities and of the ministerial level. In order to protect a Minister from recriminations in the Knesset, a Government may invoke collective responsibility by notifying the Knesset that the defeat of a particular Minister will be considered a defeat of the entire Government.

As to the powers referred to in Article 14 of the above-mentioned Ordinance, there is a legal discussion as to whether they include the preprogative powers of the Crown, especially those in the field of foreign relations—Acts of State—such as the power to declare war, to negotiate and conclude treaties and ratify them, the recognition of States and foreign Governments, the establishment of diplomatic relations, the granting of diplomatic status to representatives of foreign States—in fact all legal acts concerning external relations. The issue of the interpretation of Article 14(a) of the above-mentioned Ordinance was dealt with in case 5/65 (A.G. *vs.* Kamiar, *Judgements of the District Court*, Vol. 51, p. 13). In that case, a request of extradiction by Switzerland on the basis of an extradiction convention between Switzerland and Israel was being considered. A question arose about the power of the Government to conclude a treaty and to ratify it. The judge was of the opinion that Article 14(a) refers only to the law which was in force in Palestine. However, in his view, it includes the British Foreign Jurisdiction Act of 1890, which is the basis of the jurisdiction of the Crown over dependent territories including the mandatory territory of Palestine and, through that Act, the prerogative powers of the Crown have become a part of the legal system of Israel. Other authorities base the incorporation of the prerogative powers of the Crown in the legal system of Israel through the Common Law, which is binding in Israel as long as recognised by the courts. Others claim that these powers are inherent to any Government according to international law. (For the different views, see A. Rubinstein: *The Constitutional Law of the State of Israel*, 3rd ed., 1980, pp. 350-361). In the appeal of the above-mentioned case [Kamiar *vs.* A.G. Criminal Appeal 131/67 22 *Judgements of the Supreme Court* (2) p. 89], the Supreme Court based the power of the State to conclude treaties and to ratify them on its general powers to conduct the affairs of the State and the constitutionally consistent usage in Israel according to which all the treaties subject to ratification were in fact ratified by the Government without the participation of the Knesset. In this respect Justice H. Cohen rejected the approach of those who appeal to the pre-State powers of the British or Mandatory Governors in order to find the general and basic powers of the authorities of the State. Practice over the years has confirmed the existence of these executive powers in the Government of Israel (See Michael Brechner: *The Foreign Policy System of Israel: Setting, Images, Process*, 1972, pp. 126-133).

In what follows, we shall concentrate on the foreign-policy powers of the executive in Israel and especially on its general foreign policy power, its power to conclude and ratify treaties and its relation in this regard with the legislative body—the Knesset.

The Powers of Conclusion and Ratification of Treaties

The position of the Government of Israel with respect to

the powers of conclusion and ratification of treaties was stated in its Memorandum of 11 March 1951 addressed to the Secretary General of the United Nations (United Nations Legislative Series, *Laws and Practices Concerning the Conclusion of Treaties*, New York, 1953 ST/LEG/Ser. B/3 pp. 67-72) and is summarized as follows:

(a) The legal power to negotiate, sign, and ratify international treaties on behalf of Israel is vested exclusively in the Government of Israel and is in the charge of the Minister of Foreign Affairs.
(b) Where the Knesset has given its approval to the ratification of the treaty, the act of ratification is signed by the President of the State.
(c) Where the President of the State performs acts connected with the treaty-making power, the documents have to bear the attesting signature of the Minister for Foreign Affairs acting on behalf and under the authority of the Government.
(d) General parliamentary control over the actions of the Government in the sphere of treaty-making power is exercised by means of the procedure of performing motions of non-confidence.
(e) If the international treaty necessitates changes in the domestic law, the Government will not normally ratify the treaty until it is apprised of the attitude of the Knesset.

While the power of the Government to conclude treaties has not been challenged, several attempts have been made in the Knesset to restrain its power of ratification or at least to insure more involvement of the Knesset in this sphere. The challengers of the Government's position generally base the power of the Knesset to ratify treaties on Article 6 of the Transition Law, 1949 (*Laws of the State of Israel*, vol. 1, pp. 9-10) which provides that "the President of the State shall sign treaties with foreign States which have been ratified by the Knesset." This provision has since been repealed by Section 26 of "Basic Law: The President of the State". It has been reproduced, however, almost word-for-word, in Section 11(a)(5) of said Basic Law (see

R. Lapidoth, *La Conclusion des Traites Internationaux en Israel*, 1962, p. 73, and A. Rubinstein, *op. cit.*, p. 370). The Government opposes this view and gives a restrictive interpretation of that section. As stated in the above-mentioned memorandum: "...[It] means that when in fact the Knesset has expressed its approval to the ratification of the treaty, the act of ratification will be signed by the President. In other cases, the act of ratification may be signed by the President or by the Foreign Minister...." The issue arose in the Knesset in 1949 when the Government introduced the Crime of Genocide Bill. The Minister of Justice made it clear that the Government intended to deposit its Instrument of Ratification of the Genocide Convention after the adoption by the Knesset of the domestic bill. Mr. Warhaftig, M.K., challenged the practice followed by the Government and tabled a motion providing that "the Knesset resolves to ratify" the Genocide Convention (*Divre HaKnesset* 3, pp. 315, 321). This was countered by the Government's own motion saying that "the Knesset recommends to the Government to ratify" the Convention. The compromise formula finally adopted by the Knesset provided that "the Knesset resolves that ratification be given" to the Convention (*op. cit.*, p. 345). This compromise formula left open the question as to the true meaning of the provision contained in section 6 of the Transition Law, and the Government could thus continue to apply its restrictive interpretation.

The whole issue was raised again in 1962 when Mr. Riftin MK tabled a Private Member's Bill to amend the Transition Law by adding a new section which would have provided for international treaties to be ratified by the Foreign Affairs and Defence Committee of the Knesset or, upon the request of at least one third of the Knesset Members, by the Knesset Plenary (*Divre HaKnesset* vol. 35, p. 782). In the explanatory note to his Bill, Mr. Riftin stated that Israel's existing practice constituted a serious departure from the accepted democratic patterns and that his Bill was aimed at a practical solution to the problem. In the discussion in the Knesset on 7 January 1963, the then Minister of Justice Dr. Dov Joseph reiterated the Government's position on this matter by pointing out that the Knesset's supervisory authority over the Government's activities through its power of bringing down the Government by a vote of confidence was a sufficient safeguard. He also made the point that treaty-making as such fell exclusively within the sphere of the Executive and any encroachment by the legislative branch on the executive responsibilities would greatly affect the separation of powers essential in any democratic state. At the same time, the Minister of Justice pledged the Goverment to inform the Knesset about the contemplated conclusion of treaties by bringing the text of such treaties to the knowledge of the Knesset after they had been signed and prior to their ratification, provided that they are not mere "routine" treaties having no special significance or only little significance (*ibid.*, p. 773). The Minister did not, however, specify what treaties he regarded as falling within these categories and he proposed to distinguish between "important" and "less important" treaties. The Knesset defeated the Bill by a vote of 42 to 26.

The matter was brought up again in 1964, when Section 11 of the "Basic Law: the President of the State" (which, as already mentioned, is similar to Section 6 of the Transition Law) was debated. Prof. I.H. Klinghoffer, M.K., severely criticized the Government's practice in the field of treaty ratification and characterized it as illegal (*ibid.*, p. 2034). He suggested that the possibility of "tacit ratification" be also recognized in those cases in which no request to discuss a treaty was forthcoming from at least 15 Members of the Knesset within three months after the treaty had been brought to the Knesset's knowledge. Likewise, Mr. E. Meridor, M.K., criticized the Government's practice and said that if the Knesset's powers remained a dead letter, it would be more dignified to delete them from the new law. Mr. Kushnir, M.K. preferred that a treaty be signed on behalf of Israel only after it had obtained the Knesset's approval. The Knesset defeated all the amendments. On the following day, Mr. Riftin, M.K., reintroduced his Private Member's Bill, with the same result as in the previous year. The Knesset by a vote of 31 to 14 refused to place the matter on its agenda (*Divre HaKnesset* 40, pp. 2048-2051). On this occasion the Minister of Justice once again pledged the Government to its earlier undertaking to communicate to the Knesset, whenever possible, the text of "important" treaties about to be concluded by Israel, prior to their ratification by the Government (*ibid.*, p. 2050).

Practically, until 1974 the Government's statement had been almost totally disregarded. The only instance of a treaty that was laid on the table of the Knesset until then concerned the amendments to the Charter of the United Nations relative to the enlargement of the Security and Economic and Social Councils. These amendments were ratified by the Government on 25 April 1965 and laid before the Knesset on 24 May 1965. However, even in this case the amendments were communicated to the Knesset after, and not prior to, ratification by the Government.

In 1974, the Disengagement of Forces Agreements between Israel and Egypt and between Israel and Syria were brought by the Government to the Knesset for its approval prior to their entering into force (*Divre HaKnesset* 69 p. 12, p. 60, p. 74; *Divre HaKnesset* 70, p. 1509). In 1975 the Interim Agreement with Egypt was brought to the Knesset for approval prior to its full signature (*Divre HaKnesset* 74, p. 4134).

In 1978 and 1979, two important agreements and a treaty were brought by the Government for the approval of the Knesset prior to their ratification: the Camp David Accords (The Framework for Peace in the Middle East; and A Framework for the Conclusion of a Peace Treaty between Israel and Egypt) between the Governments of Israel and Egypt, signed in Washington on 17 September 1978, and the Treaty of Peace between Israel and Egypt, signed in Washington on 26 March 1979 (*Divre HaKnesset* 83, pp. 4058, 4192; *Divre HaKnesset* 85, p. 1898). (For the English text, see "*Israel's Foreign Relations, Selected Documents*, Vol. V, pp. 544,685.)

On 28 July 1981, the Protocol between Israel and Egypt on the Establishment of a Multilateral Force in Sinai, together with its annexes and letters, was brought by the Foreign Minister for the approval of the Knesset prior to its ratification. On 11 May 1983, the Agreement between Israel and Lebanon was brought by the Foreign Minister for the approval of the Knesset prior to its ratification. Also, some international economic agreements were brought to the knowledge of the Knesset: the Agreement between Israel and the European Community of 1975 (*Divre HaKnesset* 73, p. 2730); and the Free Trade Agreement of 1985 between Israel and the United States of America. An additional attempt was made in 1983 and 1985 to legalize the Knesset's involvement in the ratification of treaties. In 1983, Mr. A. Rubinstein M.K. presented a Private Bill according to which the Government would put on the table of the Knesset every treaty subject to ratification and then Members of the Knesset would have the right to ask for debate on that treaty. Mr. Rubinstein withdrew his Bill following a recommendation to the Government by the Minister of Justice which was adopted as an amendment to the Government Regulations regarding the procedure for international treaty ratification, according to which an international treaty, prior to its inclusion on the agenda of the Government for the purpose of being ratified, will be sent by the proposing Minister to the Secretariat of the Knesset for the information of the Members for a period of two weeks, unless the proposing Minister's opinion—with the approval of the Ministers of Foreign Affairs and Justice—is that such forwarding is impossible for reasons of urgency or security. The Government may decide that a specific treaty, due to its importance, shall also be submitted to the Knesset for approval or ratification. Any action taken by the Knesset in respect of the treaty, according to the Knesset Rules shall be reported to the Government by the Minister responsible during the debate on the ratification of the treaty in the Government session (Government Resolution 534 of 25 March 1984).

During the debate on Mr. Rubinstein's Bill the Minister of Justice reiterated the position of the Government that the conclusion of treaties is an integral part of the responsibility of the Government to conduct foreign relations, which power is exclusively vested in it and that there is no place to involve the Knesset in this process except for instances when the Government, at its discretion, decides that a treaty of special importance will be brought before the Knesset for approval, as was done in the case of the Camp David Accords and the Peace Treaty with Egypt.

This new procedure is now generally followed.

The Knesset and General Foreign Policy

Even though the Knesset has no direct role in foreign policy—because of its interdependence with the Government, the system of elections and its composition as a House of parties, rather than a House of individual representatives of the electorate—the Governments of Israel have taken care, even when not asked, to regularly inform the Knesset Foreign Affairs and Security Committee (hereafter, the Committee) of its activities and eventually to ask for the Committees's support and approval. Whenever information is requested from the Government by the Committee, it is accurately provided. The Committee usually meets weekly when the Knesset is in session, but special meetings are also held during the parliamentary recess and when circumstances so require. The Committee pledges its Members to secrecy and this secrecy is generally kept. It has always exerted intangible influence on Israel's foreign policy and its participants are as a rule highly qualified. It reflects the Knesset's pulse in foreign affairs and when considerable opposition is reflected in the Committee's debates, the Government will generally withdraw its intention to adopt or apply the measures sought and will not try to bring the matter to a vote at the Plenary of the Knesset. Important issues are also brought directly to the knowledge and for the approval of the Knesset plenary. Whenever dissatisfied with the information provided, Members of the Knesset do not hesitate to resort to the parliamentary means embodied in the Rules such as motions for the agenda, urgent motions, motion for a debate, and, as a last resort, motions of no-confidence.

Opposition blocs which present motions for no-confidence do not really believe that they will succeed in upsetting a Government. Such actions are generally considered to be a way of showing strong opposition to the policy of the Government in a certain field or, sometimes, an attempt to divide the coalition on a issue in which there exist contradictory views within the coalition itself. However, in spite of the fact that the results of a vote of no-confidence are generally predictable, there is always tension in the coalition parties when such a move is made and preparations are made to block this move.

During the first twenty years of the State's existence, foreign policy issues have not been a major obstacle to coalition-building of Israeli Governments nor has foreign policy been decisive in the general elections. This has also been reflected in the Knesset's debates. However, in the last nineteen years, foreign policy issues have had a considerable impact on general elections and this was accordingly reflected in the Knesset's work, especially in the increasing consultations between the Government and the Committee and in the long debates following Government statements to the Knesset on foreign policy. Some important Government decisions on foreign affairs have also been brought by the Government to the Knesset for approval. For example, the Government's decision to endorse the United Sates Peace Initiative and the text of its reply to the United States was brought to the Knesset for approval on 4 August 1970. It was approved by a vote of 66 to 22 with 9 abstentions. On that day, the Ministers from the Gahal bloc submitted their resignation to the Prime Minister, thereby bringing to an end the existence of the Government of National Unity, which had been instituted on 1 June 1967, on the eve of the Six Day War.

The seriousness with which Governments of Israel regard the Knesset and the Committee is reflected in the following words of Prime Minister Rabin, which are part of his statement of 16 July 1975, given in reply to a motion calling for a foreign policy debate :

> The Knesset in Israel does not suffer from a paucity of foreign policy debates. This applies to the Plenary and especially to the Defence and Foreign Affairs Committee. The Government takes pain to supply a continual flow of detailed information, including classified information, on matters of foreign and defence policy. It is only natural that discussions, both in the Defence and Foreign Affairs Committee and in the Plenary, have focused on the question of the Interim Agreement beetween ourselves and Egypt. Since the end of March, the problems connected with an Interim Agreement have been reviewed and discussed in the Defence and Foreign Affairs Committee eight times with my participation and twice with that of the Foreign Minister, and I am glad to note the fact, a welcome one in the life of a democratic society, that the Government feels itself under the watchful eye of the Defence and Foreign Affairs Committee and willingly accepts the situation.

> No one can have any doubt that the Government will take

the initiative for a comprehensive foreign policy debate when the negotiations on the Interim Agreement reach a stage that will enable it to submit to the House a decision and all the data serving as a basis for it. We have not yet reached such a stage. I should like to assure you that the Government needs no reminders on the need for a foreign policy debate. (*Israel's Foreign Relations, Selected Documents*, vol. III, p. 254)

As foreseen, the agreement was indeed brought for the approval of the Knesset by Prime Minister Rabin on 3 September.

The Sri Lanka Parliament and Foreign Policy

SHELTON U. KODIKARA

Foreign policy is not a subject that can easily be brought within the purview of parliamentary control. The necessity to ensure secrecy in diplomatic negotiations, the need for quick responses to international crisis situations and for foreign policy decisions to be made even when Parliament is in recess or under dissolution, have all subordinated the role of Parliament in democratic politics in the matter of foreign policy decision-making.[1] The ineffectiveness of democratic decision-making in foreign policy has been commented upon since Alexis de Tocqueville averred in his classic *Democracy in America* that foreign policies demanded scarcely any of those qualities which a democracy possessed, but required, on the contrary, all the faculties in which they were deficient, a sentiment which has been echoed by a number of more recent writers as well as practitioners of the art of diplomacy. Pointing out that objective information about power, institutions, outlook and policies of other States were vital to foreign policy formulation, Max Beloff, for instance, held the view that "it is not clear that democracies normally appreciate the significance of this factor... and it is probable that their institutions are often ill-designed to give it proper weight."[2]

Democratic decision-making in foreign policy is under compulsion to cater to the public mood, to present foreign policy in terms which are believed by the power elite to be acceptable to public opinion, and decision-makers tend to pose as the advocates of public preferences in foreign policy even more than actually might be the case. It was Joseph Frankel's view also that "as large clumsy bodies, parliaments cannot effectively exercise initiative, and [that] their participation upsets diplomacy."[3] The case against democratic decision-making in foreign policy was especially that public opinion might be peculiarly subject to making emotional preferences rather than rational choices (the assumption being that elite decision-making must necessarily be rational), that public opinion is often misinformed about the facts of a given case, and that such decision-making entails delays which might defeat the pursuit of a State's interests. As Walter Lippmann pointed out :

> Even when there is no deliberate distortion by censorship propaganda, which is unlikely in time of war, the public opinion of masses cannot be counted upon to apprehend regularly and promptly the reality of things. There is an inherent tendency in opinion to feed upon rumors excited by our own wishes and fears.[4]

Whatever the drawbacks of democratic decision-making in foreign policy, legislatures in democratic polities do enter into the decision-making process, to a greater or lesser extent, depending on the nature of the Constitution, the nature of the issues involved, and the personalities involved in the decision-making process. Congressional participation in foreign-policy decision-making in the United States may be an exceptional case, but in general terms the Eastonian formula of "input-output-feedback" can be regarded as the norm determining the decision-making process.[5]

For thirty years, from 1948 to 1978, the Prime Minister stood at the apex of the foreign policy decision-making process in Sri Lanka. Section 46(4) of the Independence (Soulbury) Constitution required that the Prime Minister should also hold the portfolios of Defence and External Affairs, and even when this constitutional requirement was done away with under the First Republican Constitution in 1972, the then Prime Minister Mrs Bandaranaike, continued to hold these portfolios until the change of Government in 1977. After the July elections, Mr

J.R. Jayewardene as Prime Minister retained the office of Minister of Defence but but for the first time appointed a separate Minister of Foreign Affairs. When the new Government, first by a constitutional amendment, then by an entirely new (Second) Republican Constitution, instituted a Presidential form of Government in place of the Westminister model, Mr. Jayewardene as first executive President, Head of State as well as Head of Government, continued to impart initiatives, and give direction on important foreign policy issues apart from conducting personal diplomacy in his official capacity, as when he led the Sri Lankan delegation to the Sixth Non-Aligned Summit held in Havana in 1979.[6]

In this regard President Jayewardene was merely continuing a long established tradition in foreign policy decision-making in Sri Lanka, where the Head of Government has customarily had a large, perhaps the largest say in the formulation of foreign policy. The situation was not unlike that which obtained in India, where Nehru combined the offices of Prime Minister and Minister of External Affairs in his person for the first seventeen years of Independent India, becoming during this period "the philosopher, the architect, the engineer and voice of his country's policy towards the outside world."[7] Since 1948, eight different persons have held the office of Prime Minister in Sri Lanka and one of these the office of executive President since 1978. If we exclude the present Prime Minister who has no formal foreign policy responsibilities, and the caretaker administration of W. Dahanayake (September 1959 to March 1960), every other Head of Government in Sri Lanka has had his or her personal style and personal influence on foreign policy decision-making. From a decision-making point of view, this holds good even for the various administrations of Dudley Senanayake (1952-53, March-July 1960, 1965-70), which generally adopted a low profile in foreign policy. D.S. Senanayake's foreign policy, for example (1948-52) veered towards strong support of the Commonwealth, the connection with which was considered to be the essential condition of Sri Lanka's security, Sir John Kotelawela's term 1953-56) was marked by a strident anti-communism, S.W.R.D. Bandaranaike (1956-59) articulated an eloquent, often rhetorical Nehru-style non-aligned philosophy, while Mrs Bandaranaike developed a special relationship with

China but at the same time emerged as one of the Non-aligned Movement's most ardent advocates. The quiet diplomacy of the present Minister of Foreign Affairs (Mr A.C.S. Hameed) has been especially adept in his dealings with the Arab world, but the special links forged by this Government with Japan, to some extent also the revival of the old partiality towards Britain and, of course, the pronounced 'tilt' towards the United States, are clearly due to decisions and attitudes emanating from the President's House.

No approximation to the Congressional-style committees on the American model were set up in Sri Lanka's Parliament after the adoption of the Presidential Government under the Second Republic in 1978, and in fact, all executive powers including defence remain firmly vested in the President of the Republic. However, by the expedient of the amendment of Standing Orders of Parliament, Sri Lanka has, since 1978, established Ministry Consultative Committees on the Indian and French models, though if we are to go by the Indian experience, this departure is not likely, and in fact has so far not had, any visible impact on foreign policy decision-making.[8]

Even so, it is in Parliament that the most important discussions on foreign policy take place. A specific issue of foreign policy might lead to the discussion of a substantive motion; or a foreign policy statement of the Prime Minister/Foreign Minister may lead to debate; or foreign policy generally may be discussed in the context of the debate on the Throne Speech or President's Address, or the appropriation Bill when the votes of the Ministry of Foreign Affairs are being discussed; or an Opposition Member of Parliament may move the suspension of Standing Orders to discuss a current topic of international affairs. Further, the Foreign Minister, or someone on his behalf, is obliged to reply to the Opposition at Question Time, and on all these occasions the Prime Minister/Foreign Minister and other Members of the Government are called upon to defend their policies. The Minister of Foreign Affairs, therefore, will not easily expose himself to the criticisms of the parliamentary Opposition by espousing a controversial foreign policy unless it is an important article of faith in the party programme. During the period 1948-56 there existed a fundamental divergence of approach between Government and Opposition on important foreign policy issues in Sri Lanka, and the parliamentary debates highlight this divergence.

The divergence existed both in respect of the Defence Agreement signed on the eve of Sri Lanka's independence by the United National Party (UNP) leadership with Britain and the pronounced anti-Communist, pro-Western bias in Sri Lanka's foreign policy during this period. UNP foreign policy was based on an articulated antipathy to Communism and on perception of a threat to the newly established parliamentary institutions from communist subversion in the island. Preservation of Western-type parliamentary institutions was, therefore, a basic factor which determined relations with the West. "As far as the United States is concerned", said D.S. Senanayake, first Prime Minister of Sri Lanka, "there is not the slightest doubt that she holds the view that we hold. That is, they are for democracy."[9] J.R. Jayewardene, then Finance Minister in the Senanayake Cabinet put the case even more unequivocally:

> In this world today there are really two powerful factors, the United States of America and the USSR. We have to follow either the one or the other. There can be no halfway house in the matter. We have decided, and we intend as long as we are in power, to follow the United States of America and its democratic principles.[10]

However, it was not the United States that Sri Lanka looked to for guidance and leadership in her foreign policy during this period; it was the Commonwealth, particularly Britain, which became the sheet-anchor of Sri Lankan policy. The policy laid down by D.S. Senanayake, that friendship with Britain was Sri Lanka's greatest security, was closely adhered to by both his UNP successors during this period, who tended to regard the Commonwealth as a kind of third force in a world of power blocs headed by the United States and the USSR, in which Britain's role was seen as that of mediator and preserver of the peace. The fact that Britain was herself a member of the North Atlantic Treaty Organization and, therefore, an integral part of the collective security arrangements in the Western world did not appear to deflect Senanayake from this view. Nor did any UNP Prime Minister during this period consider their avowed policy of non-alignment to be contradicted by Sri Lanka's Defence Agreement with Britain.

By this agreement, it had been provided that the Governments of the United Kingdom and Sri Lanka would give to each other "military assistance for the security of their territories, for defence against external aggression and for the protection of essential communication," and for this purpose the United Kingdom was authorized to base in Sri Lanka naval and air forces and land forces "as may be mutually agreed," including the use of naval and air bases and ports, etc. At the time of its negotiation there was hardly any threat to the military security of Sri Lanka, and Jennings' view that D.S. Senanayake signed the Defence Agreement rather as an inducement to Britain to hasten Sri Lanka's independence than for any military purpose seems plausible.[11] However, the British bases in Sri Lanka acquired for UNP Prime Ministers an unintended value as an insurance against a vaguely formulated threat from India, and there is no doubt that they also regarded them as strengthening Sri Lanka's role as a bastion of anti-Communism in Asia and providing the necessary military security in case of an overt Communist threat. In Sri Lanka opinion against the Defence Agreement and the maintenance of British bases was not confined to the Marxist opposition parties. Especially after the establishment of the South East Asia Treaty Organisation in 1954, there was a wide consensus outside UNP government circles that the bases were inconsistent with the policy of neutralism professed by the Government and that they would inevitably draw Sri Lanka into the conflict with the power blocs. In February 1955, C. Suntheralingam, an Independent M.P. gave notice of a motion of No Confidence in the Government for its failure to terminate the Defence Agreement with Britain.

UNP Prime Ministers of this period insisted that Sri Lanka's defence commitments with Britain were not a permanent arrangement and that, as Prime Minister Sir John Kotelawela put it, "we are masters of our own naval and air bases and we can certainly ask Britain to quit them at a moment's notice."[12] But this claim was dubious. Though technically the use of the bases was subject to prior permission of the Government of Sri Lanka being obtained, Opposition spokesmen frequently charged that British fighter plane bases on Trincomalee were being used, without the Sri Lanka Government's specific permission, for action against Malayan Communists in 1948.[13] In 1950, Sri Lanka granted harbour facilities to an American flotilla on its way to Korea, and when asked whether this did not conflict with the policy of non-alignment professed by the Government, D.S. Senanayake declared :

> I do not see any reason why facilities which were available to the Americans in the past should not be available now.[14]

And in 1954, during the later stages of the battle of Dien Bien Phu, the Kotelawela Government granted the United States permission to route American military aircraft carrying French paratroops between France and Hanoi through the airbase at Katunayake. On all these issues, there was a wide gulf between Government and Opposition both inside and outside Parliament. The anti-Communist orientation of Governments of this period culminated in Sir John Kotelawela's celebrated assault on "communist colonialism" at the Bandung Conference in April 1955. When Sir John returned home from that Conference, he had to face a vote of No Confidence in Parliament.

Another dimension of foreign policy on which divergence was reflected in Parliament was in respect of Sri Lanka's attitude to India, and the role of Trincomalee bastion of the island. Government spokespersons generally tended to lump India together with the Communist powers as a threat to the independence and integrity of Sri Lanka, and therefore regarded the Defence Agreement and the connection with Britain as affording the island a security from both kinds of threats. This was well reflected in the statement attributed to Kotelawela in a public speech made in 1955 that "the day Ceylon dispensed with Englishmen completely, the island would go under India".[15] In September 1954, Kotelawela had given expression to his fears of India in a speech in Parliament referring to the scholar-diplomat K.M. Panikkar's alleged statements that India "must have Trincomalee for her safety:"

> I have also heard that Mr Panikkar is supposed to speak

for Pandit Nehru. He is supposed to know Pandit Nehru's thoughts and has said that India, Ceylon and Burma must have a Monroe Doctrine, that India will be the father of the two children, Burma and Ceylon. We do not want that. We do not want that fatherly advice nor their protection. We want Trincomalee for our use.[16]

Panikkar denied having made any statement claiming Trincomalee for India. Pandit Nehru himself repudiated the suggestion that Panikkar spoke on his behalf or on that of the Indian Government.[17] As far as he was aware, no one had said so far that India must have Trincomalee, nor was it correct that any kind of Monroe Doctrine had been put forward either by himself or on his behalf.[18] Despite these denials, however, apprehensions of India continued to exist in UNP circles, and the view that India had designs on Trincomalee was shared by prominent politicians even outside these circles.[19]

However, all sections of the parliamentary Opposition were strongly critical of the UNP policy towards India. Until 1951, the parliamentary Opposition consisted mainly of the Trotskyite Lanka Sama Samaja Party (LSSP), the Communist Party (CP), the Tamil Federal Party, and the Ceylon Indian Congress (CIC, now CWC denoting Ceylon Workers' Congress). In 1951, S.W.R.D. Bandaranaike, until then a Minister in the UNP government, crossed the floor and formed a parliamentary group of a new political party, the Sri Lanka Freedom Party (SLFP) consisting of several erstwhile Government supporters, and after the 1952 elections, he became the Leader of the Opposition.

Bandaranaike had been a Minister in the UNP Cabinet when it passed the basic legislation dealing with the citizenship status of persons of Indian origin in Sri Lanka. But while subscribing to the underlying purpose of that legislation, which was to restrict the number of Indians admitted to Sri Lanka citizenship, Bandaranaike criticised that handling of the issue by the UNP, especially under the premiership of Sir John Kotelawela. He was particularly concerned about the impact of the citizenship question on general political relations between India and Sri Lanka and accused Kotelawela of having "dissipated that degree of close friendliness that existed between us here and the Prime Minister of India."[20] He stated it as his opinion that "amongst all those in authority in India the one friend that Sri Lanka has over this issue is the Prime Minister of India Pandit Jawaharlal Nehru,"[21] and thought that UNP Governments were losing valuable time and opportunities in not negotiating a solution of this problem.

Other Opposition parties were unanimous not only in rejecting the basic principles of the Government's citizenship and connected legislation as being rigid, restrictive and discriminatory to persons of Indian origin in Sri Lanka, but they firmly believed that successive UNP Government were relying on their friendship with Britain to safeguard themselves against India. As the Leader of Opposition (Dr. N.M. Perera) but it in 1948 :

> There is a feeling among sections of the Government and the UNP that we have to safeguard ourselves against India, that we have to fight against India, and that therefore, it is necessary that we must lean upon Britain for the purpose. There is a feeling like that throughout the country among certain sections of the population. I say that it is political myopia of the worst type.

There were, no doubt, other grounds as well for the Opposition criticism of the British bases in Sri Lanka. The inconsistency of these bases with policy of neutralism professed by UNP Governments was one such consideration, but their significance in the context of Indo-Sri Lanka relations was a factor particularly important in the genesis of Opposition attitudes. A former Secretary of the CIC wrote in 1950 :

> It would indeed be a sad commentary if Ceylon entertains such apprehensions [of expansionist designs by India] and attempts to bang the door against India by keeping Great Britain pitched against the Indian sub-continent.[23]

The fact that the bases could hardly have been seen in this light by Britain herself is irrelevant to the point at issue. The statements of UNP spokepersons, as well as those of Opposition critics, support the view that the Commonwealth link, that is to say the Defence Agreement of 1947, was seen by the Sri Lanka Governments of the period 1948-56 as affording, among other things, a measure of security against India.

The election of S.W.R.D. Bandaranaike to power in April 1956 therefore signified a momentous change in Sri Lanka's policies, especially in its foreign policy orientation. In his very first Statement of Policy to Parliament, Prime Minister Bandaranaike declared:

> In its foreign policy, my Government will not align itself with any power blocs. The position of the bases at Katunayake and Trincomalee will be reviewed. Every endeavour will be made to establish close collaboration and cooperation with other countries. Consideration will be given to the exchange of diplomatic representation with countries in which Ceylon is not at present represented.[24]

And Bandaranaike forthwith proceeded to exchange diplomatic representatives with the Soviet Union and the People's Republic of China, and in 1957 took over the bases at Trincomalee and Katunayake from Britain. Nor did Bandaranaike entertain suspicions about the designs of 'international Communism' or fears of India, as his predecessor in office had done. The SLFP inaugurated an era of a balanced relationship with India, based largely on the personal rapport between Jawaharlal Nehru and Bandaranaike and, later on that of Indira Gandhi and Mrs. Bandaranaike. On the eve of his taking office as Prime Minister, Bandaranaike had said:

> I visualise much more friendly relations and closer cooperation between myself as Prime Minister of this country and Pandit Nehru as Prime Minister of India in dealing with not only problems affecting our two countries and Asia but general world problems.[25]

Later, he stated publicly that "in many matters conncerning international affairs, I happen to hold views not dissimilar to those held by Mr Jawaharlal Nehru,"[26] and during the short tenure of his premiership (1956-59), Bandaranaike attempted to give content to the policy of non-alignment, or neutralism as he sometimes called it, in Sri Lanka's approach to world affairs. The divide between Government and Opposition in foreign policy gradually began to lose its sharpness, with the major political parties adopting a consensus position that non-alignment was the basic foreign policy orientation of Sri Lanka, a position which was symbolised by the succession of President J.R. Jayewardene to the Chairmanship of the Non-Aligned Movement after Mrs Sirimavo Bandaranaike's own tenure of that office until she was defeated at the polls in April 1977.

This consensus was well illustrated during the debate on the suspension of US economic assistance to Sri Lanka in 1963 in retaliation against the Sri Lanka Government of Mrs Bandaranaike when it nationalised the import and distribution of petroleum in the island. All political parties represented in Parliament were strongly critical of the US action, and the UNP leader Dudley Senanayake went so far as to say that the US would be "well advised to take some lessons in the manner of dealing with these questions from other nations in the world who have done so for a much longer time and who would, I think, certainly not have rushed in this hasty manner . . ."[27]

It was not that the party consensus now extended to all issues of foreign policy. One particular issue of political controversy in the party during the first adminsitration of Mrs Bandaranaike (1960-65) was her "special relationship" with the Peoples' Republic of China, which became a feature of her non-aligned diplomacy, but which was in effect a continuation of the opening to the PRC initiated by S.W.R.D. Bandaranaike in 1957. One feature of this diplomacy was her non-aligned stance over the India-China border dispute and in the India-China war of 1962, a stance which did not detract from the good relationship which she always maintained with India and Prime Minister Indira Gandhi personally, and which also enabled her to take the initiative in convening a six-nation non-aligned Afro-Asian Conference in Colombo on 10 December 1962 to mediate in the dispute.[28] When Mrs Bandaranaike visited Beijing in January 1963, she signed a Joint Communique with the Chinese Premier Chou En-lai which stated, among other things, that Sri Lanka and China were "bound by many ties of friendship, economic co-operation and cultural and religious exchanges" and that the two Prime Ministers were "determined to strengthen these ties, further develop economic co-operation between the two countries and to work together in international relations in the cause of Asian-African solidarity and world peace."[29]

In pursuance of this policy Sri Lanka and China entered into a Maritime Agreement in July 1963, which gave most favoured nation treatment to the contracting parties in respect of commercial vessels engaged in cargo and passenger services to and from the two countries or from a third country. A similar agreement had been entered into between Sri Lanka and the Soviet Union in Febuary 1962, and a Sri Lanka Government spokesman, denying anything sinister or circumspect in these agreements, had expressed the willingness of the Government "to sign similar agreements with any country with whom we had diplomatic relations and who wished to conclude such agreements.".[30] Notwithstanding these explanations, the Maritime Agreement with China became a big issue of party political debate in Sri Lanka and the debate widened into a divergence between Government and Opposition on the general issue of relations with the PRC itself. The Leader of the Opposition, Dudley Senanayeke, made much of the fact that the 'vessels' mentioned in the agreement were mercantile vessels only, and that it required six months notice of termination, the implication being that Sri Lanka was entering into what amounted to a security relationship with China, and that China was virtually being permitted to establish a bridgehead in the strategic port of Trincomalee. This issue, and the larger one of the alleged increasing Chinese influence in Sri Lanka were actually important debating points in the general election of March 1965, which led to the return of the UNP to power under Senanayake for the next five years, although the Senanayake Government did nothing during the entirety of its five years in office to revoke the Maritime agreement which had been so sharply derided while the party was in opposition.

During the late sixties, and certainly with the inauguration of Mrs. Bandaranaike as Prime Minister and Minister of Foreign Affairs for the second time, in July 1970, a greater all-party consensus on foreign policy issues was emerging in Sri Lanka. This was reflected in the parliamentary debates, and the greater emphasis given, within the Non-Aligned Movement itself, to economic issues and problems of development in Third World countries, implying a greater measure of all-party agreement on the basic issues of non-alignment. This was symbolised by the fact that Sri Lanka's Chairpersonship of the Non-Aligned Movement (1976-79) straddled the tenure of power by Mrs. Bandarnaike (SLFP), as well as that of J.R. Jayewardene (UNP). In handing over the Chairmanship of the NAM to President Castro at the Sixth Non-aligned Summit in Havana, President Jayewardene said:

> In our own national and historical context, [therefore], the choice of Non-Alignment as the guiding principle of our foreign policy was an obvious one. Successive governments in Sri Lanka have adhered to this principle because it is rooted in a set of fundamentals which no government can vary or seek to vary, unless it chooses to destroy our political and philosophical heritage.[31]

At the Seventh Non-aligned Summit in New Delhi in March 1983, Jayewardene reiterated these views, declaring that "our commitment to the principles of Non-Alignment remains undiluted and our unity in defence of these principles unimpaired."[32]

There were, to be sure, new areas of disagreement and party political debate which cropped up between the UNP and SLFP after the UNP's return to power, which had coincided with the advent of the Janata Government in India, leading to a kind of euphoric identification of interests between the two parties, a euphoria which was shortlived, however, because Mrs Indira Gandhi and the Congress Party made a dramatic comeback to power in 1980. Mrs Gandhi had not taken kindly to the imposition of civic disabilities on Mrs Bandaranaike by the Jayewardene Government. She could hardly forget the derogatory allusions to the cow and calf election symbol of the Congress Party, allusions which were widely believed to be snide remarks about the role of mother and son in the politics of India as well as Sri Lanka. The soured relationship was spoilt still further by the pronounced pro-American tilt which marked the foreign policy of the Jayewardene government. When the ethnic problem flared up into crisis proportions in and after July 1983 therefore, India began to take a close interest in developments in Sri Lanka, which in turn led to allegations by Sri Lanka of Indian 'interference' and 'intervention'. Whether Mrs Gandhi was really seriously considering a military option against Sri Lanka in the context of the island's ethnic crisis will remain a matter of controversy. But certainly at the time of her death she was taking a hard line against the Jayewardene Government. Things have changed with the advent of the Rajiv Gandhi Government, but only marginally. From India's point of view, the big obstacles to restoring the former good relations with Sri Lanka are first, the continued existence of Tamil refugees from Sri Lanka in India; second, the continuing stalemate in the negotiations for a political solution of the ethnic problem in Sri Lanka; and third, Sri Lanka's attempts to obtain outside assistance for the prosecution of the military campaign against terrorist Tamils, e.g., from countries such as Israel and Pakistan, which are interpreted as the establishment of a 'security nexus' between Sri Lanka and these countries, From the Sri Lanka Government's point of view, the big grievance against India is its affording of sanctuary, and the status of political refugees to large numbers of Sri Lanka Tamils who have made Tamilnadu their base of guerilla operations against targets in Sri Lanka, and India's continued insistence on a quick political solution of the crisis when in fact militant leaders in Tamil Nadu are not really interested in any political solution of the ethnic crisis short of the attainment of the separate state of Eelam.

Since July 1983, parliamentary debates have increasingly begun to reflect the overriding importance of relations with India, and the two major parties are again on opposite sides of the divide, with the UNP seemingly harking back to its old pre-1956 stance of anti-Indianism, and the SLFP sounding the cautionary note and advocating the necessity of a balanced relationship with India.

In April 1984, for example, Leader of the Opposition, Anura Bandaranaike moved a Vote of No-Confidence against the Government on the grounds that it had failed to observe the principles of non-alignment, particularly by the manner of voting at the United Nations General Assembly on the debate on the issues of the Falkland Islands and Grenada (Sri Lanka having been lukewarm in its criticism of the US action in Grenada, and having voted on Britain's side on the Falklands issue). The debate turned out to be a slanging match between Government and Opposition spokesmen on Indo-Sri Lanka relations, the former being critical of the Indian tolerance of militant Tamils on its soil, and its dependence on Tamilnadu opinion on its basic approach to the ethnic crisis in Sri Lanka, and the latter stressing the vital importance of preserving friendly relations with India and personally with Prime Minister Indira Gandhi.[33] The Opposition allegation was that the Jayewardene Government were looking out for defence pacts to counter potential aggression from India, whereas as the Leader of the Opposition put it, "India was the best friend of SriLanka in the world today." The Government position was that the Tamilnadu Government, without any restraints from the Centre, had not only given asylum to Sri Lanka Tamil militants but also encouraged and allowed them to organise themselves against the established Government of Sri Lanka, and that allegations of defence pacts, of "selling Trincomalee to the Americans," were all without foundation.[34] Foreign Minister A.C.S. Hameed, attempting to place Sri Lanka's ethnic crisis in its geopolitical setting pointed out that a number of factors over the years since 1975 (the year of the first political assassination of an SLFP Tamil Mayor of Jaffna by terrorists) had 'soured' the relationship between India and Sri Lanka, that opinion had built up in the island that Sri Lankan Tamil terrorists were finding a haven in South India, that the Sri Lanka Government itself was veering towards the West, towards the US, and that the future status of Trincomalee was involved.

"In this basket," said the Minister, came the return of the US Peace Crops, the VOA agreement with the US, which was nothing new but which "had come down from 1951," so much so that he was not the creator of the problems with India, only their inheritor.[35]

And the Minister fully endorsed the proposal emanating from the Opposition Leader that Sri Lanka should enter into a Friendship Treaty with India, even on the lines of the Indo-Soviet treaty, and he expressed his willingness to enter into such treaties with all the countries of South Asia.

The current position in Indo-Sri Lanka relations was expressed on the floor of the House by Prime Minister R. Premadasa himself, ordinarily a strong critic of India's inaction in respect of the sojourn in India of Tamil terrorists, but who after talks with Rajiv Gandhi when they met at Harare to attend the Eighth Non-Aligned Summit, appeared to express a greater appreciation of India's role and attitude towards the Sri Lankan crisis. Declaring that he had requested Prime Minister Rajiv Gandhi to 'warn' terrorists to stop their activities against Sri Lanka from Tamilnadu soil, Prime Minister Premadasa said that Rajiv Gandhi himself found it difficult to help Sri Lanka without the support of Tamilnadu, and that was why he was anxious that a political solution of the crisis should be reached as soon as possible.

> There were good reasons for us to explain to the Indian Government the situation in Sri Lanka and how we feel about terrorist activities in Tamilnadu affecting us.[36]

Accordingly he had elucidated the Sri Lanka position in writing to the Indian Prime Minister, and he was sure that "we will receive the support of India to solve this problem through the political discussions now taking place in Sri Lanka.

In Parliament, as well as outside it, Indo-Sri Lanka relations have assumed primacy of place amongst all foreign policy issues facing the Government and, in the best traditions of parliamentary democracy, no opportunity is lost to clarify these issues and to debate them. What emerges from these debates and discussions is that in foreign policy there is a tendency to reach a bipartisan consensus, if not on the broad orientations, at least as far as the big neighbour to the north is concerned. At the same time, in Sri Lanka as among some other neighbours of India, the attempt to balance power with India in some way or other is also a continual quest among decision-makers.

Notes and References

1. For a more general discussion of foreign policy decision-making in Sri Lanka, see my *Foreign Policy of Sri Lanka: A Third World Perspective* (New Delhi, 1982), pp. 1-20
2. Max Beloff, *Foreign Policy and the Democratic Process* (Baltimore, John Hopkins Press), pp. 85-86.
3. Joseph Frankel, *The Making of Foreign Policy: An Analysis of Decision-Making* (London, 1963), p. 25.

4. Walter Lippmann, *The Public Philosophy*, p. 27.
5. Cf. *A Systems Analysis of Political Life* (New York, 1965).
6. The President does not sit in Parliament, though he can address it on occasion, and he therefore does not participate directly in foreign policy discussions at the parliamentary level, though as Head of State and Head of Government, in which capacity he presides over Cabinet meetings, his initiative is all-important on some issues of foreign policy.
7. Michael Brecher, *Nehru: A Political Biography* (London, 1959), p. 564, quoted in K.P. Misra, *Foreign Policy and its Planning* (Bombay, 1970). Misra writes that till 1962 or so, foreign policy remained Nehru's monopoly, and not much parliamentary or scholarly attention was devoted to it, "though traces of the tangential impact of certain individuals and institutions might be detected here and there". *ibid*, p. 20.
8. See Misra, *op. cit.*, pp. 34-44. An approximation to the American model, however, is provided by the creation of a Select Committee of Parliament to review higher Government appointments, including ambassadorial appointments.
9. House of *Representatives Debates*, (9150), Vol. 8, col.487.
10. *ibid*, col. 293.
11. See Sir Ivor Jennings, *The Approach to Self-Government* (Cambridge, 1956), pp. 50-51.
12. *Asian Recorder*, Vol. I (8) : 85.
13. See e.g., *House of Rep. Deb.*, (1948) Vol. 4, coll. 2007-08;, col. 1060.
14. *ibid*, (1950), Vol. 8, coll. 1856-60.
15. Reported in *The Times*, 26 May 1955.
16. *House of Reb. Dep.* (1954), Vol. 20, coll.50-52.
17. See *The Hindu*, 10 September 1954. Panikkar had, however, made a speech in Bombay about 2 weeks before Kotelawela's speech in which he had declared that India had made clear to foreign Big Powers that she would not tolerate any interference in the affairs of Nepal, Burma or Ceylon as countries lying within India's area of primary and strategic importance. *ibid*, 26 August 1954. See also M.S. Rajan, "Indian Foreign Policy in Action 1954-56", *India Quarterly*, 16:228-29 and n. 100, July-September 1960.
18. *Lok Sabha Deb.*, (1954), Vol. 4, Part I, coll. 1202-04.
19. See, e.g. *The Times*, 2 October 1956; R.G. Senanayake, a Cabinet Minister under UNP as well as SLFP regimes shared this view. See *Indian Express*, 18 July 1963; *Ceylon Daily News*, 16 July 1964.
20. *House of Rep. Deb.*, (1955), Vol. 253.
21. *ibid*.
22. *ibid*, (1948), vol. 4, col. 1696; see also vol. 5, col. 450
23. H.M. Desai, "Ceylon and India" *United Asia*, 2 : 374, April 1956.
24. *House of Rep. Deb.*, (1956), vol. 24, col. 25.

25. *The Hindu*, 8 April 1956.
26. *Ibid*, 7 October 1956.
27. *House of Rep. Deb.*, (1963), vol. 50, col. 2156. For J.R. Jayewardene's speech, *ibid*, 2033-61; and for the Government point of view, *ibid*, Coll. 1635-43 and *Senate Deb.*, (1963), vol. 18, coll. 1766-67.
28. For details, see my *Indo-Ceylon Relations Since Independence* (Colombo, 1965), pp. 55-58.
29. See *China Today*, No : 15, February 1963, p. 2.
30. *Times of Ceylon*, 11 March 1965.
31. *Tolerance, Non-Aggression and Mutual Respect. Text of Speeches by J.R. Jayewardene, President of Sri Lanka.* Department of Information, Sri Lanka, Colombo, 1979, p. 13.
32. *The Seventh Non-Aligned Summit, New Delhi : Statement by His Excellency J.R. Jayewardene, President of Sri Lanka, 8 March 1983.*
33. See *Parliamentary Deb.*, (1984), Vol. 28, coll. 1041 et seq.
34. *ibid.*, col. 1145.
35. *ibid.*, coll. 1150-54.

The European Parliament and Foreign Policy

JULIET LODGE

The European Community (EC) neither pretends to have nor seeks to devise a common foreign policy. Its 12 member States merely agree on the desirability of their consulting each other and exchanging information on their own national views of and intended actions in respect of foreign policy and international developments. However, the European Parliament's own role-perception in international matters is based on the premise that even in default of a common EC foreign policy, it should act as if there were one or as if one were possible. The European Parliament takes very seriously indeed its assumed role as the conscience of the European Community. Nowhere is this more evident than when it becomes the grand forum for debating matters of international moment.

In order to understand how the European Parliament's role in foreign policy has evolved, it is necessary first to ask why it should have felt that it should play any role at all in this area and second to place its development within its historical and political context.

Many parliaments in Western Europe have a minimal role in either scrutinising or influencing Governments' intended foreign policy actions. Many debate foreign policy and play a grand forum role but few are able to influence the actual elaboration, direction or content of foreign policy.

By and large, parliaments in Western Europe have less

extensive opportunities to survey and influence foreign policy than their counterpart in the United States of America. Indeed, since foreign policy-making is an executive process par excellence where the demands of international bargaining place a premium on secrecy and the sensitive handling of often delicate issues, it is hardly surprising that national parliaments should have no more than a peripheral role in the day-to-day conduct of foreign policy.

However, this does not mean that they are denied any role. Many covet their special links with sister parliaments overseas, and inter-parliamentary delegations and committee meetings are a useful means of reinforcing diplomacy or of circumnavigating other channels where communication may be fraught with or blocked for political reasons in the short term. Moreover, many parliaments do have formal constitutional roles to play in the ratification but not the negotiation of international treaties. As will become clear, the European Parliament's role in international affairs reflects national practices. But it also goes beyond them.

Perhaps the most important reason for this is that the European Parliament is one of the institutions set up with a unique international organisation whose working method is geared towards supra-nationalism and the ultimate integration (however that may be defined) of member States following the elimination of national barriers between them. Moreover, a foreign policy decision on the part of the member States led to the creation of the EC and its institutions. The latter's subsequent EC activities, however, ceased to be regarded simply as part of a State's foreign affairs. Instead, whole areas of policy have become domesticized and internalized.

The process of domestication has itself generated a new set of foreign policy issues. These have often been linked to trade matters. Indeed, as progress towards the customs union and the common external tariff was made, the member States insisted on maintaining the somewhat artifical and increasingly untenable distinction between 'external relations' and 'foreign policy'. This distinction has found expression in the divisions between 'low politics' and 'high politics' respectively. External relations embraced trade and technical matters often related to the international effects of the EC's commercial policy, the common agricultural policy, and other policies including steel and textiles for example. Foreign policy related to diplomatic relations, security and defence issues were pursued individually by the member States.

The distinction was clearly the product of the historical circumstances within which the member States operated when the EC was created. It seemed appropriate therefore during the 1950s when the establishment of the EC succeeded NATO and the failure to create the integrated European Community. Then, even more than now, States were more wary about undermining the EC's claim to be a 'civilian power,' devoid of imperialistic military intentions, through involving themselves in an organisation having clear-cut strategic implications and common foreign policies with all that implied for political integration. States like the Federal Republic of Germany were very sensitive to claims that the EC was the economic wing of NATO and others keen to attract additional members were anxious to ensure that neutral states would not be alienated.

The distinction between external relations and foreign policy was also useful in the context of the EC's member States' policies of decolonialisation; their reappraisal of their own positions in a bipolar international system; the creation of special relationships with former colonies and developing countries under the supra-national umbrella of the Yaounde, Arusha and Lome agreements; and the enlargement of the EC itself.

The significant weaknesses of that artifical distinction have become increasingly acute and the boundaries between external relations and foreign policy have become more penetrable and susceptible to erosion. The European Parliament has played no small part in accelerating this process. However, this erosion owes perhaps less to the 1970s idea of pentapolar diplomacy than to the difficulties the EC experienced in trade and aid links with both the developed and developing world. The Middle East and oil crisis underlined the inter-connectedness of security (high politics/foreign policy) and trade (low politics/external relations). It is no accident that the European Parliament's role in foreign policy should have grown since then. Nor is it unimportant that this growth coincided with a deliberate strategy on the part of Members of the European Parliament (MEPs)—

notably since the first direct elections to the European Parliament in 1979—to increase the European Parliament's role, influence and formal powers in the EC. What then is the European Parliament's role?

The European Parliament's Role

The increase in the European Parliament's role and activities in foreign policy spheres must be put in the context of the member States' attempts to institutionalise their own interests in exchanging information, consulting each other on, and where desirable coordinating, their own national foreign policy pronouncements and actions with their EC colleagues.

For some States, like the Federal Republic of Germany, the 'Europeanisation' of national foreign policy goals was a useful means of legitimizing and strengthening them. For others, like France and the United Kingdom, the EC has been as a means of maintaining a capacity to influence international affairs and to act on the world stage. The EC is an integral part of a design to maximize independence in an era of uncertain interdependence (outside the EC) and to balance the consequences with a lessening of the sponsor-client relationship with the USA.

France and the United Kingdom accord the above elements different emphasis and their tactics differ markedly. However, they share a commitment to the EC arena and, like the Germans, see it as a useful instrument of foreign policy. The smaller EC States, too, use the EC to enhance their European and international profiles. Moreover, as the world outside the EC has come to expect an EC voice on international developments, (and EC is represented within international organisations like the United Nations) the member States have become sensitive to the need to minimize the chances of others exploiting internal division or dissent. They have also felt it important to establish the distinctiveness of EC policies from those of the USA. This has been particularly important given large-scale overlapping memberrship between the EC and NATO and the diametrically opposed positions of the EC and the USA (even before the Mediterranean enlargements of 1981 and 1986 which accentuated such divisions) on several critical international developments.

There can be little doubt that the activities of the European Parliament and MEPs have contributed to this development. MEPs have helped to increase awareness of majority EC position, transcending national boundaries, on many issues. They have assisted the articulation, and to a lesser extent the formulation, of EC positions particularly when their own views and resolutions have presaged formal EC decisions.

While the European Parliament's role in elaborating EC positions must not be overstated, it must be noted that the timing of Plenary sessions, where international issues often figure prominently, rarely coincide with or precede relevant meetings of EC Foreign Ministers meeting either in Political Cooperation (EPC) or as the General Council. Nevertheless, such debates subtly shape EC positions and they always underscore the EC's commitment to its 'civilian power' image.

In examining the European Parliament's role in foreign affairs, it is necessary to differentiate its role in EC external relations matters from its role in respect of Political Cooperation (EPC). In both arenas, its roles are respectively defined either in the Rome treaties establishing the European Communities, or in the various agreements concluded since the inception of EPC up to the Solemn Declaration on European Union (Stuttgart 1983) and more recently the Single European Act (SEA). The latter was to enter into force in early 1987. In addition, the European Parliament is unlike many of its national counterparts in being able to set its own agenda. It has fully exploited this right to deal with foreign policy matters traditionally regarded as the distinct preserve of national diplomacy.

A further distinction needs to be made concerning the European Parliament's role in foreign policy. This relates to the international composition and activities of its political party groups. MEPs are, moreover, drawn from national parties—the major ones of which are themselves involved in international political movements and organisations that transcend EC and European boundaries. Moreover, the formation of 'inter-groups' (such as that on European Union created in September 1986 comprising members from several different party groups) could be significant in the longer term. Inter-groups may well seek to influence particular aspects of foreign policy on a deliberate, organised and sustained basis. They are effective in aggregating and articulating consensus views against Governments, and when general consensus seems elusive or ill-defined. This would offer the opportunity for a more directed, sustained, pro-active rather than reactive input into the policy process. While such activities may be limited to certain key issues they could be important as they would bolster and complement the present system of coalition-building on a rather ad hoc issue-specific basis.

The European Parliament's Formal Powers

The Rome Treaty stipulates instances where consultation of the European Parliament is foreseen. These are limited to accession and association agreements (articles 237 and 238 respectively) and to the conclusion of agreements between the EC and other States (article 228). The European Parliament has no right to be consulted on the common commercial policy and the elaboration of common policy in the field of external trade. However, the 'Luns-Westerpterp' procedure covering articles 113 (on the negotiation of commercial agreements) and 238 means that first the Commission (during the negotiation phase) and then the Council (after the agreement has been signed but before its entry into force) has to inform MEPs about the progress of negotiations via the appropriate committee of the European Parliament.

In practice, this means that the European Parliament has a negligible role. Even if it holds an 'orientation debate' before negotiations with third countries begin, the outcome neither binds the Commission or the Council nor necessarily influences in any way what follows.

The Single European Act (SEA) does little to alter the European Parliament's peripheral formal role in this field. Indeed, the new legislative cooperation procedure is limited in application to a few amended articles of the Rome Treaty (7; 8; 49; 54; 57; and 100). It excludes articles 28, 59, 70 and 84 which are amended to replace the unanimity requirement by qualified majority in the Council. Even though the European Parliament is given the right now to approve accession and association agreements, it is unlikely that new ones will be concluded in the foreseeable future. Therefore, its position is not greatly enhanced.

The SEA contains a separate title (Title III) regulating provisions on European cooperation in the sphere of foreign policy. This Title does not amend the Rome Treaty but it does codify and extend slightly the inter-governmental system of European political cooperation (EPC). Unlike in external relations, the European Community as such has no formal competence here. However, the Commission does participate in the quarterly meetings of the Ministers of Foreign Affairs; it is 'fully associated' with EPC, and shares responsibility with the EC Presidency for ensuring consistency between EC external policies and EPC matters.

The European Parliament (but not the EC Court of Justice) is recognised by Title III of the SEA. It is referred to as 'the European Parliament' rather than as 'the Assembly' implying a small but not completely insignificant upgrading of its status. The European Parliament is given the right to be 'closely associciated' with EPC. The Presidency is obliged to inform the European Parliament regularly about foreign policy issues being examined in EPC and has to 'ensure that the views of the European Parliament are duly taken into account.' This means that colloquies with the European Parliament's Political Affairs Committee are likely to become more important and their operation even more refined and streamlined than suggested even by the European Parliament's series of reports in 1977 and 1980-81 on aspects of inter-institutional relations and EPC matters. It is probable that the European Parliament's influence will be felt, at least informally, on EPC as a result. Moreover, the position of one or more Governments will inevitably enjoy a moral boost at least if supported by the majority of MEPs. Alternatively, Governments may allude to unsympathetic majorities in the European Parliament to justify their position in the Council.

While the European Parliament's role in EC external relations and EPC is limited, its actual activities in respect of foreign affairs is extensive. Part of this activity flows naturally from special consultative assembly arrangements set up under the Lome conventions between the European Parliament Members and Members drawn from Lome countries' parliaments. Part follows from the European Parliament's expansive interpretation of its own Rules of Procedure and its unique right to set its own agenda. Much follows from MEPs' appropriating the role of public 'conscience of the European Community' and from the various activities that reinforce this.

Moreover, the party groups themselves use their international contacts to advantage. This will be probed in a little more detail. The examination of foreign policy-making within party groups helps to elucidate and accentuate problems in creating consensus on foreign policy issues among a diversity of States whose Governments may change (and with them, the State's foreign policy) while policy is being elaborated simultaneously within a major party group like the European People's Party or the Socialist Group and other groups within the European Parliament.

It must be stressed that party group activity underlies all the work of the European Parliament. However, there can be little doubt that since the direct elections in 1979, the European Parliament's work and activities have become increasingly politicized and subject to party competition. This is true of all issue areas, whether concerned with domestic matters internal to one or more States, or concerned with specific EC issues relating either to existing internal policies, external policies or foreign policy cooperation. Moreover, the foreign affairs arena is one in which MEPs have sought to increase the European Parliament's role. This has happened either intentionally or sometimes unintentionally as the European Parliament's international standing has grown.

It will be useful to consider this increase in Parliament's role with reference to (a) its own agenda setting, (b) the work of its inter-parliamentary delegations, and (c) the elaboration of positions by the party groups.

Agenda-Setting

The most important opportunity that MEPs have to ensure that the European Parliament accords international matters a high profile is the right to hold debates on urgent topics. Questions to be dealt with under urgent procedure are given priority over other items on the Agenda. The latter include matters relating to EC legislation on which the European Parliament must issue its opinion; and committee reports (usually 30 per plenary); oral questions with debate; and Question Time sessions involving the Commission and the Council.

Strict time limits are imposed on speaking time and debate is regulated according to the Parliament's Rules of Procedure and by agreement with the President and the party groups. Question Time theoretically provides a vehicle for MEP's questions on international matters. However, for a variety of reasons, the Council representative replying to such questions may be less than forthcoming. MEPs have frequently complained about the evasiveness of answers from the Council compared to the Commission. Moreover, under EPC, questions are not admissible if they raise issues not already discussed in EPC; if they relate to the foreign policy of a particular EC State; if no EC common line exists; or if secrecy is necessary. Before the close of Question Time, however, any political group or at least five MEPs may request that a debate be held immediately on the answer given by the Commission, or Council of the Foreign Ministers meeting in Political Cooperation on a specific matter of general and topical interest. This debate is limited to one hour but does provide a means by which MEPs can try and influence the course of international affairs' deliberations and member States' foreign policies. Such interventions lack any legal effect, however.

Inter-Parliamentary Delegations

Relations between the EC and overseas countries and territories (OCT) were originally governed by Part Four of the EEC Treaty, in conjunction with implementing conventions where appropriate and later by the various protocols annexed to Acts of Accession. Indeed, enlargement negotiations have often boosted the role of the European Parliament vis-a-vis States seeking association and/or accession in that special parliamentary committees have been established, revivified and used until accession was completed. Thus, the committee with Greece (set up in 1962) was dissolved upon Greece's accession to the EC in 1981. That with Turkey (set up in 1964) ceased to meet when the Turkish parliament was suppressed. Provision was made for parliamentary relations with other Mediterranean countries but no formal procedures have been instituted.

Parliamentary arrangements have been set up with non-EC states having either pre-existing special relationships with a 'new' EC Member (for example, Australia and New Zealand in the case of British accession to the EC) or seeking a more wide-ranging dialogue with the EC through political as opposed to simply diplomatic channels.

The European Parliament has followed the example of national parliaments in establishing inter-parliamentary committee to foster good relations with parliaments in other countries of the world. Foremost among these is, of course, the Consultative Assembly established with the African, Caribbean and Pacific signatories to the Lome convention. This comprises two representatives per ACP State and an equal number of MEPs and ACP parliamentarians. Its meetings are prepared by the Joint Committee which meets twice a year, once in Europe and once in one of the ACP States.

Apart from the institutionalized parliamentary dialogue with the ACP countries, the European Parliament has also established a dialogue with two other groups of States : those who are members of the Association of South-East Asian Nations (ASEAN) and the ASEAN Inter-parliamentary Organization (AIPO), and more recently, with members of the 'Latin American Parliament'. The latter comprises delegates from Mexico, the Central American States, Brazil and members of the ANDEAN Parliament. This delegation has 36 members in all whereas most joint-parliamentary delegations comprise 10 members. Exceptions to this are those with ASEAN, China, Japan and Canada which comprise 18 members: and that with the USA which has 21 members.

Joint inter-parliamentary committees have often been set up on the initiative of parliaments outside the EC. Links are maintained by periodic meetings of delegations which examine matters of common commercial and/or political interest. For example, following Britain's accession to the EC, the New Zealand parliament set up links with the EP and talks take place on a regular basis, often coinciding with important junctures in the Council of Ministers' deliberations on butter quotas and prices for dairy and sheep meat exports. Inevitably, New Zealand's trading interests—particularly arrangements for the continued access at higher prices of its butter exports to Britain, and sheep meat exports—assume a high priority. In addition, French nuclear testing in the Pacific and the Greenpeace, 'Rainbow Warrior' affair along with other matters of common strategic interest have been discussed.

The range of issues discussed by joint-parliamentary delegations and committees is invariably broad and typically covers energy questions, agricultural trade, textiles, steel and international affairs. Inter-parliamentary meetings can help to stimulate and improve mutual understanding. At the same time, there can be little doubt that non-EC Governments see them as a useful way of reinforcing their own lobbying of the EC on issues. Indeed, it is not just the joint parliamentary committees and delegations that are lobbied but, increasingly, specific committees of the European Parliament and MEPs in general. Sometimes, inter-parliamentary committee meetings are preceded by a visit of the President of the European Parliament to the country in question for initial talks which can prove useful and productive. On other occasions, presidents of national parliaments and heads of state, including US President Reagan, President Sadat of Egypt (in 1981) and President Eanes of Portugal in 1978, have visited the European Parliament.

The first joint parliamentary delegation to be set up with a country that was not directly linked to the EC by virtue of association agreements, or agreements consequent upon the accession to the EC of a State like Britain, was that between the Congress of the United States of America and the European Parliament. This came into being in 1972 when the first of its twice-yearly meetings was held. Since then, the European Parliament has established parliamentary links with most countries having a system of parliamentary democracy. It also has links with other countries who are members of the Inter-Parliamentary Union. As of 1982, the following joint delegations (excluding those with the Spanish Cortes and Portuguese parliament) included :

EUROPE

—the Northern European countries (Sweden, Norway, Finland, Iceland) and the Nordic Council

—Switzerland
—Austria
—the Committee of EFTA Parliamentarians
—Yugoslavia
—the countries of Eastern Europe
—Malta
—Cyprus

NORTH AFRICA, the NEAR and MIDDLE EAST

—the Maghreb countries (Algeria, Morocco, Tunisia)
—the Mashrek countries (Egypt, Jordan, Lebanon and Syria)
—Israel
—the Persian Gulf States

THE AMERICAS

—the USA
—Canada
—Latin-American Parliament

ASIA and AUSTRALASIA

—the countries of South Asia (Bangladesh, India, Pakistan, Sri Lanka)
—the member States of ASEAN and AIPO
—the People's Republic of China
—Japan
—Australia and New Zealand

The European Parliament's influence on foreign policy is not, however, exercised exclusively or even primarily through these joint parliamentary committees and delegations. Rather, it must be remembered that the European Parliament's own committees which broadly parallel the responsibilities of the Commission, play a pivotal role in all aspects of the European Parliament's business.

At present there are 18 standing committees whose members are drawn from all party groups. Their membership is renewed half-way through the European Parliament's term of office, that is, 30 months after the direct elections. Fierce inter-party competition accompanies election to key political committees and characterises the election of committee chairmen and up to three vice-chairmen. These people form the committee's bureau. The party groups are able to appoint a number of substitutes (or supplements) equal to the number of their members on the committee. Other MEPs may attend all committee meetings as observers unless the committee determines otherwise.

Given the committee's major roles in the exercise of the European Parliament's advisory and supervisory functions and its wider role in the EC's legislative process, the role of rapporteur in each committee on subjects coming before it can be crucial. MEPs of certain nationalities endeavour to get onto committees where they can make their weight felt or where they can do their most—possibly as rapporteur—to ensure that the European Parliament's opinion on legislative matters reflects both their own country's concern and that of any third country whose interests may be involved. Thus, for example, British Labour MEPs were keen to ensure that they would furnish the rapporteur for deliberations on New Zealand butter imports when discussed in the Committee on Agriculture. Similarly, MEPs were heavily lobbied by business, American and corporation interests anxious to dilute the Vredeling proposals on industrial co-determination.

While it is likely that most, if not all, the committee will have interests in international affairs, a few committees naturally play a more prominent role. These include the committees on the following areas: Development and Cooperation; Agriculture; External Economic Relations; Political Affairs; Environment, Public Health and Consumer Protection; Energy and Research; Economic and Monetary Affairs.

The committees deal primarily with matters referred to them by Parliament meeting in Plenary session or, in-between part-sessions (as plenaries are called) by the President acting on behalf of the Bureau. They may also draft 'own initiative' reports on all manner of topics if so authorized by the Bureau. With the prior authorization of the enlarged Bureau they may appoint one or more sub-committees; and set up working parties to undertake specific studies or fact-finding missions. They may also invite experts and representatives from national and international institutions to participate in their meetings and hearings. Thus, the scope is enhanced for a two-way channel of communication between the European Parliament and third country interests.

Moreover, the Political Affairs Committee is entrusted with responsibilities that are very wide-ranging and include not only matters falling under the general rubric of political cooperation, but relate also to political and institutional aspects of relations with other international organisations and third countries; the political aspects of international problems; and problems concerning human rights in countries.

Such matters are frequently the subject of topical and urgent debate in the European Parliament. A political group or at least 21 MEPs may ask for a debate on a topical and urgent matter, and there has been a significant increase in the amount of time now given over to such debates and to discussions on 'own initiative' reports. About one third of requests for urgent debates are turned down, and between 33 and 45 per cent of such debates result in the adoption of resolutions under the 'urgent' procedure.

There can be little doubt that the European Parliament's international stature and profile has increased since 1979. Non-EC States and groups accord it more importance than internal groups and lobbying of the European Parliament by both domestic and foreign interests has grown. Since the European Parliament's ability to significantly influence, let alone alter, EC policy has been modest, the fact that it has become a lobbying point owes something to its image as a European Parliament independent of any particular national bias. Its foreign policy is not, therefore, simply a reflection of one dominant national position but rather mirrors a European consensus which itself is shaped by the multinational political forces within the European Parliament.

Party Groups and European Parliament Policy

When examining the role of the party groups in the formulation of positions that may eventually translate themselves into the European Parliament's 'policy' on a given international matter, it is necessary to distinguish carefully between EPC and external relations matters. As already indicated, although the MEPs are extremely active on matters of high politics and topical international issues, their influence on them is modest. Indeed, some MEPs now fear that with the Single European Act's introduction of a special secretariat for EPC and the continuing division between EPC and external relations matters, the European Parliament may be even more marginalized in the foreign policy sector. Now, more than in the past perhaps, it will indeed be necessary for MEPs to work with and through national governments and especially the Council Presidency in EPC in order to influence high political international issues on which the Community members wish, or need to be urged, to articulate a distinctive EC line. By contrast, the more technical aspects of external relations matters should remain slightly more amenable to influence from the European Parliament.

The crux of the problem for political groups wishing to influence policy is that the European Parliament's powers in international relations are largely declaratory. It may be convenient for the EPC President to be able to allude to MEPs' support for a given policy line but such support is rarely necessary. EPC Ministers are responsible to national parliaments, not to the European Parliament. The latter's need for information on foreign policy questions is extensive and not met in the same way that national foreign offices meet those of national governments. Therefore, the European Parliament and the party groups have an information deficit. This gap can only be partially closed by the efforts of party groups working both on their own account, sometimes competitively so, against other groups but also in accord with them. In addition the party groups have had some impact on persuading EPC Presidencies to provide information to MEPs on EPC deliberations shortly after EPC meetings so that MEPs would not have to rely on the press for such briefings.

Annual reports and European Council reports certainly provide an overall picture of EPC work but the more streamlined and focused colloquies have proved far more useful. Moreover, since 1982 Presidents of the European Council have followed the example of Belgian Premier Martens in April 1982 and British Prime Minister Thatcher in December 1982 in addressing the European Parliament immediately after Summit sessions. However, the importance of such addresses should not be overstated. They were started off, moreover, during the Falklands crisis and the Governments involved acted in a self-interested manner rather than primarily with the intention of keeping MEPs informed or informing foreign ministers of MEPs' views. Indeed, it would be unrealistic to expect much more given the nature of international diplomacy and the marginal role assigned by national governments to national parliaments. If this is the case, why do party groups in the European Parliament endeavour to influence EPC and external relations issues?

One of the answers to this question lies with the parties' self-image and own role conceptions. Another lies with their genuine desire to try and promote where feasible and desirable a genuine European policy line. Sometimes such a line will reflect virtually an all-party position. On other occasions, nuances or major policy splits will divide the main parties. An example of the former arose in February 1985 when six different reports on combating terrorism were tabled. Together they approximated a coherent whole but no single compromise text could be elaborated.

However, it is in the European Parliament's interest to secure consensus where possible, no more so than in respect of inter-parliamentary delegation meetings. For it is not just the opportunity for a formal exchange of views between parliamentarians that is important, but also the opportunity of visits (either in this context or in the context of working groups or fact-finding missions) that afford for informal meetings with others. For example, during visits to the US, contacts are maintained with the staff of the White House, the State Department, Treasury, functional ministries (like commerce and agriculture) and with trade and industrial organisations. These parallel and complement those which the ambassador to the US of the State holding the Presidency has. His role vis-a-vis other EC ambassadors is not unimportant.

How then do the major party groups operate with a view to influencing foreign affairs? If one takes party rivalry as a starting point, then there will be competition between the main parties to determine the European Parliament's line or to mobilize a committee in a certain direction, for example, in calling for an urgent debate. If one party group is better prepared than others, it may try to capitalize on its tactical advantage.

However, the mere existence of a party group does not imply that it will be easy to secure consensus within that group as to what the official party line should be on a foreign or domestic issue. Component national parties as much as the group itself usually want to make clear in public what their particular viewpoint is, so differences have first to be reconciled. Moreover, where deep-seated divisions exist between or within party groups, the Council's position can influence the European Parliament crucially. The converse is rarely, if ever, the case : MEPs' do not critically influence or alter the Council's position.

It must be said that party groups are in a weak position to influence foreign affairs. They have organisational problems that are exacerbated by information deficits in often fast-changing areas of international diplomacy. The cycle of the European Parliament's business complicates matters still further. Whereas the Council can convene within 48 hours for urgent business (as in the case of the US raid on Libya in early 1986), the European Parliament's cycle of plenaries in Strasbourg and committee meetings (mainly in Brussels) is fixed.

Before Plenary sessions and committee meetings, the national component parties of the European Parliament's party groups have to determine among themselves what their own position is. For instance, the British Labour Group within the EP Socialist Group, will be guided by national Labour policy as announced at their Conference or the National Executive Committee. The British Members of the European Democratic Group will be expected (by the British Government) to take their cue from the Government—an expectation that is not always fulfilled.

Assuming that the component delegations have decided a line, the EP party group has to determine its line. Internal discussions on different proposals may take place, working parties may be set up or called in for views, and the various party group leaders may then get together to see whether a multi-group resolution is possible. The likelihood of a successful outcome depends in part on the ability to muster majority support and hence to devise multi-party or all-party resolutions.

Clearly, the chance of a resolution either being noted by Council or influencing Council foreign policy deliberations is enhanced if significant majorities can be managed within the European Parliament.

Whereas so far, discussion has centred on the party groups' own efforts and personnel, it must be noted that the outcome depends as much upon successful manoeuvering by individual MEPs and the various national contingents as on EP party group officers. In addition, the party groups can and do avail themselves of the considerable expertise of the European Parliament's Secretariat. The latter provides not only administrative and drafting services and those of a general bureaucratic nature but is able to act politically in a discreet manner. This can be useful to the party groups in the development of a consistent line on a given foreign policy issue.

The development and maintenance of consistency and continuity in foreign policy are difficult to achieve both for the reasons outlined above and because foreign policy inputs by the European Parliament are typified by ad hoc arrangements in response to situations outside. However, there is growing evidence of a desire by MEPs to develop clear and consistent lines on a number of domestic and foreign policy issues. To this end, inter-groups comprising members from the European Parliament's party groups have been set up. Inter-party compromises can be elaborated within these groups with the aim of producing high profile, publicly visible consensus on important issues. This is no mean achievement for a number of reasons.

First, it demands that individual MEPs and national component contingents of party groups subordinate their individual particularistic desire to secure publicity for their own rather narrow positions to the projection of a European majoritarian consensual position. Second, it demands that positions are both policy-relevant and timely. Third, it means that worthy though declaratory statements may be, a prescriptive element has to be introduced that is realistic and practicable. Fourth, attention has to be paid to the possible reception outside the European Parliament and outside the EC to any pronouncements on international affairs by MEPs. This means that statements must be consistent with past statements where appropriate and that given policy arenas be closely monitored to allow for speedy additional parliamentary intervention if necessary. The administrative work consequent on this is great since a premium is placed on data collection and analysis and on forward policy planning and coordination.

Forward policy planning by the party groups has further implications for the European Parliament and for the general politicization of MEPs' political behaviour. Party groups vie for position and compete for majorities on major issues (for example, security) irrespective of whether or not the EC itself has legal competence for that area. They work also in non-EC international bodies in pursuit of objectives they wish to realize within the EC. Questions that may have had particular significance for a national contingent within a party group may become Europeanized so that it becomes possible to pursue parallel aims at the national, supra-national and international levels. Inter-parliamentary delegation meetings can assist this. For example, regular Conferences of the Presidents of European Parliamentary Assemblies are held. These involve not only the EC's national parliaments but also representatives from the Parliamentary Assembly of the Council of Europe and the Assembly of Western European Union. Cross-fertilization of ideas and the simultaneous pursuit of major issues can be valuable as has been shown recently in respect of EC measures to combat terrorism.

Conclusions

It is difficult to quantify the European Parliament's influence on foreign policy. However, even though its formal powers are very limited, the European Parliament expends a lot of effort in attempting to influence foreign policy inputs made by the EC. This involves a great organisational investment of time and resources and makes increasing demands on the administrative and research facilities of the party groups, their national components and the European Parliament's Secretariat.

Moreover, since the EC system is a fluid rather than a fixed one, the European Parliament's party groups have to be ever vigilant of the potential opportunities for influence that any procedural changes, budgetary amendments or domestic or international developments may afford them. It also means that the European Parliament and the party groups have to develop a 'foreign policy memory' so that changes in the European Parliament's composition consequent upon direct elections every five years do not result subsequently in contradictory policy statements or partial institutional amnesia. Moreover, where the European Parliament has had some impact upon foreign policy matters—such as on combating world hunger—MEPs must ensure that they reinforce any achievements.

The European Parliament's Development Committee heightened the profile of combating world hunger when, following the 1979 Euro-elections, it instituted a special study of the problem. Public hearings were held and a report published in September 1980. This did indeed influence both the Commission and the Council who followed in large measure many of the Report's policy guidelines. The then President-in-Office of the Council, Lord Carrington, even quoted the Hunger in the World Report as an example of the European Parliament having substantial influence over subsequent EC policy. For its part, the Commission in 1981 proposed an action programme with an exceptional grant of 40 MECUs. Following on from this, the European Parliament used its power to create a new item in the 1983 EC budget entitled 'The Programme for the Fight Against Hunger in the World.' The administration of such a programme by a special (non-parliamentary) committee, however, meant that MEPs' had no control over the next stage.

The problem of combating world hunger is one example of how MEPs may try to influence a foreign policy matter and how domestic constraints (bureaucratic, political or financial) can seriously and unintentionally undermine their achievements simultaneously. It illustrates moreover the problems consequent upon the disjunction between policy-initiating and legislative bodies (that is, the Commission and the Council of Ministers respectively) in the EC. The European Parliaments' good intentions can too easily be eroded unwittingly by the Commission and/or the Council. They can also be undermined by MEPs themselves oblivious to linkages between various intertwined policy sectors such as the Common Agricultural Policy, Development Policy and Expenditure. Making linkages clear and keeping them before MEPs can be facilitated by interparliamentary links. MEPs clearly need a vast amount of

The European Parliament and Foreign Policy

information to make decisions and to weigh up the costs of the sometimes incompatible choices they make. However, if the European Parliament's international stature is to grow and if the European Parliament is to effectively influence and contribute to the development of the independent European foreign policy consensus that is recognised as such by outsiders, then MEPs must use all the means at their disposal to exploit potential channels of influence and assist EC Member Governments in their attempts to do likewise. Whether the Single European Act will help this endeavour remains to be seen.

The New Zealand Parliament and Foreign Policy

RAMESH THAKUR AND ANTONY WOOD[1]

Modesty of involvement and influence of legislatures and legislators in foreign policy matters is typical of a parliamentary system of government. The reasons for this are well known. In the Westminster tradition, foreign policy has generally been regarded as the preserve of the executive. Furthermore, since foreign policy involves the affairs of state and the defence of the realm, a bipartisan approach to foreign policy has been encouraged on the argument that such matters should be shielded from the rough and tumble of party political polemics. National Interest, it has been argued, should prevail over narrow political advantage. Foreign policy has been seen to be the prerogative of the executive, and the executive has customarily been allowed unfettered latitude in the discharge of this function. The conduct of foreign policy, including overseas military engagements, declarations of war, and the negotiation and ratification of treaties, is the exclusive prerogative of the Crown advised by the executive government.

Responsibility for the conduct of New Zealand's foreign policy rests with the Minister of Foreign Affairs, and, acting under him, the Ministry of Foreign Affairs, the functions of which include "co-ordination between departments in all matters affecting New Zealand's interest overseas "(*Directory of Official Information*, 1983: 601). Parliament need be involved only if legislation is required or desired, and for voting funds. Only the

Crown can propose to Parliament any form of expenditure and, of course, rejection by Parliament is equivalent to a vote of no confidence. But if government requires or desires legislation, or needs supply, then it must go to Parliament.

In practice in foreign affairs there is very little legislation that can serve as the focus of parliamentary activity on a foreign policy issue, insulating much of foreign policy from the process of debate and scrutiny that bills encounter in Parliament. Apart from oral question period, or a special debate, that leaves debate on the government's estimates in committee of the whole as the occasion for executive-parliament dialogue, with a minister "in the chair" for his estimates, and his advisers close by, next to the Speaker's chair. For direct contact and exchange between advisers and parliamentarians there is the venue of the parliamentary select committee, which also provides opportunity for input to Parliament from both groups and individual citizens.

But perhaps the most important role of Parliament in foreign policy is that deriving from the basic character of the institution, as the forum for national debate, the educative body, processing and spreading information and declaring issues. For much of New Zealand's history, however, dependency and distance from world trouble spots meant that questions of defence and external relations rarely impinged upon domestic politics. The New Zealand Parliament's involvement in foreign policy was "negligible," wrote a Member of Parliament (MP) in 1976 (Marshall, 1976 : 75).

Only ten years later, Helen Clark, a Labour Government backbencher, could count "being influential in Labour's foreign policy" as one of her major achievements (Myers, 1986: 173). An increasingly active assertion of Parliament as the centre of foreign policy choices resulted from international issues impinging upon the consciousness of political parties and MPs to a greater extent than previously. While Parliament has always had several avenues of discussion of foreign affairs open to it theoretically, it is only relatively recently that it has chosen to travel down these avenues and confront the electorate with major foreign policy issue-oriented choices.

Background

It was not until 1947 that the New Zealand Parliament had extraterritorial jurisdiction, and before 1943 there was no annual vote specifically for foreign affairs. The sole, if long-standing overseas post, in London, came under the vote of the Department of Internal Affairs, and the only administrative unit for conduct of foreign affairs was, from the 1920s, a small Prime Minister's department.

The one significant aspect of external affairs which did come regularly before Parliament was the administration of overseas territories, principally the Cook Islands and the mandated Western Samoa, which until decolonisation in the 1960s involved both legislation and voting of supplies. There was a further major area of New Zealand responsibility, the Ross Dependency in Antarctica, claim to which New Zealand took over from the British in 1923; but for this territory government used its regulatory powers.

It was during the war years that modest steps were taken to create the formal administrative structures necessary for the conduct of foreign policy. In the war the United States assumed the role of protector, and Australia was New Zealand's most important regional ally: New Zealand opened posts in those countries in 1941 and 1943 (and also in Ottawa, 1942). The Prime Minister's department acquired a second, and more important, statutory identity as Department of External Affairs (renamed the Ministry of Foreign Affairs in 1970) with a separetely designated minister. It was not until 1975 that Foreign Affairs and Prime Minister's Departments were completely separated. The Prime Ministers of New Zealand have not uncommonly also held the Foreign Affairs portfolio: until 1949, and again 1957-72, 1972-75, 1984-87.

For much of the post-war period, as New Zealand developed new bilateral and multilateral relations—including a period of major expansion of overseas posts in the 1960s and 1970s—the ministry had a special status as principal adviser to the leader of the government, including over many years being the Prime Minister's own chosen major portfolio responsibility. The head of the department, in both his capacities (Secretary of External Affairs, and Head of Prime Minister's Department), was amongst the select group of top officials appointed by the government and not the public service commission: a status conferred in 1946 and lasting until all offices came under the commission in 1962. The department was located in Parliament Buildings, on the same floor as the Prime Minister's suite. In Parliament, both administratively and in policy, for many of the post-war years foreign affairs was the direct responsibility of the Prime Minister (who also, until the late 1970s, was House Leader).

It was in keeping with a special prime ministerial interest— and recognition of a low level of information of the world overseas—that in 1947 the government promoted establishment of a nine-man (later eleven-person) foreign affairs committee of Parliament. Unlike the several other parliamentary committees (all known as "select" committees), this one did not have specific chores to undertake —consideration of bills or recommendations to government on the prayers of petitions—but was simply a venue for discussion and briefings, sometimes of a confidential or quasi-confidential nature. Hence it did not report back to Parliament. A liaison officer from External/Foreign Affairs acted as committee secretary while his minister sat as a committee member. The committee could be a venue for government-opposition dialogue, and for the government it had the great merit of encouraging a bipartisan approach to foreign affairs, an approach well influenced by officials.

Bipartisanship and Division

Bipartisanship partly explains limited parliamentary involvement in foreign affairs in the years after the second world war. From the late 1960s, however, there were not only increasingly significant differences between the major political parties on key foreign policy issues, but also heightened awareness of such issues in the community at large.

In the post-war years, under the long-term Labour Government until 1949, and then the more conservative National Government of 1949-57, the principal issues were the relationship with the United States and New Zealand's involvement in South East Asia. In the early 1940s the war in the Pacific had shown that without the United States, New Zealand was defenceless; the danger, of course, came specifically from Japan, although it was communist expansionism which prompted introduction of compulsory military training in 1949. Hence, there was bipartisan support for the ANZUS Treaty of 1951 which linked Australia, New Zealand and the United States in a formal security pact. To the United States, ANZUS was part of a policy of ringing the Soviet Union and China with treaties, while for Australia and New Zealand, it was a protective alliance against Japanese resurgence. Hence, too, New Zealand participated in the United Nations action in Korea (1950-53), joined the South East Asia Treaty Organisation (SEATO) in 1954, supported Great Britain in the Malayan Emergency (1955-60), and fought alongside the United States for much of the Vietnam war (1965-72).

In the 1950s government, officials and opposition adjusted to the decline of Great Britain. Britain was not a party to the tripartite ANZUS Treaty, which for decades was deemed to be the cornerstone of New Zealand defence and foreign policy. New Zealand followed United States not British policy on recognition of the People's Republic of China. Nevertheless, in the Suez crisis of 1956, New Zealand backed its traditional protector and friend and not the United States. By cautious balancing of old loyalties with new, and by using the parliamentary committee for briefing interested MPs (as well as showing confidential exchanges to the opposition leader), governments were able to use Parliament not for debating and airing differences, but for sustaining bipartisanship and giving low salience to foreign policy issues. One of the most important steps taken by New Zealand, acting as a sovereign state with its own recognised special interests, was negotiation and signature of the Antarctic Treaty of 1959. Yet this prompted little interest or discussion within Parliament, or without. The national consensus on Antarctica would no doubt have been helped by the fact that the Antarctic Treaty system included New Zealand's most important friends and allies: America, Australia, and Britain.

In time, the experience of the Vietnam war was to lead to increasing recognition that New Zealand's current perceptions and future interest could diverge significantly from those of the US, and consequently to a questioning of the entire basis of the alliance with the US. The tradition of bipartisanship in foreign policy was abandoned in New Zealand's Parliament as the

Labour Party, under the leadership of Norman Kirk (1965-74), attacked the prosecution of the US war in Indochina and the National Government's support of US policy. There were two inter-related strands to the differences in the foreign policy positions of the two major parties. Firstly, the Labour Party was expressing the New Zealand public's disenchantment with the Vietnam war. Since 1949 the Labour Party had held office only during the three-year parliamentary term, 1957-60. It had a long tradition of greater nationalism than its more conservative rivals, whether that be showing independence from pre-war Great Britain, or from post-war United States. Years of unease at close identification of New Zealand policy with that of its protecting ally grew in the 1960s. As the long-term governing National Party was being drawn further in its support of the United States in Vietnam, the now long-term opposition Labour Party increasingly distanced itself, while protest mounted in the country. Secondly, and perhaps more importantly, Kirk used opposition to the Vietnam war to articulate his sense of what New Zealand's role in the world should be in the context of its values, location and size.

It was the Vietnam war, then, which, from the mid 1960s, ended bipartisanship. The war heightened public consciousness of foreign relations; it politicised the universities. Division was expressed in mass demonstrations and confrontations between protesters and authority, a style of political debate which was to be adopted for other issues in following years. In particular, there was the question of New Zealand's sporting contacts with South Africa. This issue, dating from the early 1960s, had profound effects on New Zealand society in the 1970s and 1980s, and confirmed that this was a society bitterly divided, with contrasting perceptions of the outside world.

Sporting contacts with South Africa was a question which cut to the core of New Zealand. For generations New Zealand had been the model society where two races—indigenous Maoris and immigrant Europeans—could live together in harmony and equality. For New Zealand and white South Africa to continue to play their national sport, rugby, with each other was to do more than condone apartheid. To many New Zealanders it was to symbolise and confirm how their much-boasted harmony and equality at home were in fact a sham.

For government conduct of foreign relations, the rugby

tour issue also had particular significance. In 1975 the issue appeared to be settled, at least for a time, by normal electoral processes. The National Party, committed to permitting sporting contacts, regained power. In 1976 that government learnt—through an African boycott of the Montreal Olympic Games—that however small and insignificant New Zealand might be, it was not ignored by the rest of the world. Nor could it ignore the world: New Zealand negotiated and accepted the Commonwealth Gleneagles Agreement for Governments to discourage sporting contacts with South Africa.

In other ways, too, the outside world intruded upon New Zealand in the 1970s. With a declining market for New Zealand meat and dairy products in Europe once Britain joined the Common Market, and with New Zealand's dependence on imported Middle East oil, the oil shock of the early 1970s had quickly led to re-assessment of a simple pro-Israel policy and to recognition of market potential in oil-rich Arabia and Iran. Decolonisation in the South Pacific and the appearance of new mini-states (including from the 1960s Western Samoa and the Cook Islands) not only gave New Zealand a region with which it naturally associated, but one in which it could, and happily did, play a leadership role. Massive migration from the islands to New Zealand reinforced this new regional perspective as well as creating for it new domestic problems. New Zealand's regional perspective was further developed by a changing relationship with Australia—one in which Australia both offered closer inter-governmental cooperation and encouraged closer trading ties through free trade association.

With the possibility of British entry into the European Common Market in the 1960s, and actual entry in the 1970s, New Zealand had both to engage in constant lobbying and negotiating to retain part of its traditional British market, and to diversify its trade. It opened new posts in continental Europe, in the Middle East and Latin America, and in the People's Republic of China. At the end of the 1950s, New Zealand had opened posts in the United Kingdom, USA, Canada, Australia, and also in France, Japan, and three South East Asian countries. The number of posts had nearly doubled by 1970, and almost doubled again by 1980 to a total of about 50.

There had been, too, an opening up of government in the 1960s, a process which continued in later years. It was government policy to release its senior advisers from traditional anonymity and allow them to explain policies in their own names. In foreign affairs the government saw value in a better educated public and through ministerial speeches as well as those of officials it sought better understanding of New Zealand's foreign policies. It encouraged the small non-partisan New Zealand Institute of International Affairs, with branches in the several main cities, and eventually supported the Institute's educational work with a modest annual grant.

As with other parliaments, overseas travel became one of the perks of parliamentary service. By the 1980s, it was a rare cabinet minister who had not had several overseas trips within months of taking office. From the early 1970s, the leader of the opposition, too, had annual publicly funded overseas tours. Like their counterparts in other countries, New Zealand MPs have the opportunity to travel other countries on familiarisation or study trips. They may be courted by foreign governments wishing to create favourable impressions, or they may be ambassadors of their own country's policies. MPs may travel to the United Nations to see how the organisation works, or to gauge the strength of feelings on issues such as apartheid. While Britain, America and Australia remain the favourite destinations, proportionately more MPs have begun to travel to the South Pacific island countries in recent times. Overseas exposure can also be provided through such bodies as the Commonwealth Parliamentary Association, or affiliations with conservative or socialist groupings of parliamentarians around the region or the world.

The world view of New Zealand MPs of the 1980s, therefore was very different from that of a generation earlier. There was likely to be more interest, and better informed interest, in foreign affairs. In the post-war years the educational levels of MPs steadily rose; particularly in the Labour Party there was an increasing preponderance of members drawn from the professions, including significant infusion of idealists on foreign policy issues, drawn into the party by opposition to the Vietnam war.

Equally significant was change in the extra-parliamentary

Labour Party. Traumatised by their defeat in 1975 which was as conclusive as had been their victory only three years earlier, the Labour Party which came to power again in 1984 was in many respects a new party, its organisation restructured, its membership more than quintupled. The membership increase gave weight in party conferences and executive elections to party activists, activists committed to breaking all remaining contacts with South Africa and strongly representative also of the peace movement which had burgeoned in numbers. The peace movement could mount impressive demonstrations against the occasional visits of United States warships which, by US policy, might be free or full of nuclear arms.

The new Labour Government quickly showed that in the domestic sphere it intended to jettison traditional Labour economic policies. The result was to harden the party position on its most important foreign policy goal : the exclusion of nuclear-powered and nuclear-armed, or potentially nuclear-armed ships. But—as with the previous National Government a decade earlier—the Labour Government promptly discovered that sanction of policies by the electorate did not mean acceptance outside the country. The United States responded with bluster, criticism, and eventual ouster of New Zealand from the tripartite ANZUS alliance.[2]

It also soon learnt that even New Zealand legal processes did not obtain automatic acceptance abroad. On 10 July 1985 the French security service blew up the Greenpeace vessel the *Rainbow Warrior* in Auckland harbour, killing a crew member. Two French agents were caught and—after pleading guilty of manslaughter—were convicted and sentenced. The French demanded their release. This was unequivocally and resolutely refused—until French sanctions began to bite.

The Parliamentary Opposition

In the 1970s and into the 1980s the Labour Party had made sporting contacts with South Africa a major policy issue of dispute with its National rivals. A South African rugby tour in 1981, permitted if not formally condoned by the National Government, had provoked violent confrontations and a city/country cleavage, with Labour opposition gaining support in the cities and National Government holding support in the rural and provincial centres. From 1984 the parties were equally clearly divided on the ANZUS/nuclear ships issue and—uncertain in its response to Labour economic measures—the National opposition began by making defence of ANZUS the principal ground of criticism.

As the forum for party debate Parliament had become a centre for exposing and expounding foreign policy issues. Nevertheless, foreign policy debates are rare. (For a time, in the 1950s and 1960s, there used to be a government-initiated discussion of foreign affairs, once or twice a session.) The infrequent ministerial statements on foreign policy are not debatable apart from a brief reponse by an opposition spokesman. In 1986, Prime Minister David Lange did, however, read a statement on the UN Secretary-General's ruling in regard to the France-New Zealand dispute over the sinking of the *Rainbow Warrior*. The statement was constantly interrupted by exchanges across the floor of the House. The bizarre character of the occasion can be gauged from the fact that four opposition members were evicted from the House by the Speaker before Lange had finished reading his statement (*Hansard*, 8 July 1986: 2707-11).

With an overloaded legislative calendar a government itself only occasionally moves a debatable motion and, with specific exceptions, government controls Parliament's agenda. In a small House (80 to 97 members in the twentieth century), since the 1930s parties have operated tightly organised teams in Parliament: discipline rarely shows any signs of weakening and is most apparent on procedural matters. No independents have been elected for forty years, the MP who has quit party has invariably been punished by the electorate, and the third party— Social Credit, from 1986 Democratic—has never placed more than two members at a time in Parliament.

Apart from local authorities with limited housekeeping functions, the New Zealand Parliament is the only forum for elected public figures, and its members are the sole elected representatives for their respective constituencies. In short, New Zealand's unitary constitution gives to its Parliament and central executive responsibilities which elsewhere might be undertaken at sub-national level, and single member constituencies reflect the localism which is a distinctive feature of

New Zealand politics. Abolition of an appointed upper house in 1950 reinforced the parochial, partisan character of political debate. There is no place in the New Zealand Parliament which is free from constituency-concern and tight party obligations, or from govenment-determined debating and work priorities.

Traditionally, the length if not the timing of Parliament's two major set debates has not been subject to government control, and once begun these debates have taken precedence over most other business. Debate on the annual address-in-reply to the speech from the throne, at the start of a session, gave members opportunity to speak—and most did. But with a quorum of but 20 (reduced in 1985 to 15), the debate might serve only for the recording in *Hansard* of personal interests and opinions. The Labour Government elected in 1984 found it could gain parliamentary time by rushing the annual debate through under urgency, or (in 1987) by cutting it out altogether and carrying a session through a second year.

However, the government could not dispense with the annual budget debate, and it remains the one open-ended debate, in which members have twenty minutes to raise issues and to ignore those raised by previous speakers. There are also four-hour general debates on two Imprest Supply bills a year, granting government interim supply pending passage of annual Appropriation acts.

Under a change adopted in 1985, normally two hours each fortnight are set aside in which, in ten minute speeches, members "may take note of miscellaneous business" : private members notices of motion, ministerial answers to questions, ministerial statements, and reports of inquiries by select committees (Standing Order 92). This change broadened existing general debates, as a move to guarantee time for private members. The list of matters which may be discussed is indicative of what at other times is unlikely to be discussed. Perhaps inevitably, the occasion is an invitation for parties to orchestrate a debate and tempts front benchers to join in at the expense of time for backbenchers. It is the least edifying part of the parliamentary calendar.

Occassionally, the pre-arranged business of the House will be set aside for a two-hour debate on a motion that the House take note of a "definite matter of urgent public importance"

(Standing Order 89). A member wishing to move such a motion for a "snap" debate must submit a written statement to the Speaker at least one hour before the House meets, although in exceptional circumstances this requirement can be waived. To accept the motion, the Speaker must be satisfied that the case is of recent occurrence, that it requires the immediate attention of the House or government, and that it involves the administrative or ministerial responsibility of the government. The letter of application should deal with only one subject for debate, and can include a succinct statement of explanation. It is not necessary for the government to be informed by either the MP lodging the application or the Speaker; the practice is to keep it strictly confidential. There can be only one motion under this rule on any one day (McGee, 1985 : 415-16).

There were, for example, two snap debates on foreign affairs in 1986 : on the *Rainbow Warrior* affair, and on the ANZUS alliance. The opposition forced a debate following the Prime Minister's statement on the release into French hands of the two French agents convicted of involvement in the bombing of the boat *Rainbow Warrior* in July 1985 (*Hansard*, 8 July 1986 : 2720-40). The opposition attacked the government's and the Prime Minister's credibility in no uncertain terms.

A month later, US Secretary of State, George Shultz met Australian Minister of Foreign Affairs, Bill Hayden, in San Francisco on 10-11 August 1986. In the communique issued at the conclusion of their meeting, the US announced that it was "suspending its security obligations to New Zealand under the ANZUS treaty pending adequate corrective measures" over nuclear ship visits (*New Zealand Foreign Affairs Review*, July-September 1986 : 24). In a snap debate in Parliament, opposition leader, Jim Bolger accused the Prime Minister of "duplicity" in insisting for two years that the government's anti-nuclear ships policy was consistent with ANZUS membership. The government's policies had left New Zealand with no capacity to defend itself, and with no allies to provide a security umbrella. A future National government, he said, would take the necessary steps to return New Zealand to a fully operational ANZUS alliance. Deputy Prime Minister Geoffrey Palmer retorted that the National Party was clearly pro-nuclear and an uncritical supporter of the United States, acting as the spokespeople for the US government in New Zealand's Parliament (*Hansard*, 12 August 1986 : 3778-99).

Passage of private members' bills, although not unknown, is uncommon—especially given statutory prohibition of legislation involving expenditure unless it has been recommended by the Crown. Nevertheless, oppositions have found introduction of bills of some propaganda value, especially since the Speaker does not rule a bill out of order until after a two hour introduction debate. A private member's bill must be printed and circulated to all members before leave to introduce it is moved, and once a fortnight private members' business normally takes precedence over government orders of the day. In its opposition years after 1975, for example, the Labour Party introduced several bills to exclude nuclear weapons from the country (as did also the Social Credit MPs), a bill to write into law the Commonwealth Gleneagles agreement against sporting contacts with South Africa, and a bill for any free-trade agreement with Australia to require parliamentary ratification.

It is customary for the opposition to select which classes of estimates shall be debated, although the order in which they are presented are at government's discretion, and estimates not approved in the allocated 13 days are all passed together without further debate. From the early 1970s estimates debates widened to include general policy, but in the mid-1980s debate was once more restricted more closely to particular items of expenditure. Speeches are short, five minutes at a time, but members may speak up to four times.

The New Zealand parliamentary entertainment period, the 45 minute daily question time, has the unusual feature that questions are presented on written notice. This reduces opposition ability to embarrass ministers, who come briefed for the occasion—to the extent that a minister has no difficulty responding on behalf of an absent colleague. The Speaker normally allows several follow-up supplementary questions, provided they are closely related to the original question and answer. But opposition exploitation of the occasion is further limited by firm tradition that with both questions on notice and supplementaries, a strict alternation is maintained between the two sides of the House, with prime minister and other cabinet members joining in to assist their colleagues. Since 1985 fifteen minutes have been allocated to "questions of the day," for which ministers have only a few hours notice; for other questions they have at least two days. With proposed questions (up to 16 a day) passing through the hands of respective party whips, it is possible for the opposition to see that an issue is kept alive, as in the mid-1980s when the ANZUS/nuclear ships issue was a principal matter of party debate.

Questions do not serve to catch ministers ill-prepared and off-guard, but to draw out or air facts and matters which put government at a disadvantage or advantage as the case may be. Hence it is no great loss if some questions are not dealt with and receive written response later in the day, and the game also is played with questions presented for written answer. In both cases replies appear in *Hansard*. But questions for written answer have superseded motions for returns and on occasion may elicit detailed information—as for example an itemised list of warship visits to New Zealand over a thirty year period or, of lesser moment, the complete appointments schedule of a minister travelling overseas.

Since 1936 Parliament has been broadcast on state radio as an avowed (and probably partially successful) attempt by a new Labour Government to counteract media bias against it. In practice, in much of the country reception for evening sittings has been lamentably weak, but there is quite good afternoon coverage which includes question period, snap debates if they occur, and the fortnightly miscellaneous business debate. Irrespective, then, of the impact television has had on New Zealand political news coverage since the 1960s, MPs have long been assured of at least some audience for their views (although until 1984 Parliament might go off the air when, under urgency, sittings continued beyond regular hours), and the opposition has had some guarantee that the media will not blanket or blatantly distort issues it chooses to hammer in Parliament. Parliament could be a constraint upon governments of the 1940s and 1950s as they attempted to maintain bipartisan support for their foreign policies, and as bipartisanship broke down it became the principal forum for the parties to debate their differences. (It had also been a platform for Labour criticism of Conservative governments before 1935, but without benefit of a radio audience).

Parliamentary Select Committees

The contribution of Parliament to foreign policy depends significantly on the degree of ministerial encouragement given. With the development of a department of foreign affairs with a clear organisational mission, and expansion of New Zealand representation overseas, there was in the immediate post-war years conscious effort to put information before Parliament. In later years, along with the increasing importance of Parliament as a forum for debating foreign affairs, there was significant procedural change enhancing the parliamentary role outside the sphere of partisan debate.

During the Second World War, New Zealand was involved in allied planning for peace, and with its bolder appearance on the world stage, both sides of the House saw the value of having the informational, consultative and deliberative External Affairs Committee set up in 1947. With it, along with tabling and publication of international agreements, the government introduced an annual report by the Department of External Affairs as a parliamentary paper. (Previously neither as Prime Minister's department nor as External Affairs had it produced such reports, nor until 1950 was there a report from the other department of external responsibilities which from 1943, until its eventual phasing out, was named Department of Island Affairs). Since 1943 there had already been a separate annual External Affairs vote. From 1951 External Affairs published its monthly or quarterly *Review* (eventually named *New Zealand Foreign Affairs Review*), a widely distributed summary of speeches, statements, and other records of activities and developments.[3]

Starting in 1961-62 there has been a succession of reviews of Parliament's standing orders, with the main thrust of consequent changes being to increase the role of the private member. The daily oral question period was revived in 1962. There was experimentation with short adjournment debates. A new and powerful select committee both reviewed government estimates and was empowered to carry out post-expenditure studies. More legislation was sent to an appropriate subject select committee before second reading, and it became increasingly common for committee hearings to be open to the media.

As, then, foreign policy questions became a matter for

partisan debate and New Zealand's trade and hence diplomatic relations diversified and as, too, new questions of sovereignty arose, Parliament through its select committees could and did become increasingly involved in foreign policy. The External Affairs Committee had had legislation before it in 1957 and 1959 with moves towards decolonisation of the Cook Islands and Western Samoa. It was twenty years later, however, before it again reviewed legislation—this time in open session. There was legislation creating a 200 mile exclusive economic sea zone in 1977, on Antarctica in 1981, and reversing a decision of the judicial committee of the British Privy Council giving New Zealand citizenship to a large number of Samoans in 1982. With the Public Expenditure Select Committe adopting a policy of parcelling out estimates for review, the Foreign Affairs Committee from 1976 might have that task also. It had petitions too for nuclear disarmament, on French nuclear testing, on sporting contacts with South Africa...

The several committee's tasks involved receiving submissions, questioning, seeking official response, reporting back and in the case of estimates, with associated annual departmental reports—questioning officials on their department. . . . and its finances.

By the 1970s, the estimates review had greater significance for parliamentary examination of external relations. There was a wider range of public servants advising government, especially from Defence (with a Ministry established in the 1960s) and Overseas Trade, a division of the Department of Trade and Industry but with a separate Minister of Overseas Trade, and with its estimates reviewed by the Foreign Affairs Committee.

Parliament's Defence Select Committee from the mid 1970s had its estimates to consider. It had a long history, since the close of the First World War, when its principal and often only function was to consider petitions arising from war service, relating to pensions, or expressing grievances of past or present members of the services. On one occasion, in the late 1950s, it had a joint meeting with the Foreign Affairs Committee; at least once, in the mid 1960s, it had a tour of inspection of New Zealand's defence establishments; occasionally it reported on bills, relating to the military and its administration or to war pensions.

In 1982 when the Labour opposition brought forward one of its bills to ban nuclear ship visits, an unsympathetic government was pushed by a backbencher (it had a one vote majority) into referring the question to a select committee. The special task of such committee, and the limited brief of the existing Defence committee, prompted creation of an ad hoc Disarmament and Arms Control Committee, with significant overlap in membership with Defence and Foreign Affairs Committees. Completion of its task by the new committee, however, was frustrated by a premature parliamentary dissolution in mid-1984, and then subsequent change of government and consequent change in party balance on the committee. (Normally, Parliament maintains a committee, albeit with possible change of members, over an election period: in 1984 the snap dissolution necessitated reconstitution instead when the new Parliament met.) Nevertheless, when all committees were restructured in late 1985, a changing committee membership had meant that almost one-fifth of the House had at some time been exposed to information and discussion on the issues.

Committee Restructuring 1985

Major committee restructuring in 1985 had the contradictory effect of both increasing and decreasing MP involvement in foreign policies. Committees had been created over the years and with some seventeen permanent select committees (including committees on private bills and housekeeping committees), together perhaps with further ad hoc committees like the Disarmament and Arms Control Committee, each normally numbering seven or more members, the House was stretched to keep them manned, even with most cabinet ministers included. Pressure was increased from the end of the 1970s when it became a rule that all bills, other than money bills, should normally be referred to a select committee after introduction/first reading.

In 1985, under the Labour Government, the standard size of select committees was cut back to five members (three government, two opposition MPs). The committee system was revised to give thirteen subject committees which as well as considering the bills, petitions and estimates referred to them, were empowered to "examine the policy, administration and expenditure of departments and associated non-departmental government bodies related to" their respective areas. There was also a new requirement that committees should henceforth table a report on the estimates they considered.

The intended change was to create small groups of specialists with power to initate inquiries, in contrast to the former more restricted committee role, with members dashing from one committee to another, or turning up only to provide the necessary numbers for a committee vote. There was thus a reduction in possible occasional exposure of an MP to a committee's work, and disappearance of the old large Foreign Affairs Committee, meeting in camera for briefings and talks for interested members. Ministers, too, no longer were to be committee members, and thus formally associated with committee deliberations (although in some domestic-oriented committees an associate non-cabinet minister, or "under-secretary," might be chairman).

So drastic was the reduction in committee places, that there was no longer the right, and obligation, of every private member to serve on a select committee. It was the opposition which missed out. With a twenty-person cabinet and six under-secretaries, the government had fewer private members than the opposition, but the opposition had two committee seats for every three government seats. The opposition found extra places by putting up alternate members of the Foreign Affairs and Defence Committee—giving two to sit on foreign affairs matters, and the other two on defence matters.

Despite their new powers, committees are unlikely to lose their close ties with the party caucuses and party caucus committees, and in their standard work—on bills, estimates and petitions—to embarrass the government or run counter to party caucus decisions and policies. (A new right to present minority reports does not extend to reports on bills and petitions.) Membership and membership changes are arranged by the respective party whips. The government continued to choose chairmen (although the Labour Government experimented after 1985 with having an opposition MP chair a new regulations review select committee). The broad inquiry powers, however, did invite committee involvement in policy formation.

The changes were particularly significant for parliamentary involvement in foreign policy. A new Foreign Affairs and Defence Committee combined the work of the former Foreign Affairs, Defence and Disarmament Committees with an enhanced status for both committee and chairman. There was no under-secretary in the relevant portfolios to be chairperson: as in the constituent former committees, she was a government backbencher, Helen Clark. And the committee was cast in the role of keeping the Labour Party conscience in the one field— exclusion of nuclear-armed ships—in which hitherto the government had been held to party policy.

It was the Foreign Affairs and Defence Committee which— shortly after its formation—presented the results of the labours of the 1982-84 and 1984-85 Disarmament and Arms Control Committees, in a relatively brief 32 page report, but with solid information appended. The Committee's first major task, however, was consideration of the government's anti-nuclear bill (see the following section). This bill apart, the Committee could anticipate having little other legislative work to undertake, and it immediately took advantage of its new investigative powers to carry out inquiries into New Zealand's relations with China (1986) and then with Canada (1987).[4] Before tabling its 60-page China report, the Committee, aided by a clerk and advisory officer, held fifteen meetings, heard or read 46 submissions from individuals and government agencies, and read background papers from nine government departments (all reprinted as a report Appendix). 1985 Standing Orders make provision for debating reports of inquiries, and a 1986 Standing Order (352A) requires government to table a response to committee recommendations within 90 days (although the report on relations with China was more notable for its substantial content than its modest recommendations).

The extent to which the changes of 1985 will increase the role of the backbencher cannot yet be assessed. As well as the Foreign Affairs and Defence Committee, several other select committees also promptly exercised their inquiry powers, and it is unlikely that a future government would revert to the former restricted committee role. Labour Party policy, with support from a royal commission on the electoral system, is to increase the size of the parliament and this would alter executive/backbench relations. At present talent is thinly spread and a committee chairmanship can be seen as a step towards ministerial office in a not distant future. It was an unusual circumstance that for a period before the 1984 election, the then Foreign Affairs Committee chairman, P.I. Wilkinson, was a former minister, who had retired from cabinet for health reasons. Cabinet ministers cling to office, and dismissals are extremely rare.

Actual backbench influence on foreign policy through committee work is likely to be modest, and committee activity is likely to have more importance in promoting discussion and in educating future government ministers. The resources available to committees and to individual MPs have improved immeasurably in the post-war years. But they are unlikely to go beyond provision of clerical assistance, a committee research officer and a small publicly funded research unit attached to each political party. The place for MPs to influence government undoubtedly will continue to be in the privacy of weekly party caucus meetings and not in committee hearings in the presence of both opposing MPs and the media. Governments' close association with caucus, however, does mean that as well as legislation requiring caucus acceptance before introduction in the House, governments seek caucus endorsement on major partisan issues—such as on contacts with South Africa and nuclear ship visits.

Undoubtedly, changes will affect the educative role of Parliament, giving more substance to the messages taken by MPs into the community. Mass membership built up in the 1970s in both major political parties, in particular, gives MPs a means of communicating back from Parliament to the electorate. Universities and voluntary organisations provide a platform for the MPs, and with the free air travel available to them, they have little difficulty responding to invitations if they so desire. (They also have substantial discounts if they wish to travel abroad.)

Anti-Nuclear Legislation

In a most notable instance of parliamentary impact upon foreign policy, the immediate cause of the dissolution of Parliament in 1984 and the calling of early elections was a private member's Nuclear Free New Zealand Bill, sponsored by Labour MP, Richard Prebble. During the introductory debate on the Bill, Prime Minister Sir Robert Muldoon told Parliament that the National Party could not remain the government if the Bill became law (*Hansard*, 12 June 1984: 266). The Leader of the House, David Thomson declared that such a bill, even if passed by Parliament, would not become law because the Governor-General's formal assent was required, and the government would not advise assent (*Hansard*, 12 June 1984: 259). In the event, the Bill was refused introduction by a vote of 39-40, despite two government MPs voting in favour, because a couple of Labour-turned-independent MPs voted with the government (*Hansard*, 13 June 1984: 318). Shortly afterwards, one of the rebel government MPs resigned from the party, although declaring that she would continue to support the government. Muldoon immediately sought and obtained dissolution of Parliament by the Governor-General.

As part of its 1984 election platform, the Labour Party had promised to emplace an anti-nuclear policy on a legislative basis in order to give it relatively greater permanence. Despite the fact that the initiator of the doomed 1984 Nuclear Free New Zealand Bill was now a senior cabinet minister, the Labour Government was noticeably tardy in introducing anti-nuclear legislation. A year after having taken office, Deputy Prime Minister Palmer was still saying that the government would hold discussions with Australia and Britain before bringing in anti-nuclear legislation (*Otago Daily Times*, 6 August 1985). The Democratic Party threatened to bring in its own bill if the government did not act soon (*Otago Daily Times*, 10 August 1985)—a threat it made good a month later. Prebble said that the government would allow the Bill to be introduced, but that it would then "rot" at select committee level (*Otago Daily Times*, 20 September 1985).

The New Zealand Nuclear Free Zone, Disarmament and Arms Control Bill was introduced to Parliament by the government finally in December 1985. The Bill banned the entry and stationing of nuclear weapons and nuclear-powered and nuclear-armed warships in New Zealand. The responsibility for implementing the Bill would rest with the Prime Minister acting on the advice of an advisory cammittee on disarmament and arms control. The National Party promised to oppose the Bill in Parliament, and, if it became the government, to repeal those sections of the law which banned the visits of nuclear-powered or armed ships. In National's view, the Bill violated and guaranteed the end of ANZUS, and would benefit the Kremlin more than New Zealand. The Bill was introduced by a vote of 48-30 (*Hansard*, 10 December 1985: 8910-30). The United States reacted immediately by warning that enactment of the Bill would lead the US to review security obligations to New Zealand under ANZUS (*Otago Daily Times*, 12 December 1985).

The Bill was held up in select committee for a very long time. The Committee on Foreign Affairs and Defence had to consider more than 1,200 submissions supporting, strengthening, opposing and modifying the Bill's provisions. In September 1986, the government indicated that passage of the Bill could be delayed until the following year, even though the policy of opposition to nuclear ship visits would remain in force (*Otago Daily Times*, 16 September 1986). The Committee reported back to Parliament in October 1986. Given firm party positions for and against permitting entry to US ships, the role of the Committee was to educate its members and permit a belief in public participation, not to exercise its powers to make amendments to the Bill. It only made a few drafting alterations.

In the second reading debate in February 1987, Lange supported the Bill by arguing that it reflected New Zealand's commitment to nuclear disarmament and New Zealand's refusal "to be a doormat for anyone else's nuclear aspirations." Bolger opposed it because it did not at all make New Zealand any safer, it did not affect the mix of nuclear weapons in the world, but it did destroy the country's alliance relationship. The Democratic Party supported the Bill, but would have preferred a stronger version (*Hansard*, 12 February 1987: 6978-7022). Ruth Richardson of the opposition National Party went on to attack the Bill for being hypocritical and designed to reap cheap electoral advantage at the expense of the nation's security. (*Hansard*, 17 February 1987: 7088-90). Subsequently, Bolger suggested in London that the government was dragging out the progress of the anti-nuclear legislation in Parliament in order to maximise political advantage (*Otago Daily Times*, 9 March 1987).

Interest Groups

As is to be expected in a Westminster system, groups and interests have to concentrate their political pressure on government and government officials—although select committees offer a specific point on which to apply pressure on Parliament. But, trade apart, bodies concerned with external relations are unlikely to have close and continuing consultative links with officials.

On trade matters, MP involvement is likely to be one of being briefed and persuaded. Negotiations leading up to the free-trade agreement with Australia (the Closer Economic Relations Agreement of 1983) well illustrated the close involvement of organised economic interests in policy-making, whereas the parliamentary input was exceedingly modest. The principal interest of the government was to avoid partisan debate. Opposition spokesmen received high-level official briefings; joint parliamentary study groups were sponsored to travel across the Tasman Sea; the draft heads of agreement were presented and explained to the Foreign Affairs Select Committee.

On issues of human rights, overseas aid and arms control, however, Parliament can be an important instrument for putting pressure on the government. Churches, charitable organisations and protesters turn to the media and to MPs rather than to the bureaucracy. MPs are recruited into an activist body like Amnesty International, or an educational one like Institute of International Affairs. MPs can be prodded to put down questions (such as on the arrest of a well-known churchman in South Africa), and to air concerns in general debates. There was, for example, pressure on the government to ratify the United Nations Convention for the Elimination of All Forms of Discrimination against Women (which it eventually did).

The parliamentary party caucus elects, and therefore can dismiss, the party leadership. In the Labour Party, the caucus also elects the Cabinet, although the Prime Minister allocates portfolios. The tradition of party discipline ensures that MPs debate and vote on issues on the floor of the House along party lines. MPs who have strong convictions on foreign policy issues can raise the matter at the regular caucus meeting each week. The caucus is also an effective target for lobbyists of all persuasions on foreign policy matters. In early 1985, when the US requested a port call for the USS *Buchanan*, there were fears in some quarters that the government might succumb to American pressure. Anti-nuclear activists responded by communicating their concerns and feelings to MPs prior to the caucus meeting, which in the event took a united decision that the ship would not be allowed in unless the US was prepared to state that it was not nuclear-armed. There remains a lingering suspicion in some people's minds that Lange could possibly have been prepared to strike a compromise deal with the US, but that the strength of caucus feeling ruled out any such option. Certainly "the Americans had the impression that the proposed visit by the USS *Buchanan* . . . "would be accepted" (*Defence and Security*, 1986 : 89).

Conclusion

Like legislatures in Westminster style governments in general, New Zealand's Parliament cannot be said to have a policy-making role in external affairs. By and large, Parliament's role is reactive rather than formulative. It is the chief forum for ratifying the government's foreign policy decisions and explaining their rationale, or for embarrassing the government over the conduct of foreign policy in any particular instance. Nor can the Select Committee on Foreign Affairs and Defence be said to provide either an effective check or a stimulus to the government on foreign policy issues. The primary determinants of foreign policy are the Prime Minister and the Cabinet; Parliament can have but a derivative role of influencing Prime Ministerial and Cabinet preferences by various means and through various channels.

Party positions of both the government and opposition groups are determined in confidential caucus meetings, not on the public floor of the House. What Parliament does do is to act as an open forum for the articulation, attack and defence of alternative positions. Secure in its own caucus, the Labour Government has been able to adhere to the anti-nuclear policy despite the objections of the National Party opposition in Parliament. But the House has enabled both parties to state their policies, point to the differences with each other, justify their respective positions, and appeal to the electorate on the basis of their promise and performance in Parliament. The extent to which Parliament can legitimise foreign policy decisions, affect foreign policy outcomes, or alter the context of foreign policy choices will depend upon such factors as the political strength and conviction of the Prime Minister and his cabinet colleagues, and the balance of parties in the House; a minority or slim majority government must perforce be more sensitive to the nuances of parliamentary opinion than a government which has a comfortable majority.

In previous decades, the established assumptions of foreign and defence policy, the dedication to bipartisan and compromise in foreign policy, and the pragmatic approach to the conduct of foreign policy served to insulate the realm of foreign policy from changing international circumstances and shifting public priorities. The Vietnam war broke the prevailing consensus on foreign policy in New Zealand's Parliament; the Southern African and nuclear issues have widened party cleavages. During the years of the third Labour Government (1972-75), and then again during the years of the National Government (1975-84), the party in opposition used Parliament to debate and question a whole range of foreign policy matters which then became issues in the 1975, 1978, 1981 and 1984 general elections: the threat of a growing Soviet naval presence in the Asian-Pacific region; the visits of nuclear-powered and nuclear-armed warships to New Zealand; the subject of sporting contacts with South Africa and fidelity to the Gleneagles Agreement; immigration policy and the status of Pacific Islanders in New Zealand.

The recent years have been traumatic ones for New Zealand, with challenges to fundamental assumptions both about the society and about foreign policy, and Parliament mirrors the change. Decades of complacency about successful intermingling of two races have ended. There is now perception of a society which has been racist domestically and racist in its external relations. Since British settlement in the mid-nineteenth century, whether the threats were from France, Russia, Japan, or China, New Zealand saw need for protection by the world's major naval power, and in international forums its role was that of a small, loyal ally—if sometimes expressing a high moral tone. In the 1970s the old protector removed the economic security given by its open market; in the 1980s the new protector declared New Zealand had lost the privileges and status of loyal ally.

Foreign policy issues have caused bitter confrontations, cleaving country from city and becoming the focus of partisan debate. In 1951, it was a domestic issue, a long, divisive strike—leaving scars for years afterwards—which prompted the first snap election of the twentieth century. In 1984, it was a foreign policy issue which prompted the second snap election of the century, after a government MP had quit her party on the issue of nuclear ship visits. A South African rugby tour was a principal issue in the 1981 election. The ANZUS alliance and nuclear ship visits were principal issues in the 1987 election. These issues may continue in future years, or others arise and a government again find a foreign policy issue bringing people on to the streets. But the likelihood is that in time, foreign policy will drop lower on the agenda of public debate. Legacies will remain, however: greater national awareness and recognition that New Zealand has a place in international affairs, better informed parliamentarians, and a parliament which has a continuing involvement in foreign policy.

Notes

1. The authors are grateful to Charles Littlejohn for helpful comments upon an earlier draft.
2. The ANZUS Treaty, signed in 1951, has no provision for denunciation or expulsion. Its abrogation would require the unanimous consent of all three partners. Since this would affect the basis of its defence relationship with Australia, and rule out a return to the fold of a more pliant New Zealand in the future, the United States has not moved towards such a course of action. But the "ANZUS alliance" has come to be used to refer to the entire range of military cooperation between the three countries. In retaliation against the New Zealand ban on nuclear ship visits, the US has progressively withdrawn from all military cooperation with New Zealand, culminating in the formal withdrawal of the US security guarantee to New Zealand under ANZUS in August 1986. While ANZUS still

functions bilaterally between Australia and New Zealand, and between Australia and the United States, and while the ANZUS Treaty still remains technically intact, the tripartite alliance has been rended inoperative with New Zealand's ouster.
3. 2500 copies of the *New Zealand Foreign Affairs Review* are printed at a cost of $4.40 each. They are distributed, free of charge even in these user pays days, to public libraries, educational institutions, diplomatic missions, government departments, MPs, individuals, organisations and firms.
4. These were the topics to be considered in those years in the prestigious annual University of Otago "Foreign Policy School," organised in cooperation with the Ministry of Foreign Affairs.

References

Candy, G.I. Parliamentary Scrutiny of Foreign Policy in New Zealand. (Master's Thesis, Victoria University of Wellington, 1986.)

Defence and Security : What New Zealanders Want. Report of the Defence Committee of Enquiry (Wellington : Government Printer 1986.)

Directory of Official Information (Wellington: Government Printer, 1983.)

Eayrs, J. *The Art of the Possible : Government and Foreign Policy in Canada.* (Toronto: University of Toronto Press, 1961.)

Henderson, J. "The Foreign Policy Decision-Making Process," in J. Henderson, K. Jackson and R. Kennaway (eds.), *Beyond New Zealand: The Foreign Policy of a Small State.* (Auckland: Methuen, 1980.)

Kember, J.L. "The Select Committee on Foreign Affairs: Foreign Policy and the Legislature." *New Zealand International Review*, 1978, 1(6): 25-6.

Marshall, C.R. "The New Zealand Parliament and Foreign Policy." *The Parliamentarian* 1976, 57(2) : 75-9.

McGee, D. *Parliamentary Practice in New Zealand.* (Wellington: Government Printer, 1985.)

McIntosh, A. "Origins of the Department of External Affairs and the Formulation of an Independent Foreign Policy, "in *New Zealand in World Affairs.* (Wellington: Price Milburn, for the New Zealand Institute of International Affairs, 1977)

Myers V. *Head and Shoulders.* (Auckland: Penguin, 1986.)

New Zealand. Appendices to the Journals of the House of Representatives (Parliamentary Papers) Departmental Reports, Estimates of Government Expenditure, Reports of Select Committees).

Parliamentary Paper, 1986 I.5A (Report on New Zealand-China relations).

Parliamentary Papers, 1983 I.20, 1985 I.19 (Reports of D'sarmament and Arms Control, and Foreign Affairs and Defence Committees).

Parliamentary Paper, 1985 I.14 (Report of Standing Orders Committee).

New Zealand Foreign Affairs Review.

New Zealand. Journals of the House of Representatives (Schedules of Select Committees).

New Zealand Parliamentary Debates (Hansard).

New Zealand Standing Orders of the House of Representatives brought into force 28 June 1951, with subsequent amendments and re-numbering.

New Zealand. Standing Orders of the House of Representatives brought into force 1 August 1985 (incorporating amendments made in 1986).

New Zealand. Statutes.

Otago Daily Times.

Thakur, R. "A Dispute of Many Colours: France, New Zealand and the Rainbow Warrior' Affair." *The World Today* 1986a, 42(12): 209-14.

—. *In Defence of New Zealand : Foreign Policy Choices in the Nuclear Age.* (Boulder, Colorado: Westview Press, 1986.)

—. and H. Gold "The Politics of a New Economic Relationship : Negotiating Free Trade between Australia and New Zealand." *Australian Outlook* 1983, 37(2) : 82-8.

Wallace, W. *The Foreign Policy Process in Britain.* (London : Allen & Unwin, 1977, for the Royal Institute of International Affairs.)

Wood, G.A. "New Zealand's Patriated Governor-General." *Political Science* 1986, 38(2) : 113-32.

Coping with Super Power Pressures on Indian Foreign Policy : An Assessment of the Indian Parliament's Performance

MANOHAR L. SONDHI

Political Dynamics : Parliamentary Resources and Political Culture

Any assessment of the performance of the Indian Parliament must rely on : (a) the need for a political culture within which the diverse elements of the Indian polity can interact while retaining a high degree of autonomy—more than is evident in other countries of the Third World; (b) the relative ability of Indian party politics to use the Indian Parliament as the political expression of civil society by articulating and aggregating interests, while bypassing controversies which could shake the political system to its foundations (the breakdown during the Emergency in 1975-77 may have served the purpose of removing some of the flaws and the rebirth of democracy was a decisive verdict in favour of a viable democratic parliamentary system); and (c) the capacity of the legislators to maintain their ties with the people, to develop parliamentary skills and utilise the shared values and feelings of solidarity which have resulted from the socialisation and mobility of the Indian political elite since the freedom struggle. Both the electoral process and the political dynamics of conflict and negotiation within parliament suggest that in four decades, India has achieved a form of interaction between political socialisation and political organisation which is unique in the developing world.

The centrist political culture of the Indian Parliament has clearly been shaped by the liberal convictions of politicians who continue to be nourished by the Gandhian tradition, which is equidistant from the ideologies of the Right and the Left. The absence of a proportional electoral system has also helped to frustrate both the Left and the Right in the electoral results. The first Prime Minister, Jawaharlal Nehru, who preferred the predominant political discourse of the left began to shift centrewards as he developed a more realistic vision of India's role in world affairs. He continued to adhere to a statist vision of the economic transformation of India induced in a generation brought up on Sidney and Beatrice Webb's "Soviet Communism—a New Civilisation", but renouced Third-World vanguardism and took little trouble to conceal his disagreement with Sukarno and other Third World leaders who fiercely attacked liberal democracy and advocated a catch-all mobilisation against the capitalist West. In domestic politics, Nehru would time and again launch intemperate attacks on those who wanted constitutional prerogatives to hold the Executive in check. He showed a sense of outrage over the role of the veteran statesman C. Rajagopalachari's efforts to discredit Nehru's *permitlicence raj* and for demanding a shift to Gandhian ideas about state and society for restraining power-intoxicated ruling party politicians and *dirigiste* bureaucrats. Nehru's adherence to the liberal-democratic order and his key role in strengthening the Westminster style of parliamentary politics does not at all imply that he supported the vision of the classical liberals. His predilections on democracy did not run parallel to those of Congress Party stalwarts like Sardar Patel, Rajendra Prasad and Maulana Azad, some of whom he regarded privately as politically retrograde. There is some evidence that Nehru overcame his anti-pluralist propensities and was astute enough to protect his authority and competitive position through mass electoral campaigning. His commitment to Parliament was addressed not so much to the development of a healthy competition among Indian political parties; he socialised into the Indian parliament because it helped him to take advantage of the values, presumptions and role-conceptions of the British parliamentary system. It was not expedient to disrupt the shared set of expectations which the Indian political elite had on the Westminster model, although Nehru knew that many of his supporters from the left did not express a confident view on the future of bourgeois democracy.

Nehru's successor Lal Bahadur Shastri attempted to reduce tensions between the Congress Party and the non-Communist Opposition by discarding some of the ideological tenets which were channelling the expression of political interests in a sharply polarised manner. In his short but eventful tenure as Prime Minister, Shastri introduced constructive bargaining through a non-acrimonious home-spun political style.

The return of power to the Nehru family and the installation of Indira Gandhi as Prime Minister had the extraordinary effect of providing varying yardsticks for measurement of democratic performance. Indira Gandhi had a Janus-like quality : on the one hand, she used the distinctive symbols of the world's largest democracy and tried to develop a far-reaching consensus on national security and foreign affairs, while on the other, she gradually legitimised dynastic rule. She encouraged the expression of political interests transgressing the framework of moral principles and thus produced a vicious circle of competitive politicking and social violence.

The Emergency had fateful consequences both for Mrs. Gandhi and for the Congress Party. When the General Elections were held the Indian electorate was in a punitive mood and the non-Communist opposition was able to build a new identity as the People's Party—the Janata Party, which gained an ascendency in the Parliament and in the Northern states. Although its peak of popularity faded on account of rank-and-file dissatisfaction with factional conflicts, the threat posed by the Emergency was defused through a Contitutional Amendment, and the two non-Congress Prime Ministers, Morarji Desai and Charan Singh, both fostered participatory attitudes both in party democracy and parliamentary leadership.

The return of Mrs. Gandhi to power after the collapse of the Charan Singh government, her assassination and the massive sympathy vote in favour of Rajiv Gandhi did not solve the Congress Party's deeper structural problems. A systematic analysis of these problems and the complex constraints which have been created for Rajiv Gandhi's parliamentary leadership in 1987 with the eruption of the Bofors Scandal is beyond the scope of this essay. Recently, there has also been much academic discussion on the need for electoral reform to reduce the influence of money on Indian politics.

The crucial point, however, is that the consensual basis of the Indian political system has survived the realignment of electoral attitudes and appears to be successfully facing the test of the decline of the Congress Party and the emergence of a new structural environment in which regional demands are strongly articulated e.g. Andhra Pradesh, Karnataka, Kerala and West Bengal.

The potential for blunders like Mrs. Gandhi's Emergency remains, but even taking into account factors of uncertainty in the future, Indian political culture provides most of the preconditions for the continued viability of the parliamentary system. In terms of political scenarios that stretch into the future, the parliamentary arena alone encompasses the common dimension for the integral forces of society to overcome both authoritarian and divisive tendencies. The expectations which Members of the Indian Parliament attach to their roles combined with the electoral resistance of Indian voters to anti-democratic pressures constitute important contextual assumptions which help reinforce India's self-image as a functioning democracy.

Motivations to Maintain Limits of Involvement with the Super Powers

The extent of problems faced by most Third World leaders as a result of Super Power competition can best be described in the historical context of the manipulation of several Third World politics. On the pretext of denying access to the opposing Super Power, the Third World has been penetrated by both the United States and the Soviet Union. If India has shown the capacity to stand up to the Super Powers with a considerable degree of autonomy—apart from temporary setbacks—the role of Parliament can help explain certain peculiarities of the form and content of Indian foreign policy towards the Super Powers. A significant dimension of Super Power interference in Third

World countries has been the direct and indirect ways in which they have gained access to internal bureaucratic politics. Indian parliamentary activism has enabled national exposure to foreign policy issues against the polarising compulsions of Super Power diplomacy. Indian foreign policy-makers have been helped by the broad parliamentary support against over-involvement with either Super Power; this support which has extended across the political spectrum may be summarised as follows :

(1) *Development Cooperation.* The Indian Parliament has been strongly involved in questions of development assistance as part of its performance in the area of economic planning. Parliamentary pressure on the Government takes the form of ensuring that the development process is not made the target of economic domination from outside, by any one power. Members would not hesitate to ensure government accountability through debates and interpellations if the economic involvement with either USA or the Soviet Union runs counter to national requirements of economic independence. Particularly pronounced problems like the Rupee Trade with the Soviets and the gross violations of national rights by US based multinationals have been the subject matter of regular discussion in Parliament.

2. *Security interests.* Although India has not been able to avoid external dependency for military supplies, the debates in Parliament have tried to strike a balance in the analyses of security issues. India's security concerns with China and Pakistan, and the corresponding value which for a variety of reasons is now attached to Indo-Soviet cooperation, has not prevented objective references to the shifts in power and influence of the Super Powers. Members of Parliament are aware that India has to cope not only with the differences but also the convergence of security interests between them. For example, the Non-Proliferation Treaty which is not in line with India's contemporary strategic thinking reflects the joint security interests of the United States and the Soviet Union. Parliament has continued to stress the negative consequences of Super Power rivalry and the dangers of Super Power confrontation. The Indian debate on the security environment is primarily directed towards political responses and the signing of the Indo-Soviet Treaty has not led most Indian MPs to adopt Soviet lines of argumentation.

3. *Conflict Resolution*: At the parliamentary level the impact of India's peace-keeping practices in Korea, Congo and Indochina continues to be salient inspite of the high level of violence in India's neighbourhood and in certain parts of the country. Although adversely affected by the oil crisis, Indian parliamentary opinion was totally opposed to US plans to protect its oil interests through armed action. Similarly, Indian parliamentary opinion has not supported intervention by the Soviet Union to preserve its Socialist Camp. Although the Indian Government has become, over the years, skilled in adversary diplomacy, debate in Parliament will often betray an earlier set of shared expectations of an Indian role to probe for amicable relations between parties in protracted conflict.

4. *India's Anti-Nuclear Discourse*: After the Pokhran test, the Indian Government has perhaps changed its nuclear stance dramatically and permanently. Since its inception, the Indian Parliament has seriously considered functional alternatives to nuclear war and its anti-nuclear discourse has buttressed its role in the global disarmament community. The regulation of world peace through the two nuclear-armed Super Powers has a restricted appeal to the Indian political mind, and the pronuclear discourse whether it emanated from Moscow or from Washington (or from Beijing) has few takers in Parliament.

5. *Controlling India's Professional Military Establishment*: Both the US and Soviet Union have sought to influence the political regimes in the Third World by gaining influence in the armed forces. India has not permitted this to happen so far, and the ground rules of Indian parliamentarianism appear to be resilient enough to resist the armaments culture of either Super Power. The reinforcing capabilities of Indian political culture have so far proved an effective barrier to the dominant external interests which would like the professional military establishment to see itself installed as a political conscience as is the case in Turkey, Indonesia, and Ethiopia.

6. *Rapprochement and Relaxation of Tensions between the Soviet Union and the United States*: Among the broad range of possibilities of a transformative vision for India, the one that suggests a breakthrough to Indian legislators is the intentional or accidental rapprochement between the two Super Powers. China's competitiveness has often expressed itself as a wish for

a catalytic crisis between the Soviet Union and the United States. In the Indian perspective greater Super Power interdependence is seen as a pre-condition not only for a new peace order but also for reducing India's military dependency. The acceptance of such a broad perspective provides the necessary basis for the Indian Parliament to support a mediator-orientation, and to question any move which may lead to over-involvement with either Super Power, and a possible disruption of India's non-aligned status. Although there are few traces left of the euphoria for the Non-alignment of Nehru's days, the changing perceptions of the policy agenda in Parliament remain largely immune from alignment with either Super Power. Any Indian Government which becomes over-submissive to either Super Power would find itself courting disastrous failure in Parliament.

Case Studies of Legislative Responses to Super Power Pressures

Several trends and events form the backdrop to our assessment of the Indian Parliament's performance in coping with Super Power pressures on Indian foreign policy. A scrutiny of important foreign policy debates in Parliament shows that problems that appeared reasonably simple to the Executive took on new dimensions and complexities when examined within the broader context of the parliamentary domain. Two sets of cases have been selected: (*i*) the Soviet intervention in Czechoslovakia, the Indo-Soviet Treaty of Friendship, and the Soviet intervention in Afghanistan—to show how the parliamentary process affected the outcome for Indo-Soviet relations; and (*ii*) U.S. intervention in Vietnam, the Nuclear Non-Proliferation Treaty, and the supply of US arms to Pakistan—to identify their impact on Indo-U.S. relations. It will be argued that although both the Super Powers play active roles in encouraging shifts in Indian foreign policy, the Indian parliament is led by the logic of its approach to question and uncover the games the Super Powers are playing. Parliamentary checks on the Executive ensure that what at first appear to be self-explanatory and clear standards for formulation of Soviet or American foreign policies, later reveal themselves as polarising compulsions to globalise the East-West conflict. The extent to which the Indian parliament has provided opportunities for meaningful political participation and open and articulated protest has helped to narrow the ruling elite's margin for appeasement of either Moscow or Washington.

a. Soviet Intervention in Czechoslovakia

To review the partiamentary response to the Czechoslovak crisis of 1968 may serve a number of analytic purposes: first, it can be of interest in showing how India while maintaining its special relationship with the Soviet Union can recapture increasing measure of freedom of action whenever there is a massive and flagrant violation of the rights of another country; second, it can show that any trend towards closer orientation with Moscow can come up against offensive postures of the Super Power when India would prefer to visibly dissociate itself from Soviet global strategy; third, it can explain the educative role of Parliament in handling conflicts which carry grave dangers of escalation and confrontation between the Super Powers.

Under Mrs. Indira Gandhi's Government there were fairly deterministic guidelines for foreign policy towards the Soviet Union. In domestic politics she was dependent on Communist support, and it was to be expected that the Soviets would make heavy demands on India when the Czechoslovak crisis began. What the Soviets and their supporters easily overlooked, however, was that Indians have prided themselves on an integrating function within the global system. The strength of Indian public opinion is evident in the text of the Private Member's Resolution adopted on 30 August 1968:

> This House hails the brave people of Czechoslovakia in their bid to liberalise and democratise the political life of their country, reiterates its faith in the policy of non-involvement and non-intervention in the internal affairs of any country and appeals to all freedom loving countries and people to extend their support and sympathy to the movement in Czechoslovakia.

Apart from factional politics within the ruling Congress party which culminated in the resignation of the Socialist turned Congress Minister Asoka Mehta, the non-Communist parliamentary opposition set general constraints on any overt support to Soviet intervention. A ceaseless battle in Parliament and outside put the Communists entirely on the defensive, and some of the controversies spilt over into intra-Communist affairs. Fully aware of these difficulties, the Prime Minister's caution reflected deepening public dissatisfaction. She tried to acquire greater credibility and legitimacy by consultation with the Opposition parties. The intense mobilisation around the Czechoslovak issue awakened parliamentary interest in the political settlement of international conflicts and the renunciation of the use of force in international relations. The spectrum of views in parliament was widened and the incompatibility between the Indian model and the Soviet system with its monopolisitic decision-making and bureaucratic centralism was emphasised.

b. *Indo-Soviet Treaty of Friendship*

The 1971 Treaty of Peace and Friendship between India and the Soviet Union has been given a high degree of attention in studies attempting to unravel the most salient relationship in India's international politics. The tendency has been to emphasise the divergence of Indian strategies since 9 August 1971 rather than to emphasise the stability of the Indian foreign policy system. The most striking aspect of the treaty relationship is clearly Article IX of the Treaty which states :

> Each High Contracting party undertakes to abstain from providing any assistance to any third party that engages in armed conflict with the other party. In the event of either party being subjected to an attack or a threat thereof, the High Contracting parties shall immediately enter into mutual consultations in order to remove such threat and to take appropriate effective counter measures to ensure peace and security of their countries.

Similar provisions in some other treaties which the Soviet Union has signed have enabled Moscow to act solely in its own self-interest and ignore the interests of the other contracting party. The pattern of questions and debates in Parliament, however, show that there is no significant shift in intellectual perspective towards Soviet political views and orientations. The following considerations help to clarify the function Parliament fulfils in the evaluation and criticism of the Soviet strategic and ideological thrust towards India.

(1) The Indian system of parliamentary government ensures that the conceptual rigidity which the Soviet Union wishes to maintain in its bilateral relations with New Delhi is diluted. The tradition-bound masses of India elect a parliament which inspite of all the consequences of modernisation remains much more heterogeneous that the orientation of proletarian socialism demands. As a school for democracy such a parliament does not easily align with Soviet sensibilities inspite of the rhetoric of the unshakeable friendship of the Indian and the Soviet peoples. The receptivity of certain Soviet ideas and forms is perhaps greater in the Indian bureaucracy. The concept and experience of a public forum like the Indian parliament is a real problem for the leadership elite of any Communist country, except perhaps of Yugoslavia. With even a few members in the Congress party who are by no means certain that the Soviet connection is a matter for euphoria, the non-Communist opposition is able to neutralise or reverse tendencies which would support the interpretation that the Soviet bloc is the naturally ally of the non-aligned.

(2) To clarify the meaning of Article IX of the Treaty using Soviet formulae hardly helps. On 29 December 1971, *Pravda* claimed that the Indo-Soviet Treaty was the shield which protected South Asia from the interference of outside forces during the Indo-Pakistan conflict. Indian officials have been understably not eager to challenge the Soviet way of assessing prospective developments. The parliamentary [history of the pre-Bangladesh period contains enough evidence to show that there was overwhelming support in both the Houses for the Indian Government to act independently, and it was the Soviet Union which worked persistently for a solution within the framework of a united Pakistan. For India, therefore, there were two sides to the matter : on the one hand she knew that

the Soviets wished to moderate Indian actions and were concerned at her operative readiness: on the other hand India could take advantage of the dilemmas of Soviet security policy vis-a-vis China and the US if there was an institutional framework for security policy cooperation. Viewed in the Indian parliamentary context Soviet backstage support certainly hastened the end of the Bangladesh war and also introduced necessary doubts in the minds of other parties. But many informed observers found Soviet pretensions ridiculous especially when for sometime they started looking at New Delhi through a special prism—that of the 1971 Treaty.

(3) Even in an atmosphere of crisis, the Indian Parliament, echoing the example of the British Parliament during the War, continues to concern itself with the wider connotations of political issues. It is difficult to find support for a parochial view against a broad system of consultations in foreign policy, cutting across the two power blocks. The Soviets have repeatedly tried to form a package which would solve their dilemmas with India. Even after signing the Indo-Soviet Treaty, New Delhi's perceptions of the role of India towards the two Super Powers have never reached the point of no return. The Soviet efforts to carefully engineer Indian support for Asian collective security have not succeeded and as far as India is concerned the issue has simply faded away.

(4) India's political pluralism is out of sympathy with the strong ideological flavour of Soviet maxims for promoting the further development of Indo-Soviet relations. Whether it is trade and economic relations, or the politics of disarmament, the 'great debates' in India cannot find common ground with Soviet political commitments and position expressed in hegemonic terms. The evolving interaction between Moscow and New Delhi has resulted in close political and economic ties but it is necessary to make a distinction between the realistic expectations at government level and the lack of a vibrantly creative relationship. Most Indian parliamentarians would shrug their shoulders if told that the relationships within the socialist bloc represent a "revolutionary" model of friendly relations on which a future world system could be built.

The differences in the historical and environmental contexts of the two political cultures explain why for the Indian Parliament the Indo-Soviet Treaty can never be an end in itself; both the elite and the public at large accept the abiding importance of the Indo-Soviet dialogue, but the Soviet role of a self-proclaimed messiah of peace and security is accepted only with reservation.

c. *Soviet Intervention in Afghanistan*

On grounds of national interest and long-term strategic planning, India should permit neither the Soviets nor the Americans to dominate Afghanistan. Mrs. Indira Gandhi's Government was under strong pressure from Moscow to buttress their position at the U.N. Moscow apparently calculated that with her belligerent outlook against the non-Communist opposition parties whom she had trounced in the recently-held General Elections, they could capitalise on the political change in India. The speech of the Indian delegate to the General Assembly on 11 January 1980 was deeply disturbing to non-aligned opinion at the U.N. At home, independent observers noted the lengths to which the Soviets could go in frustrating an independent Indian stance on a matter of vital national interest. It was hardly factual for the Indian delegate to say that India had no reason to doubt Soviet assurances that their troops would be withdrawn, coming as these assurances were "from a friendly country like the Soviet Union with which we have many close ties." This was a vastly changed position from what Mrs. Gandhi had herself adopted at the time of Czechoslovakia. The U.N. statement caused deep dismay in political circles in New Delhi and there was general agreement that the Russians had indulged in arm-twisting. Coming on the eve of the session of Parliament, Opposition moves put Mrs. Gandhi in a difficult dilemma. Surveying the situation with leaders of the Opposition parties in Parliament before the commencement of the Session, she tried to cover up the cardinal error of the U.N. statement and calm the furore it was likely to create on the floor of Parliament by indicating that she was seriously desirous of getting the Russians out and affirming that India was opposed to foreign intervention everywhere, including Afghanistan. There were at least four considerations which impelled the Prime Minister to reject the assumptions behind the statement of the Indian delegate to the U.N. : first, with Communist acclaim of the Indian position, Mrs. Gandhi wanted to seek a middle ground in Parliament so that she could stike a new balance of relationship with the Right and the Left, and project her new Government more constructively; second, opposition to the Soviet invasion of Afghanistan grew by leaps and bounds in the Indian Muslim community. To counter the general feeling of unease and alarm among Muslim members of Parliament, the Prime Minister arranged to meet many of them informally and emphasised that India's studied moderation on the Afghanistan issue was not intended to absolve the Soviets of culpability. However, India did not want to participate in the hysteria and fears of the Western world against the Soviet Union; third, the second cold war had not yet got under way and Pakistan and India were not yet engaged in the calamitous arms race that would follow US recognition of Pakistan as a front-line state. In India there was a powerful trend towards a general amelioration of relations with Pakistan and although these were not her priorities vis-a-vis Islamabad, the Prime Minister wanted to keep her options open for developing a good neighbour policy; fourth, having alienated Washington by over-accomodation of the Soviets, Mrs. Gandhi wanted to find a way out of an untenable situation. A more sophisticated explanation of India's Afghanistan Policy in Parliament would undoubtedly help to retrieve the situation.

A statement by the Minister of External Affairs, in response to a Calling Attention Motion sought to remove the impression that India was simply toeing the Soviet line. Although the efforts to counteract the mischief done by the U.N. statement were of little avail internationally, the Minister presented a clear goal:

> It is our hope that the people of Afghanistan will be able to resolve their internal problems without any outside interference. As the Prime Minister has clearly indicated, we are against the presence of foreign troops and bases in any country. We have expressed our hope that Soviet forces will withdraw from Afghanistan.

There are two contrasting images which emerge from this discussion. The Soviet Union had enough room for political manoeuvering in certain closed situations and it initially persuaded India to dilute its commitment to non-intervention. A second image points to the reduction of Soviet hegemonic expectations when parliamentary values came to the fore and the Indian Government had to justify its actions in an open forum. In her reply to the debate on the President's Address, the Prime Minister broke with some of the cliches of the Ministry of External Affairs by specifically promising that India would make every effort to ensure speedy withdrawal of Russian troops from Afghanistan.

The record of Indian policy on Afghanistan is hardly a brilliant chapter of India's external relations. Without parliament providing the opportunity for re-examination it could have become progressively worse.

d. United States Intervention in Vietnam

In the early 1960s India found itself confronted with special problems in Asia as a result of the confrontation on the Sino-Indian border. The Indian policy towards Vietnam was marked by two contradictory tendencies: while the closeness of China and Vietnam created a certain mistrust of Hanoi's intentions and encouraged a section in the Indian foreign policy establishment to view US policies in Vietnam as a necessary bulwark against Sino-Vietnamese expansionism, on the other hand the nationalism and anti-colonialism of Ho Chi Minh led to a questioning of United States interventionism in Asia.

Prime Minister Indira Gandhi's visit to President Johnson in 1966 showed that the American pressures were difficult to reconcile with a commitment to Asian peace and security. Johnson's appeal to an Indian national interest different from the common interest of the non-aligned did not overcome Mrs. Gandhi's fears of an alienated public opinion at home. Members of parliament saw with consternation that the United States, by compelling devaluation of the Rupee, had wounded national pride. It came as an even greater shock when delays in wheat shipments were used as a coercive method to secure Indian support for the US Vietnam policy. A Private Member's

Resolution (in the Third Lok Sabha) on Vietnam brought out the importance of parliamentary scrutiny of foreign policy for coping with Super Power pressures.

There were of course differing perceptions of the situation in South Vietnam and the range of Indian options, choices and policies. Rhetorical posturings by the Communist Members of Parliament were not often based on the possible long-term consequences of Sino-Soviet relations. Similarly, the enumeration of gains and losses by the non-Communist Opposition sometimes failed to assess the manipulative strategies of both the Super Powers.

The Government had wide political support not to shy away from criticising Washington after the U.S. started bombing North Vietnam. American diplomacy did not have any psychological mechanism for coping with the unbridgeable position as far as Indian parliamentary opinion was concerned: that Asians could be made victims of an inhuman type of warfare which had been ruled out in Europe and America. Moreover, with India's own perceptions of the growing Sino-Soviet rift, U.S. policy in Vietnam was perceived as ham-handed and one which was not sophisticated enough to take advantage of the Sino-Soviet tensions. Washington adopted a unitary perspective towards India after 1962 and imagined Indian policy processes to be centred on meeting the threat from China. The Indian parliament while aware of the aggressive intentions of China, could not accept the U.S. credo of intrusion into Vietnam. India progressively distanced itself from Washington and, by encouraging a normal relationship with Vietnam, found itself in a mature partnership with re-united Vietnam after US withdrawal. There can be little doubt that Parliament has helped to overcome bureaucratic inertia in dealing with radical forces in the Third World.

e. *Nuclear Non-Proliferation*

The Indian Government's decision not to sign the Nuclear Non-Proliferation Treaty in 1967 was the result of Parliamentary pressure which has rarely been explicitly acknowledged. Although official spokesmen have maintained that the NPT is discriminatory and that the underlying assessments and presuppositions of the Nuclear Powers were open to question, Mrs. Gandhi's Government would have shown little will to self-assertion if Parliament had not articulated a general disenchantment with the non-proliferention strategies of the Super Powers and chiefly the United States. In hindsight it seems clear that Prime Minister Nehru's statement in the Lok Sabha on 24 July 1957, generated a great mistrust of Indian intentions in the United States. Nehru's doctrine of nuclear development was founded on the idea of independence from external sources for the supply of fissionable materials. The strong American sentiment against India' nuclear independence increased as India built up a sizeable nuclear capacity. There was American annoyance at India building up a nuclear fuel cycle which was not subject to IAEA safeguards. Parliament was repeatedly assured that India would pursue research and nuclear testing for peaceful purposes. In May 1974 when the first underground nuclear test was carried out at Pokhran, both the Super Powers were greatly concerned regarding its consequences for the basic issues of non-proliferation policy.

That the United States had not much patience and understanding for Indian nuclear attitudes was again demonstrated when Mr. Morarji Desai, although parsonally well inclined towards the United States, found it very difficult to fine-tune India's nuclear relationship with Washington.

The United States view that the Nunclear Non-Proliferation Act of 1978 made the Indo-US agreement of 1963 inoperative was not acceptable to New Delhi which insisted that the United States was legally responsible for the supply of nuclear fuel to Tarapur. Mr. Desai also went to the extent of declaring India's disinterest in both peaceful nuclear explosions (PNEs) and nuclear weapons. This was interpreted at best as moralism and at worst as appeasement by parliamentary opinion, since the effort of both sides to work out a compromise came to nought when the Nuclear Regulatory Commission of the United States failed to give approval to the urgently required shipments. Elements of parliamentary conflict were visible even when a joint Indo-US panel of scientists was set up to find a technical solution to the problem. When Mrs. Gandhi became Prime Minister again in January 1980 she reversed Mr. Desai's negotiating posture. She reserved India's option to conduct more nuclear tests. She also made statements encompassing a solution of the unresolved issue by seeking nuclear fuel supplies from other sources and asked her officials to speculate on the possibilities of reprocessing the spent fuel which was stockpiled. Parliamentary opinion was supportive of new choices to escape the constraints from the American side. Finally during the Prime Minister's visit to Washington in 1982 it was agreed that France would act as supplier of fuel for the Tarapur reactor, while the U.S. would supply the necessary spare parts.

f. United States Arms to Pakistan

The Indian experience with US arms supply to Pakistan is not unique. Many countries in the Third World have been similarly affected by Super Power military aid which has a considerable effect on the balance of power relationship with one or the other of their neighbours. Against a background of a whole range of issues facing India since the US-Pakistan military alliance came into being, Parliament has shown a preoccupation with US security policies which, in their effect on the subcontinent, have been largely determined by global strategic considerations. As early as 1954 the parliamentary debate on US military aid to Pakistan was a challenge to the US claim of undisputed freedom of action in the sphere of military supplies. The mainstream of Indian parliamentary opinion has contiuned to see the threat of US military commitment to Pakistan as unambiguously provocative. The US Government has tried to influence Indian perceptions and policies by stressing the asymmetry in military resources between India and Pakistan. There were occasions when in the course of diplomatic discussions washington hoped that New Delhi would accept this argument, and the US and India could move into an area of pragmatic bargaining and adaptation on the question of US military aid. The presentation of external political and security issues in Parliament has over the years produced an atmosphere of vigilance on the question of the role assigned to Pakistan in US strategic needs.

In 1968, Parliamentary activism resulted in the review of some basic premises about American arms supplies. India was not convinced that the US accepted non-alignment as a natural and effective strategy. The channeling of military assistance to Pakistan was perceived as the deep-seated belligerence of Imperial America. The Indian Defence Minister told an indignant Parliament that the U.S.-sponsored agreement under which Turkey would supply 100 Patton tanks to Pakistan was an ominous step in a strategy aimed at undermining Indian defence. Moreover, Parliament was not satisfied that the US was supporting Pakistani nationalism against Communism ; it was felt that US was fostering mistrust between India and Pakistan in order to pursue a sterile policy of using military channels for dominating Pakistan.

After the Bangladesh war, the United States indicated that it wished for a more normal working relationship with India. But to Indian opinion Washington seemed to be doing just the opposite when it mooted lifting the embargo on arms supply to Pakistan. The stick and carrot diplomacy of the United States did not provide the US the leverage it had expected. In response to Parliamentary pressure, the Defence Minister in his statement in the Rajya Sabha on 14 Merch 1973 rejected the complex explanations of the American move to lift the embargo and stated emphatically that it would jeopardise the process of normalisation. Cutting across party lines Members of Parliament placed the onus on the US for initiating a spiraling arms race between India and Pakistan.

Throughout the first half of 1975, Parliament continued to be deeply concerned with the American fueling of the arms race in the subcontinent. When Mrs. Gandhi decided to crack down with the Emergency the low priority for parliamentary activity meant necessarily an interregnum of a more hierarchical handling of the foreign policy process. The interaction with the US on urgent security issues with Executive dominance took on a different character.

The Soviet invasion of Afghanistan once again resulted in the US engaging Pakistan in extended talks on military supplies. The Francis Fukuyama report prepared in 1980 for the Rand Corporation led to further Indian despair over US security policy for the subcontinent. Fukuyama stressed the danger to US interests in the Gulf and indicated that the situation was ripe for a close US-Pakistan security relationship.

It would be difficult to exaggerate the extreme tension which gripped Indian political circles when it was learned that the US think-tank envisaged Pakistan as the bridgehead for the Rapid Deployment Force, for its movement into the Gulf.

Both the Carter and the Reagan administrations gave assurances to New Delhi that they sought options of cooperation with India. Parliament had several opportunities to assess the significance of the rapidly evolving situation after the fateful events in Afghanistan. The 4.02 billion dollar American aid package to Pakistan led Members of Parliament to ponder over the capabilities and intent of the two Supper Powers with a deep sense of frustration towards American policy-making. The lengths to which the Americans could go in pursuing the logic of the Fukuyama proposals was shown in the permanent waiver of the Symington Amendment in Islamabad's favour. The basic concern of Parliament today is to scrutinise the commitments of American security planners in making Pakistan an instrument of coercive diplomacy against India.

Parliamentary Principles for an Uncertain Future

Any attempt to draw general conclusions from our two sets of case studies must relate opinion in the Indian legislature, the public debates on foreign and defence policies and the overall Indian policy-making style in foreign affairs to the needs of the future.

Inspite of the difficulties India is facing in realising the values enshrined in the Directive Principles of the Constitution and the prevelance of violence in domestic social and political interactions, India's role in the comity of nations is a growing one and calls for greater assumption of regional and worldwide responsibilities. It is clear that both the US and the Soviet Union affect the Third World's future in terms of both real and manufactured domestic and foreign crises. There are no panaceas available for the factors of discord between Washington and Moscow, but from the point of view of India the instabilities in the strategic, geopolitical and diplomatic relations between the Super Powers will continue to claim victims in the Third World.

Coping with Super Power Pressures on Indian Foreign Policy

The experience of the past indicates that the Indian political culture and the Indian parliamentary system provide a certain measure of strength in the relationships between India and the two Super Powers. If the Super Powers have not succeeded in imposing the sort of attitudinal constraints on India as they have imposed elsewhere in Asia, Africa and Latin America, it is not only on account of the personality factor. The durability of India's parliamentary system and its central role in the Indian Constitution have provided a high quality of public scrutiny of foreign policy either through the tug-of-war between Government and Opposition or through a consensus on what is politically feasible. When the US or the Soviet Union have tried to impose their point of view on India through multilateral or bilateral channels of communication, the common stock of political discourse in the Indian parliament has played a uniquely important part in generating a creative tension for coping with Super Power pressure and threats to independence and autonomy.

Several lines of action suggest themselves for the Indian Parliament to transform the resilience of the Indian democratic system into strong political postures vis-a-vis the two Super Powers.

First, in the wider context of India's international relations, the Indo-Soviet relationship remains important in terms of economic, political and strategic interests. An overall view of General Secretary Mikhail Gorbachev's problem-solving framework, particularly towards China, indicates that for India to rely on historically conditioned stereotypes would be politically disadvantageous. The situations and relationships of the past eras may not be relevent to the era of *glasnost* and *perestroika*. The Russian and Indian political elite need to develop new patterns of relations if mistrust and misunderstanding are to be avoided at this transitational stage. India has substantial political resources for developing further interdependence between Moscow and New Delhi and yet avoid weakness in the relationship. It is India's political culture that can point to new ways in which the interaction might be streamlined. The Gorbachev visit to India showed that the "managerial" solutions adopted by Prime Minister Rajiv Gandhi are inadequate to deal with the new political thrust of the Soviet Union. The process of accomodation to the new Soviet realities on the part of India will be difficult unless New Delhi is seen as assigning a higher priority to political issues than to ritualising joint commitments on technical issues, like the Soviet offer of a Third World centre in India for training astronauts. Rajiv Gandhi's failure to discuss the geo-strategic significance of Tibet and Central Asia and his acceptance of Gorbachev's ambiguous statements on the Sino-Indian boundary dispute point to the dangers of secret dialogues largely insulated from political debate. If parliamentarians are to carry out their function they must actively work to increase the political content of India's relationship with both the Super Powers. Political summitry should not be allowed to be used for hynotising the Indian public media through quick fixes which are essential ingredients of managerial solutions but do not always develop workable options in dealing with global powers. Parliament should receive more information from the Prime Minister whenever either of the Super Powers mounts pressures to overrule India's policy goals. It should not be enough for the Prime Minister to gain a bureaucratic consensus. MPs specialising on foreign policy issues should insist on demanding a parliamentary consensus and the fullest expression of the nuances across the political spectrum, before serious issues like Indian support to Asian-Pacific security are decided.

Second, there is need to pay greater attention in Parliament to the interconnection between different policy areas like education and culture and science and technology in addition to foreign policy and security issues in developing the overall context for functional collaboration and political and economic agreements with the US and the Soviet Union. Parliament should not hesitate to highlight conflict of the Super Powers with Indian interests and values, and should establish a clear framework of action reflecting national interests. More efforts should be made to communicate to the public Parliament's resolve that the Super Powers will not be permitted to make India an arena for their mutual rivalry.

Third, there is a strong case for changing the character of the Consultative Committee attached to the Ministry of

External Affairs. Steps to make this change should be initiated without waiting for modifications in the strutcture of Committees attached to other Ministries. The specialist parliamentary committee dealing with foreign policy should be able to deal effectively with the dysfunctional aspects of bureaucratic politics, and have adequate sources of information on the major determinants of foreign policy decisions. There is urgent need to reduce the traditional prejudice and lack of confidence in the interaction between the officials and the politicians. Ministry of External Affairs officials should explain and defend their roles before the Committee. An analytical and exploratory approach in place of the present consultative opproach will encourage both the Executive and the legislature to overcome the present compartmentalised structure.

Fourth, it is necessary for Parliament to make some conscious effort to deal with lobbying on foreign policy questions. Both the Soviet Union and the United States have well-financed lobbies in New Delhi which are both active sources of political corruption and seek to distort bilateral relationships. This trend could be countered by Parliament strictly defining the norms for legitimate attention by the Embassies (especially of the US and the Soviet Union) to Members of Parliament. Parliament should also assess the behaviour of MPs who assist foreign lobbying at the expense of their legislative roles.

Fifth, as the world's biggest democracy Indian priorities in the field of human rights are quite different from those of military or civilian dictatorships. Parliament has strongly identified itself with the condemnation of apartheid in South Africa. But human rights violations in Eastern Europe and Tibet, and the violation of civic rights of American blacks and American Indians have met with lukewarm response at best. If parliamentary politics were supportive of human rights in both the power blocs, it world strength an independent orientation and a confident attitude towards Super Power relationships. There is also a good case for parliamentary initiatives on ecological measures which are being ignored chiefly because both the Super Powers are engaged in competitive expenditures on armaments.

If India's freedom of movement is not to become restricted by the changing relations of the United States and the Soviet Union in the years ahead, Parliament has to devise new techniques to augment its political resources in order to avoid both the appearance and reality of excessive dependence on either Super Power.

Parliament and Foreign Policy: A Study of the Parliamentary Discussion on the 1974 Nuclear Implosion

SHRIKANT PARANJPE

Control of Parliament on the Executive's sphere of activity flows from the idea of responsible government. Under the Indian pattern of parliamentary government this responsibility to Parliament is direct, constituting an individual and collective accountability of the ministers to Parliament. In normal circumstances such a control is sought through general debates on various issues, appointment of committees for seeking information, individual questioning by members, etc. . The primacy of Parliament can be felt through the effective use of these procedures in practice.

In the field of foreign policy, however, one observes a historical tendency to keep foreign policy issues outside the scope of public scrutiny. This tendency arises from two main reasons: the need for urgency and secrecy in decision-making and the specialised nature of the subject. This is not to say that Parliament ought to be kept in the dark on foreign policy issues. In India, while no formal limitation is placed on the role to be played by the Parliament in this field, there arise certain practical constraints. In terms of structural arrangements, there is a Consultative Committee to discuss various foreign policy issues.

Before the formation of the 'Informal Consultative Committees in 1954, Pandit Nehru used to meet a group of about twenty-five members regularly, to consult and discuss such matters which were not discussed in the House.[1] The Informal Consultative Committee on External Affairs, alongwith other such committees, was formed in 1954. Later, in 1969 the word 'Informal' was dropped. This Committee would normally meet once every session and once in between sessions to seek information on external affairs. However, the effectiveness of this Committee was limited due to the guidelines prescribed for its working. Despite the 1969 change, the guidelines maintain that the committee would remain informal in its working. Secondly, no reference to the discussion of the meeting was to be made in Parliament. Third, the Committee could not summon witnesses, send for files or examine records.[2] There are thus several restrictions on the Committee to become effective as a medium to control or influence foreign policy decisions.

The Framework

In a system that operates on the majority party mode, it is difficult to distinguish between the Executive as the Government and the legislature as the Parliament. Unlike the 'separation of powers' model, in the parliamentary system the Members of the Government are also Members of Parliament. In fact, it is the majority party in Parliament that forms the Government that later secures formal sanction from the Head of the State.

The parliamentary system works on two integrated concepts that appear contradictory: the concept of the supremacy of Parliament and the power of the Executive, as the Government, to take initiative in the formulation and implementation of policy. The former is a constitutional position while the latter has more of a political base. This Executive privilege and the role played by the Parliament in influencing the Executive in its actions forms the crux of the debate on Parliament's role in foreign policy. The Executive, which is a creature of the legislature, is kept accountable to it by a variety of structural and procedural provisions. These include, debates in the house, interpellations, questions (both written and oral), half-hour discussions, motions, adjournment motions, discussions on matters of public importance, calling attention motions, censure motions, no-confidence motions, resolutions and committees. Of these methods, debates in the house and questions are the most frequently used methods; the others have particular and more specific functions. The Executive control, on the other hand, is effected through two important measures, party discipline kept through the whip and the threat of dissolution of the House. Despite the various constitutional provisions, the tilt in the balance of the two wings depends more on political factors. These would include, the nature of the majority held by the party in power, the nature of the leadership of the Government, the strength of the Opposition, etc. . . . Crisis situations apart, a strong leadership and a strong majority would grant the Executive a sufficiently wide scope for action.

In India, ever since independence, the Congress party has played an extraordinary role in the Indian political system. Except for a brief period between 1977 and 1979 the party has held the majority in the national parliament. Such a one party dominance has all the necessary ingredients for a strong Executive. In the field of foreign policy there were two additional factors that made the executive dominate in this area. One was the traditional image of the Parliament being 'incompetent', politically speaking, in this area and the other was the phenomenol role that Nehru played in the formation and implementation of India's foreign policy. The Indian legislature, despite the development of a number of democratic institutions, has not succeeded in establishing its dominance over the Executive in terms of influence on foreign policy making. Yet, it would be misleading to term the need for 'parliamentary sanction' as mere fiction. The Indian Parliament has been active enough to make its opinions known to the Government. It must be noted here that Parliamentary influence need not always come in the form of censure of Governmental policy. In fact it would rarely do so. An adverse vote in the House would make the Government liable to resign. Influence, in this context, is to be looked at as an input in the decision-making process.

India's nuclear policy, as it came to be formulated revolved around two features: that of research and development for harnessing atomic energy for peaceful purposes and that of self-sufficiency in the nuclear programme.[3] The Sino-Indian war of 1962 and the Chinese entry into the nuclear club in 1964 brought about the first shifts in India's nuclear policy posture. Lal Bahadur Shastri announced to Parliament that India was willing to consider the use of a nuclear blast for peaceful purposes.[4] Indian policy thus became a peace policy with a peaceful nuclear explosion (PNE) capability. Indian opposition to the Nuclear Non-Proliferation Treaty (NPT) was a logical extension of this independent policy. India viewed the NPT as discriminatory and refused to sign it. The situation of the late sixties and the early seventies finally culminated in the decision to have a PNE. This demonstration was an extraordinary event in Indian domestic and foreign policy. The debate that followed raised a number of questions of far-reaching significance. These focused on both the immediate and the future implications of the Indian decision of now having a nuclear policy that was avowedly peaceful and had also demonstrated a PNE capability.

The present paper concentrates on the Parliamentary debates and questions to understand some linkages between the Parliament and foreign policy-making. The issue taken up for this purpose relates to India's nuclear policy, more specifically the impact of India's Nuclear Implosion in May 1974.

Debate in India on nuclear policy was minimal until the mid 1960s. In the late 1960s the debate focused mainly on the Nuclear Non-Proliferation Treaty. Discussion at this juncture also focused on issues like Peaceful Nuclear Explosions (PNE) and the need or otherwise to go in for nuclear weapons.

The present paper starts with certain broad hypotheses:

— that, given the nature of foreign policy decision-making, its inherent secrecy and specialisation, decisions tend to be made public only after they are taken/implemented;
— that, given this *post facto* publication, the public scrutiny then performed acts as a feedback on the Government's decision making process;
— that it is also likely, that, in some circumstances the public scrutiny is conducted before the decision is taken. This could be done for any reason: to use as propaganda to indicate indirectly to the other party the trend of Government thinking, to stall issues, etc.

Parliament and Foreign Policy:

The Policy

India conducted its first PNE in May 1974. Following that the Indian Prime Minister made a detailed statement in the House covering a whole range of issues born out of the 'fall-out' of the implosion. Later, during the Janata Party's rule Mr. Morarji Desai also explained the stand taken by his Government on India's nuclear policy. Given below are the main issues spelt out by both the Prime Ministers.

The Lok Sabha Statement of 22 July 1974 (Mrs. Indira Gandhi)

The statement made by Mrs. Gandhi on the May Implosion covers the following areas:[5]

(*i*) The experiment conducted was a part of the research and development work carried out in pursuance of the national objective of harnessing atomic energy for peaceful purposes.

(*ii*) India is willing to share her nuclear technology with other countries provided proper conditions for understanding and trust are created.

(*iii*) The reaction of the Developing Countries to the PNE was by and large favourable.

(*iv*) The United States expressed satisfaction that the International Atomic Energy Agency (IAEA) safeguard system had worked and that the material used for the PNE was not from the United States. The US Government reiterated its stand against nuclear proliferation.

(*v*) The Soviet Union noted that India carried out a research programme striving to keep level with the world technology in peaceful uses of nuclear technology. The French had congratulated India while the Japanese had expresesd regrets. China had simply noted the event without any comment.

(*vi*) The Canadian reaction had been sharp. Canada was satisfied that India had not violated any bilateral agreement. But Canada maintained that the experiment represented a severe setback to efforts being made in the international community to prevent all nuclear testing and to inhibit the proliferation of nuclear explosion technology. The Indian Government disagreed with the Canadian view and hoped that the differences of interpretation could be sorted out in bilateral talks.

(*vii*) The peaceful nature and the economic purposes of the PNE were explained to Pakistan's Prime Minister and therefore India could not understand the talk of blackmail made by Pakistan.

The Lok Sabha and Rajya Sabha Statements of July 1978 (Mr. Morarji Desai)

During the years of Mr. Desai's Premiership two issues figured with prominence in India's nuclear policy, both being the direct 'fall-outs' of the 1974 PNE experiment: the stoppage of supply of fuel to the Tarapur Atomic plant by the US and the suspension of Canadian fuel to the Rajasthan plant. Mr. Desai's statements on nuclear policy were mainly the products of this background. He made some important pronouncements about India's stand on issues like PNE.[6] His statements were then discussed in Parliament.[7] The main areas covered by the statement are as follows:

(*i*) India was using nuclear technology for peaceful purposes. But Mr. Desai questioned the need for conducting a PNE for the purpose of using nuclear energy for peaceful purposes. He regarded the results of the PNE as inadequate compensation for the jolt to international public opinion and the consequences it had on India's peaceful pursuit of nuclear knowledge.

(*ii*) Mr. Desai denied any pressure from outside powers in the decision taken of not conducting any further PNE.

To take an overview of the various discussions that took place in Parliament on the 1974 PNE, one can spell out certain areas that figured prominently, Study of these areas in the context of the debates in Parliament could help in throwing some light on the dynamics of the relationship between Parliament and foreign policy decision-making.

(i) The PNE experiment of 1974, its effects in terms of knowledge gained, uses, dependence for technology and raw material, production of atomic weapons and cooperation with other countries.
(ii) US reaction in terms of fuel supply to Tarapur.
(iii) Canadian reaction in the context of fuel supply to the Rajasthan plant.
(iv) Reaction of Pakistan and China.

The Debates

The PNE and Related Issues: Mrs. Gandhi in her statement made in the Lok Sabha on the 1974 PNE makes reference to two earlier statements on India's nuclear policy made in 1972 and 1973.[8] Answering a question in 1972, she made it clear that the Atomic Commission (AEC) was constantly reviewing the progress in the technology of underground nuclear explosions both from the theoretical and experimental angles, also taking into account their potential economic benefits and possible environmental hazards.[9] Again in 1973, Mrs. Gandhi repeated the earlier statement and went on to deny that any schedule had been fixed for conducting a PNE.[10]

The questions asked by the Members in Parliament immediately after the 1974 PNE had a very wide range. These dealt with such issues as India's capacity to produce atomic bombs[11]; the stand taken in the UNO on Nuclear tests;[12] embargo on sale of nuclear material to India;[13] peaceful uses of atomic energy;[14] and so on. The questions asked have all been basically information-seeking questions. Consequently, one finds the answers given also plainly informative. At all times, however, an attempt appears to have been made by the Government to insist on India's peaceful intentions. By 1975-76 the trend of questions turned towards gaining information on the results of the test.[15] Here too, the answers remained informative.

The tone of the debate changes after the coming in of the the Janata Government. Questioned on the External Affairs Minister's statement in New York that India would not manufacture nuclear weapons the reply given stated in detail the

Government's policy.[16] While no mention was made of the PNE, the answer stated India's opposition to proliferation of nuclear weapons. As regards the NPT, India's continued opposition to its discriminatory nature continued to hold good. The one major change that the Janata Government instituted was the abandoning of the idea of the need for a PNE. This raised questions as to whether there were pressures from the US or the USSR for taking this decision.[17] But when Mrs. Gandhi returned to power in January 1980 she once again stated her commitment to use of atomic energy for peaceful purposes. As regards conducting of PNE she maintained that it would be decided on the basis of India's national interest.[18]

Interestingly, the parliamentary discussion on major policy statements of both the External Affairs Minister and the Prime Minister of the Janata Government came about as a result of their statements made in the US. This could well be linked to the problems of Tarapur fuel supply and the American insistence on the application of the provisions of the Nuclear Non-Proliferation Act of 1978.[19]

US Reaction, Tarapur Problems : Since the 1974 PNE, the American interest in the relationship between nuclear power and potential spread of nuclear weapons started to increase. This interest was to culminate in the major policy decisions taken by the Carter administration in 1977 and 1978. The delays in supply of enriched uranium to the Tarapur plant began around 1975.[20]

Questions in Parliament on this issue were linked in such a manner as to find out the various motives for the disruption in supply of the fuel. Thus it was asked, whether the US wants India to sign the NPT or accept certain safeguards or if the US fears India producing nuclear weapons[21] At one point there was a heated debate on the US Secretary of State's statement about Indian intentions of producing atomic weapons.[22]

On the whole, one finds that there is a similarity of tone in the discussions, despite the changes in Government. The questions asked were not basically informative as they had been earlier. Here there is evident anger against the American policies seen in the various motives ascribed to the US decision. On the part of the Government there appears to be a uniformly low key approach, indicating that the Government was trying to avoid provocations. This could very well be so because the Government was simultaneously busy in establishing a dialogue in bilateral talks with the US to resolve the crisis. Very little of these talks is reflected in Parliament. What is reflected is only the assurance given from time to time that the talks were progressing.

Canadian Reaction : Indo-Canadian nuclear cooperation goes back to the 1950s. Until the coming of the NPT the cooperation between the two Commonwealth powers was fairly close. It has been claimed that in 1971 Mr. Trudeau (Canada) tried unsuccessfully to get Mrs. Gandhi to promise not to develop a nuclear device.[23] The Canadian reaction to the 1974 PNE had, as noted earlier, been sharp, and Canada suspended cooperation in the nuclear field.

It appears from the nature of questioning on the Canadian matter that the intensity of the debate was not as high as that of Tarapur. The questions asked have by and large focused on the status of negotiations and the answers have continued the hopeful note.[24] The Government made a detailed explanatory statement in 1976 giving the Indian side of the story.[25] Again, unlike Tarapur the Canadian problem was solved much earlier importing the necessary Heavy Water from the Soviet Union. Because of this substitute arrangement the questions now focused on ths safeguards imposed by the Soviet Union.[26]

Pakistan's Case : Pakistan's reaction that the Indian PNE posed a threat to Pakistan's security was in a sense not unexpected. Two moves made by Pakistan in the post-1974 period are important for South Asia. One is the public declaration made by Pakistan of its intention to enter the nuclear field.[27] and the other is the introduction in the UNO of the idea of a Nuclear Free Zone for South Asia and the Indian Ocean.[28]

Parliamentary discussion on Pakistan has by and large focused on these issues. The Government stand as reflected in the answers to questions on Pakistan's intentions of producing an atomic bomb seems to take care that the overall pattern of Indo-Pak dialogue is not harmed. Thus the answers plead ignorance of the knowledge of Pakistan's progress in this field or are simply non-committal. A similar approach is also followed about the reports of French aid to Pakistan in this field.[30] About the Nuclear Free Zone Proposal the answers are more categoric. It is made clear that Pakistan did not make this proposal out of genuine concern for disarmament, that Pakistan should have consulted India prior to moving this resolution, that India did not believe in isolating South Asia from the Asia-Pacific region for such a proposal, and that India was opposed to it.[31] Here, one gets the feeling that the Government is making public its stand on this issue with a view to educating public opinion. This must have been necessary because India's avowed peace policy and India's opposition to this proposal would otherwise appear contradictory.

Parliament and Foreign Policy : The Linkages

This paper was started with certain limitations in mind. The link between Parliament and foreign policy-making is far too complex to be understood with only one issue as a case study. For, going beyond such documentary evidence as reports of committees, debates, recorded speeches, etc., there are certain influences which essentially operate at the human level. These include the role played by certain interest and pressure groups, individual members who wield influence, academic writings, and so on. Yet, keeping in mind all such limitations, the paper tries to go into the 'give' and 'take' indulged in by the Government in Parliament.

The issue of the 1974 PNE was chosen for this study because in the last decade, starting from the creation of Bangladesh, this was the most important domestic development having serious repercussions on foreign policy. It was, therefore, expected that the Indian representatives would be adequately interested in this development. The subject of Atomic Energy which was normally not discussed was now to be discussed from a different angle.[32] From the data collected it does appear that this issue was adequately discussed, both in the immediate aftermath of the PNE and later in the context of the problems raised by the PNE.

The decision to go in for a PNE had all the ingredients to

keep it a well-guarded secret. It is true that India's intention of going in for such a test was of long-standing; it was made clear as early as in 1967 in the Geneva Disarmament deliberations that preceded the NPT.[33] Even Mrs. Gandhi had made reference to it in 1972 and 1973 in Parliament. The Government had also, time and again, made clear India's peaceful intentions in its nuclear programme. Despite all this openness, the May 1974 implosion did come as a surprise to all.

Mrs. Gandhi's first statement to Parliament on the PNE comes on 22 July 1974, at least two months after the event. Parliament was not in session on 18 May 1974 when the PNE took place. In effect therefore sufficient time had elapsed for a very lively discussion to take place outside Parliament. When finally it was reported to Parliament it had already lost its 'recent' value. Consequently, one does not find much debate taking place on the event's importance *per se*. Unlike this delay, one recalls that the statement of Mr. Desai was discussed in Parliament immediately after it was made. This 'recent' value was an important factor to be noted in the discussion that took place. However, the 'recentness' in the discussion was only one of the reasons for the sharpness in the debate. The tone of the debate had its origin in a more fundamental feature of Parliament at that time. For the first time in the history of the Indian Parliament there existed a non-Congress party Prime Minister; further, he was making a statement that had almost amounted to a shift in the stand developed over the past decade or more.

Did Parliament go beyond pure discussion? To this there could be a counter question: How far did the Government allow the scope for a more effective role to be played by Parliament? In most cases the Government's attitude was essentially informative. The Government explained its stand on Tarapur and on negotiations with Canada. On matters of atomic weapons, all direct and indirect questions were cut short with a steadfast reply about India's peaceful intentions. The only exception appears to be the reply on the questions relating to Pakistan's proposal of a Nuclear Free Zone for South Asia. Here, there appears a deliberate effort at giving reasons for a particular Indian response. Parliament was used to express the Indian stand and the reasons behind that stand to the concerned parties.

The limits of Governmental initiative and corresponding legistative role can be understood in the context of the role-design that has evolved in the practice of foreign policy over the years. First, in this context comes the role perception of the Members of Parliament. Ideal parliamentary procedure requires the Members to have a 'national' area-focus of their perception of their role. Unfortunately, while foreign policy is a matter of collective national focus, it is perceived to have only a marginal significance on the careers of the representatives, especially in matters of re-election. Consequently, the basic thrust of their perception on vital issues remains tied to their constituency/region/section.

Second, Parliament entails certain structural hurdles. Unlike the Presidential model, the Executive is the creature of the legislature. This denies the existence of competing centres of power as they exist in the Presidential model. Parliament tackles the executive not as an independent body but as a body on whose actions control is to be exercised. This implicit granting of the power to take the initiative to the Executive is further strengthened by the fact that it is the majority party in Parliament that forms the Executive.

A third role-design has emerged through the features of the Indian party system. The Congress party has enjoyed continuous majority support in Parliament. It has also been led by strong personalities. The personality factor plays a significant role in the formulation of foreign policy since the bulk of the Indian electorate are still "uneducated" enough to consider foreign policy a specialised subject requiring specialised knowledge. Nehru's position as the principal architect of foreign policy set the trend of Executive dominance. Nehru tended to treat Parliament as a forum to explain his ideas and policies instead of consulting it. Mrs. Indira Gandhi's relations with Parliament were not different from Nehru's on this ground. The little reduction, if at all, in Executive power is seen in the brief periods of Lal Bahadur Shastri and Morarji Desai. In both cases, however, the roots of such decline in power have to be traced to the respective party organizations of the times and not in the role played by Parliament. Strong party organisations caused the shift in power from the office of the Prime Minister to that of the party, not Parliament.

The Executive can use Parliament to perform two important functions: act as a feed-back and as a sounding board for policy formulation. The feed-back role is the most established function that the representatives are expected to perform. It is rare for the Executive to solicit direct advice from Parliament before the formulation of policy. In a recent session the Defence Minister sought such advice from Parliament.[34] There is also a third likely use of Parliament. The Government can deliberately introduce a question in Question Hour to explain some policy intentions. Such an 'inspired' question can be used to warn a third party/country of the likely reaction to any particular course of action.

Given the limitations of Parliament as a body, it is necessary to consider the role of the Consultative Committees. A small group sitting with an informal set-up has greater chance of influencing decision-making than Parliament with its large numbers. But studies on the role of this committee have not come to a conclusion, which would indicate the effectiveness of its influence on the Government.[35]

Finally, there exists the long-term consideration of public opinion. Parliament can become an effective forum for expression and exchange of a wide range of views which the Government can ill afford to ignore. India does not have well developed pressure and interest groups that can lobby for support in Parliament. Nevertheless, there exist a variety of loosely organised interests which can play a role in Parliament.

Notes

1. Maheshwari S.R., 'Informal Consultative Committees of the Parliament' *Journal of Constitutional and Parliamentary Studies*, Vol. II (1), January-March 1968, p. 35.
2. 'Guidelines to Regulate the Constitution and Functioning of Consultative Committees', in Misra K.P., 'Foreign Policy Planning in India' in Misra K.P., (ed), *Foreign Policy of India: A Book of Readings*, (New Delhi, Thompson Press, 1977), pp. 86-87.
3. Speech in the Lok Sabha, 10 May 1954, in Jawaharlal Nehru, *India's*

Foreign Policy: Selected Speeches, September 1946—April 1961, (New Delhi, Publications Division, 1961), p. 191.
4. India, Lok Sabha, *Debates,* Series 3, Vol. XXXV (10), Session 10, 27 November 1964, Col. 2287.
5. India, Lok Sabha, *Debates,* Series 5, Vol. XLI (1), Session 11, 1974, Cols. 264-269.
6. (i) *Asian Recorder,* Vol. XXIV, No. 28, 9-15 July 1978, pp. 14397-399.
   (ii) *U.N. Monthly Chronicle* Vol. XV (7), July 1978, pp. 67-68.
7. (i) India, Lok Sabha Debates, Series 6, Vol. XVI, Session 5, 26-7-1978, Cols. 359-79; and
   (ii) India, Rajya Sabha, *Debates,* Vol. CVI (II), 31 July 1978, Cols. 135-39.
8. India, Lok Sabha, *Debates,* n. 5, Col. 264-65.
9. India, Lok Sabha, *Debates,* Series 5, Vol. XX (3), Session 6, November 1972, Vol. 49.
10. India, Rajya Sabha, *Debates,* Vol. LXXXVI (4), 15 November 1973, Col. 138-39.
11. India, Lok Sabha, *Debates,* Series 5, Vol. XLI, Session 11, 25 July 1974, Cols. 41-42.
12. India, Lok Sabha, *Debates,* Series 5, Vol. XLVI, Session 12, 5 July 1974, Col. 78, 151-52.
13. *Ibid.,* 4 July 1974, Col. 71.
14. India, Lok Sabha, *Debates,* Series 5, Vol. XLI, Session 11, 24 July 1974, Col. 201.
15. India, Lok Sabha, *Debates,* Series 5,
    (i) Vol. XLIX, Session 13, 12 March 1975, Col. 191.
    (ii) Vol. L, Session 13; 19 March 1975, Cols. 69-70.
    (iii) Vol. LI, Session 13, 23 April 1975, Cols. 49, 193-94.
    (iv) Vol. LV, Session 15, 7 January 1976, Col. 114.
    (v) Vol. LVIII Session 16, 10 March 1976, Col. 57.
16. India, Lok Sabha, *Debates,* Series 6, Vol. VII, Session 3, 17 November 1977, Cols. 118-19.
17. India, Lak Sabha, *Debates,* n. 7 (i).
18. India Rajya Sabha, *Debates,* Vol. CXIII (3), 13 March 1980, Cols. 27-31.
19. For details see: *Facts and Figures, Nuclear Non-Proliferation,* (New Delhi, USICA, n. d.).
20. Noorani A.G., 'Indo-US Nuclear Relations', *Asian Survey,* Vols. XXI (4), April 1981, p. 415.
21. India, Lok Sabha, *Debates,*
    (i) Series 5, Vol. XLII, Session 11, 29 August 1974, Col. 101.
    (ii) Series 5, Vol. XLV, Session 12, 20 November 1974, Cols. 114.
    (iii) Series 5, Vol. XLV, Session 12, 21 November 1974, Cols. 40, 63.
    (iv) Series 6, Vol. X, Session 4, 1 March 1978, Cols. 189-190.
    (v) Series 6, Vol. X, Session 4, 23 February 1978, Cols. 213-214.
    (vi) Series 6, Vol. XII, Session 4, 23 March 1978, Cols. 215-218.
    (vii) Series 7, Vol. 1, Session 1, 30 January 1980, Cols. 71-72.

22. India, Lok Sabha, *Debates*, Series 5, Vol. LVIII, Session 16, 11 March 1976, Cols. 28-31.
23. Lyon Peter, 'The Indian Bomb' in K.P. Misra (ed), n. 3., pp. 209.
24. India, Lok Sabha, *Debates*,
    (i) Series 5, Vol. XLV, Session 12, 20 November 1974, Col. 91.
    (ii) Series 5, Vol. LVI, Session 15, 21 January 1976, Col. 114.
    (iii) Series 5, Vol. LVII, Session 16, 10 March 1976, Cols. 92-93.
    (iv) Series 5, Vol. LXIII, Session 17, 11 August 1976, Cols. 62-63.
    (v) Series 6, Vol. IV, Session 2, 14 July 1977, Col. 42.
25. India, Lok Sabha, *Debates*, Series 5, Vol. LXII, Session 16, 20 may 1976, Cols. 14-15.
26. India, Lok Sabha, *Debates*,
    (i) Series 6, Vol. VII, Session 3, 16 November 1977, Cols. 183-84.
    (ii) Series 6, Vol. XX, Session 6, 13 December 1977, Col. 60.
27. *Asian Recorder*, Vol. XX No. 42, 15-21 October 1974 p. 12248.
28. *Asian Recorder*, Vol. XX, No. 44, 29 October—4 November 1974, p. 12269.
29. India, Lok Sabha, *Debates*,
    (i) Series 5, Vol. XLIII, Session 11, 29 August 1974, Col. 117.
    (ii) Series 5, Vol. XLV, Session 12, 21 November 1974, Cols. 60-61.
    (iii) Series 6, Vol. VIII, Session 3, 30 November 1977, Cols. 66-67.
    (iv) Series 6, Vol. XX, Session 6, 7 December 1978, Col. 155.
30. India, Lok Sabha, *Debates*, Series 6, Vol. XXI, Session 6, 21 December 1978, Col. 218.
31. India, Lok Sabha, *Debates*,
    (i) Series 5, Vol. XLVII, Session 12, 12 December 1974, Col. 29.
    (ii) Series 5, Vol. XV, Session 15, 8 January 1976, Cols. 76-77.
    (iii) Series 6, Vol. VII, Session 3, 8 December 1977, Col. 45.
32. India, Lok Sabha, *Debates*. Series 5, Vol. XLI, Session 11, 22 July 1974, Col. 269.
33. Subrahmanyam K., 'The Indian Nuclear Test in a Global Perspective', in K.P. Misra (ed), n. 2, p. 189.
34. *The Hindu*, Overseas Edition, (Madras), 4 May 1985.
35. Misra K.P., 'Foreign Policy Planning in India' in Misra K.P. (ed), n. 2.

The Foreign Policy Debate in Canada*

JOE CLARK

[*Mr. Joe Clark has concerned himself over the years with the interaction of the Canadian political system with its domestic and international environment. His suggestions in this essay, which is excerpted from a speech derive from the Canadian political culture which ensures a deliberate and positive effort to discover the source of legitimacy of foreign policy in the political process of parliament. The author examines the distinctive characteristics of Candian foreign policy and takes into consideration the specific parameters of parliamentary politics within which the forces which induce change are allowed to shape policy perceptions. The essay provides an excellent example of the thinking style of a policy-maker who has to handle questions and issues of foreign policy in a political climate where parliamentary questions and debates sustain effectiveness of government.—Editor*]

We are a country of some twenty-five million extremely fortunate people, spared the poverty and disease that ravage most of the developing world. We are also free of the deep psychological scars of having had our own community torn by war, as Uganda has been; and the two Koreas, and the two Germanys, and Russia have been; as the old states of Estonia, Latvia, and Lithuania, who were "converted" to Marxist-Leninism by external conquest, have been; and as the United States, after Vietnam, had been.

We are the world's eighth-largest trading nation, with the human and physical resources to grow stronger. Our people have an interest in almost every question in the world. As a

---

*Adapted from an address to the Couchiching institute on Public Affairs.

nation of immigrants, we come from Sri Lanka and Lebanon, from the Punjab or El Salvador, from Zimbabwe and from boats bobbing in the China Sea. As a nation of traders and missionaries, we maintain Jesuit schools in Ethiopia and India and Bhutan, we run leper colonies near Yaouande, our salesmen sell computer software to the Japanese and rapid transit systems to the Mexicans; our investors are constructing bulldozers in Thailand; and our developers are building oil towns in deserts, and irrigation systems almost anywhere there is dry land.

We can also claim to have created the modern Commonwealth. We practically invented United Nations peacekeeping, and have honed our rare skills as peacekeepers in Indochina, in Cyprus and in the Sinai. We helped establish the multilateral trading system, and are currently one of its most creative defenders. We are, arguably, the developed country most trusted in the Third World, not because we utter moral verities, but because we send Candian specialists to remote parts of Thailand to teach villagers to innoculate chickens against disease; because our doctors and nurses in that country work the Khao-I-Dang camp hospitals where refugee children come daily with limbs blown off by mines set by one side or the other.

And yet—and yet—some self-consciousness shrugs off these real accomplishments by Canadians, and returns to the ritual of doubt : "Who in the world needs Canada?"

Not to belabour the point, Valentyn Moroz, Georgi Vins, the Vashchenko and Chmykhalov families and more than six hundred other people needed Canada, over the last five years to secure their exit from the Soviet Union and reunification with their families in this country. And there have been nearly 95,000 Indochinese who needed Canada, those who have been admitted to Canada as refugees since 1975. On a per capita basis, we have been the most welcoming nation in the world to the Indochinese.

600 families in the village of Mutara, Rwanda, depend on Canadian-financed irrigation for their survival. 80,000 people around the village of Nioki in Zaire depend on Canadian-built medical clinics. 12,000 people in Tabakouta, Senegal, support themselves as a result of Canadian development of their

banana farms. In 50 rural villages of the Piura and Tuubas regions of northern Peru, 40,000 people have roofs over their heads as a result of Canadian reconstruction efforts after a flood. And 30,000 people in the shanty towns around Lima now have clean water because CIDA made $500,000 available. They also needed Canada.

In Bridgetown, Barbados, there is to be a new fishing harbour because a Canadian company undertook a feasibility study with CIDA financing. In India, hydro-electric plants and new railways are being built, and staff trained to run them, because Canadians saw the possibilities and prepared the groundwork. People in these countries also needed Canada.

So did the discussions on chemical weapons at Geneva, where Ambassador Don McPhail nearly got agreement. So did the committee of like-minded nations dealing with disarmament at the U.N. in New York, known as the Barton Group, after Ambassador Bill Barton of Winnipeg.

If you need further answers to that ritual of doubt, ask children in Ethiopia; ask the Contadora countries; ask the Western group we chaired at the Nairobi Conference; ask the West Germans, who must live daily beside massive armament, and received a strong signal of common solidarity through an additional twelve hundred Canadian troops newly sent to NATO; ask the people of Holland after the Second World War. Ask the Cypriots who for 20 years have been spared the bloody ravages of civil war thanks to the few hundred Canadian soldiers making up the thin blue line in Nicosia. Ask Jamacia and Zimbabwe and the Philippines and the more than 20 other countries who would all be helped if the world accepts our Prime Minister's Third Window proposal.

We have an envied tradition of using limited resources to accomplish great ends. and the fact is that our resources and our ability, and if we wish it our influence, are growing. The fact that we—and much of the world—are looking to economic growth as the instrument of progress strengthens the position of this nation, with our humanitarian traditions and modern economy. By the way, when I say much of the world, I include Mr. Gorbachev, Mr. Deng, Mr. Kadar, Mr. Quett Masire, and leaders of other countries reforming their economies, whether timidly or boldly. Some have a certain advantage in size, or access to markets, but we are leaders in technology and in trust, currencies that count.

When I tabled the Government's Green Paper on Canada's international relations in May 1985, we aimed to start along a path towards addressing this question of using our limited resources to best effect.

In recent years, the world has undergone dramatic changes. The most salient features for Canada are that we can take our prosperity and onr securiiy much less for granted. As the Green Paper noted, where once we could rely on our natural resources for wealth and on our geogrophic location for security, neither can any longer assure us of the peaceful and prosperous future we used to assume would be ours. Instead, we are faced with international economic and political trends which, if left unattended, could seriously diminish our national wealth and perhaps even lead us and the world to the brink of disaster.

We want to be effective internationally, but that requires influence. Our influence derives in large measure from our position as a wealthy, politically-stable member of the Western Alliance. We draw on other assets as well, but we cannot avoid the hard truth that if we don't pay, we don't play.

For these reasons, the Green Paper suggested that priority attention be accorded to refurbishing our traditional assets, to improving our international economic competitiveness and increasing our influence on international political and security issues. We must be in a position not just to talk about the future but to do something about it.

In general terms, what makes foreign policy today so complex is the formidable number an sheer stubbornness of the interlinkages—linkages among countries and among issues. More than ever before, countries have been drawn into mutual dependency through trade, investment and technology flows. Problems of joint management of structural change, of resources and of cross-border environmental pollution have created a new agenda for international diplomacy. Economic and political crises interact, for example in the Mid-East, with disastrous consequences.

Economic and political issues are bound together in intimate ways. Consider the global economy. The links in the chain include high budgetary deficits and interest rates in the US and elsewhere, currency misalignments, high unemployment and slumping competitiveness, structural distortions, Third World indebtedness, and—globally—looming trade protectionism. There is a very real danger that positive economic adjustments and political accommodations may not be made. Mounting protectionist pressure may yet permanently damage the international trade and payments system. And even if that doesn't happen, competition within the system is obviously going to remain very tough, and the political pressures difficult to bear.

In looking at the problems of managing this tangle, certain realities are clear.

First, International affairs cannot be managed only by the political and economic Super Powers. They don't have the solutions; on the other hand, they do have national self-interests that may or may not accord with the general good. There is no White Knight country, Super Power or otherwise, which has the key to unilaterally managing the problems of the international system.

Second,—this is the corollary—management has to be multilateral, plurilateral, collective, or joint. Management must also be flexible and adaptable. There is nothing, no dominating or restraining force, that can replace the world order system embodied in the major international institutions and negotiating forums. These must be maintained, and strengthened where necessary.

Third—this is the conclusion—the concept of national "role" has to emerge from a critical analysis of what is needed to make this international system work, and a pragmatic examination of national vocations. It doesn't emerge from any abstract or wishful notion of what a nation might like to be seen to do, or what it once did.

What does this mean for Canada ? It means that we, like others have to start with an accurate sense of our own interests, capacities and problems—but above all our interest —as we look at the world. I want to suggest to you strongly that there is no contradiction between doing well in the world and doing good in the world. If we are not doing well economically we will be more likely to retreat into protectionism and insularity, more likely to lose the resources necessary to make a positive contribution to development and to peace-keeping, and to famine and refugees, and more likely to lose the inclination to play a positive international role, as we grow more preoccupied with economic problems at home. There is an obvious connection between sane domestic policies and a sane international system. Policy coherence is as much an international, as a domestic concern for an open country like Canada.

To really appreciate the nature of Canadian interests, in their present configuration, is going to involve rather painful reappraisal. The Green Paper that initiated the current International Relations Review began this process with a little reality therapy on current facts of Canadian life. I wanted it to emphasize our critical dependence on foreign—particularly US—markets for our prosperity; our declining share of world trade and sagging competitiveness, the importance of our getting serious about structural adjustment; the evolving security challenge facing our country. The key message I wanted conveyed through the Green Paper was simply this: we have to do better. The status quo will not work.

Doing better means involving Canadians in the international issues that bear on their competitiveness and security. It means provoking their interest and listening to their concerns. Parliament's Special Joint Committee is doing a good job of that now, in hearings across the country.

And there will be other Parliamentary initiatives. In ten months in this portfolio, I have used Parliamentary statements on motions, allowing debate and questions on five occasions so far. The former Government did not once in five years use this mechanism to allow for wider House of Commons discussion. We invited Committee debate on the North Warning System before we proceeded, in contrast to the earlier Government. We insisted on public debate of our obligations under NORAD, before the renewal date next year, and had to fight to get the Opposition to agree to the reference. So we are opening up the foreign policy process. What we have to build toward, through this kind of public consultation, is nothing less than a collective national effort to see ourselves clearly. To achieve that, the Review process will have to thrash through some difficult policy options.

But whatever specific policy recommendations ultimately emerge from the Review, the general question of Canada's place and purpose in the world is not, in the meantime, hanging in abeyance. Leaving aside questions of particular policy and strategy emphasis, two things ought to be obvious. First, what we are doing in the world—I'm talking about action, not about abstractions—is working very hard to preserve the international economic system, prevent a calamitous war, and deal with human anguish in the developing world. And second, the way we are going about this reflects some remarkable Canadian attributes and areas of experience. I say these things ought to be obvious, but sometimes they're blurred by some old ghosts of inferiority and passivity that history has left with us.

There is one other aspect of Canadian foreign policy that I think needs further emphasis. The test of whether a foreign policy is distinctively Canadian is not whether it is sharply different from the United States of America. The test is whether it serves Canadian interests and the international structures on which we depend.

Obviously our interests will often parallel those of the US. We share a common faith in democratic values, a common knowledge that those values are rejected and opposed by an armed Soviet system, and a common determination to defend our values.

Sometimes our interests will differ from the Americans, as they differ now regarding the embargo of Nicaragua.

As the Canadian policy debate proceeds, I hope people who might have seen Canadian foreign policy as a Canadian-US affair will take a wider view of the world. Of course the United States is of pre-eminent importance to us; it could not be otherwise, given our geography, our values our relative populations and power. But the United States, is important to many others also, indeed to everyone else, and for us to be blinded by our relations with that country—to let apoplexy affect our judgement each time the Pentagon says something stupid—is to deny our identity and interests.

In the next decade, our greatest growth in new trade will not be found in the United States, but in Southeast Asia, if we pay attention to Southeast Asia.

Our political influence in the developing world is strong precisely because we have demonstrated that a democratic Western nation can approach practical problems of development in a way different from the United States and, indeed, different from Britain and different from France.

Our influence in international institutions is precisely because the distinctive Canadian characteristic is to bring opposing sides together, and try to make the system work on a collective basis, as we are doing in UNESCO, as we are doing through the Commonwealth on South Africa, as we are doing with our special trade policy missions to developing countries, to seek practical agreement on the scope of a new MTN, indeed as we are doing in Contadora.

And so, finally, who needs Canada? Let's not overlook the most obvious response: Canadians want and need Canada to be active internationally. We need that, not only to have our interests protected and advanced, but also to have our collective sense of ourselves affirmed and projected. We are what we do, not only at home but abroad, and I intend to ensure that foreign policy of Canada reflects the whole of this modern and outward-looking country.

The question of "Who in the World Needs Canada" is simply another anachronism. In a complex world, it isn't a matter of identifying some hapless country in need of a friend. Our obligations and opportunities are broader. The hard-pressed international system as a whole needs us, and we need it. Skillful collective inspiration is required in order to keep the system working. If we Canadians are not qualified to help accomplish that task, then I do not know who is.

Bibliography

INDIA

Appadorai, A., "Parliament's Review of our Foreign Policy," *Eastern Economist*, Vol. 54, No. 23, June 1970.

Appadorai, A. and Rajan, M.S., *India's Foreign Policy and Relations*, New Delhi, South Asian Publisher, 1985.

Andersen, Walter K., "Domestic Roots of Indian Foreign Policy"; *Asian Affairs*, Vol. 10, No. 3, Fall 1983, pp. 45-53.

Bandyopadhyaya, J., *Making of India's Foreign Policy: Determinants Institutions, Processes and Personalities*, Bombay, Allied, 1970.

Brown, Judith M., "Foreign Policy Decision-Making and the Indian Parliament", *Journal of Constitutional and Parliamentary Studies*, Vol. 3, No. 2, April-June 1969, pp. 15-52.

Chavan, Y.B., *India's Foreign Policy*, Bombay, Somaiya Publication, 1979.

Chavan, Y.B., "India's Foreign Policy," *Indian Horizon*, Vol. 25, No. 1-2, 1976, pp. 5-12.

Chopra, Surendra, Ed. *Studies in India's Foreign Policy*, Edn. 2, Amritsar, Guru Nanak Dev University, 1983.

Congress Party in Parliament, Bureau of Parliamentary Research, *India-China Border Problem*, New Delhi, 1960.

Das, Parimal Kumar, "Myth of Consensus," *International Studies*, Vol. 17, No. 3-4, July-September 1978, pp. 789-98.

Dinesh Singh, "The Indian Parliament and Foreign Policy," *The Parliamentarian: Journal of the Parliaments of the Commonwealth*, Vol. 51, No. 3, July 1970, pp. 157-60.

Dowerah, Manjula, *Parliament and Foreign Policy Process: A Case of the Composition, Functions and Role of the Parliamentary Consultative Committee of the External Affairs Ministry*, J.N.U., 1981, (SIS Dissertation).

Dutt, Subimal, *With Nehru in the Foreign Office*, Calcutta, Minerva, 1977.

Dutt, V.P., *India's Foreign Policy*, New Delhi, Vikas, 1984.

Fartyal, H.S., *The Role of the Opposition in the Indian Parliament*, Allahabad, 1971.

Gandhi, Indira, "India and its Foreign Policy" *International Studies*, Vol. 21, No. 2, April-June 1982, pp. 95-99.

Gupta, Karunakar, *Indian Foreign Policy; in Defence of National Interest: An Analytical Study of Indian Foreign Policy*, Calcutta, World Press, 1956.

Jain, Lal Kumar, *Parliament and Foreign Policy in India*, Jaipur, Printwell Publishers, 1986.

Jetly Nancy, "Parliament and India's China Foreign Policy 1959-1963," *International Studies*, Vol. 15, No. 2, April-June 1976, pp. 229-60.

Jetly, Nancy, *Parliament and India's China Policy 1950-1964*, New Delhi, 1973 (JNU Ph. D. Thesis).

Kaile Asaiah, *Indian Parliament and Foreign Policy: A Case Study of Issues in Foreign Aid and Collaboration Agreements*, New Delhi, 1980; (JNU, SIS Dissertation).

Kamath, P.M., "Foreign Policy Making in India: Need for Committee System to Strengthen the Role of Parliament," *Strategic Analysis*, Vol. 12, No. 2, May 1987, pp. 227-39.

Kaul, M.N. and Shakdhar, S.L., *Practice and Procedures of Parliament*, Delhi, Metropolitan, 1977.

Khilnani, Niranjan, M., "The Role of Parliament of Foreign Affairs," *Journal of Constitutional and Parliamentary Studies*, Vol. 6, No. 4, 1972, pp. 32-38.

Khilnani, Niranjan, M., *Realities of India's Foreign Policy*, New Delhi, A.B.C. Pub., 1984.

Lok Sabha Secretariat, *Foreign Policy of India*; New Delhi, 1987.

Lok Sabha Secretariat, *Parliament and International Treaties*, New Delhi, 1976.

Lok Sabha Secretariat, *Report on Parliament and Foreign Policy: A Study*, New Delhi, 1971.

Madhok, Balraj, "Parliament's Influence on the Conduct of Foreign Policy," *Journal of Parliamentary Information*, Vol. 15, No. 2, October 1969.

Maheshwari, S.R. "Informal Consultative Committees of Parliament," *Journal of Constitutional and Parliamentary Studies*, Vol. 2, No. 1, 1968, pp. 27-53.

Majumdar, Asis Kumar, *Indian Foreign Policy and Marxist Opposition Parties in Parliament*, Calcutta, Netaji Institute of Asian Studies, 1986.

Misra, K.P., *Foreign Policy and its Planning*, New York, Asia Publishing House, 1970.

More, S.S., *Practice and Procedure of Indian Parliament*, Bombay, 1960.

Morris Jones, W.H., "Parliament and Dominant Party: Indian Experience," *Parliamentary Affairs*, Vol. 17, No. 3, Summer 1964, pp. 296-307.

Mukherjea, A., *Parliamentary Practice in India*, London, OUP, 1967.

Muni, S.D., "Parliament and Foreign Policy in India," *Indian Journal of Politics*, Vol. 10, No. 1, June 1976, pp. 48-60.

Narasimha Rao, P.V., Parliament and Foreign Policy, *Journal of Parliamentary Information*, Vol. 27, No. 4, December 1981, pp. 385-92.

Ratnam, P., "Policy-Making and Parliamentary Accountability with Particular Reference to India's Foreign Policy," *Journal of Constitutional and Parliamentary Studies*, Vol. 9, No. 1, January-March 1975, pp. 73-78.

Shakdhar, S.L., ed., *Glimpses of the Working of the Parliament*, New Delhi, Lok Sabha Secretariat, 1977.

Sharma, S.D., *Congress Approach to International Affairs*, New Delhi, A.I.C.C., 1970.

Singhvi, L.M., ed., *Parliamentary Committees in India*, New Delhi, Institute of Constitutional and Parliamentary Studies 1973.

Sondhi, M.L., "Future of Indian Foreign Policy After Indira Gandhi," *Asia Pacific Community*, No. 28, Spring 1985, pp. 33-53.

Sondhi, M.L., *Non-Appeasement: A New Direction for India's Foreign Policy*, New Delhi, Abhinav, 1972.

Sondhi, M.L., "Parliament and Indian Foreign Policy," *Assam Tribune*, 30 July 1976.

Subrahmanyam, K., Foreign Policy Planning in India, *Foreign Affairs Reports*, Vol. 24, No. 1, January 1975, pp. 1-12.

BRITAIN

"British Foreign Policy to 1985," *International Affairs*, Vol. 54, No. 1, January 1978, pp. 30-59, (Series of Articles).

Cogswell, Thomas, "Foreign Policy and Parliament: The Case of La Rochelle," 1625-1626, *English Historical Review*, Vol. 96, No. 391, April 1984, pp. 241-47.

Cox, Andrew and Kirby, Stephen, "Innovation in Legislative Oversight of Defence Policies and Expenditure in Britain and America," *Parliamentarian*, Vol. 61, No. 4, October 1980, pp. 215-29.

Edmonds, Martin, "British Foreign Policy," *Current History*, Vol. 83, No. 492, April 1984, pp. 157-59.

Hans A., and Wiseman, H.R., *Parliament at Work*, London, Stevenson, 1962.

Howe, Geoffrey, "International Outlook: The British View," *India International Centre Quarterly*, Vol. 13, No. 2, 1986, pp. 221-28.

Hyder, Masood, "Parliament and Defence Affairs,". *Public Administration*, No. 55, 1977, pp. 59-78.

Jack, Malcolm, "Parliament's Role as a Check on Government," *Parliamentary Affairs*, Vol. 38, No. 3, Summer 1985, pp. 296-306.

Jones, Roy E., *Changing Structure of British Foreign Policy*, London, Longman, 1974.

Klebes, Heinrich, "Parliamentary Diplomacy: A New Factor in International Relations," *Journal of Parliamentary Information*, Vol. 31, No. 4, December 1985, pp. 571-85.

Norton, Philip, "Dissent in Committee: Intra-Party Dissent in Commons' Standing Committees, 1959-1974," *Parliamentrian*, Vol. 57, No. 1, January 1976, pp. 15-25.

Richards, Peter G., *Parliament and Foreign Affairs*, London, Allen and Unwin, 1967.

Roy, Jones, *The Changing Structure of British Foreign Policy*, London, Allen and Unwin, 1969.

Russell, Conrad, "Foreign Policy Debate in the House of Commons in 1621," *Historical Journal*, Vol. 20, No. 2, June 1977, pp. 289-309.

"Specialist Committees in the British Parliament: The Experience of a Decade," *PEP*, Vol. 42, No. 564, June 1976, pp. 1-45.

Suganami, Hidemi, "Structure of Institutionalism: Anatomy of British Mainstream International Relations," *International Relations*, Vol. 7, No. 5, May 1983, pp. 2363-81.

Townsend, Guy M., "Russian-Dutch Loan in Parliament, 1831-1832," *Quarterly Review of Historical Studies*, Vol. 16, No. 4, 1976-1977, pp. 193-204.

Verrier, Anthony, *Through the Looking Glass: British Foreign Policy in an Age of Illusion*, London, Jonathan Cape, 1983.

Vital David, *The making of British Foreign Policy*, London, George Allen and Unwin, 1969.

Wallace, William, *Foreign Policy Process in Britain*, London, Royal Institute of International Affairs, 1975.

Watt, D.C., "External Affairs in the 1990s," *Political Quarterly* Vol. 51, No. 1, January-March 1980, pp. 45-56.

Young, Roland, *The British Parliament*, London, 1962.

CANADA

Canada, Standing Senate on Foreign Affairs, *Report on Canada's Relation with the Countries of Middle East and North Africa*, Ottawa, 1985.

"Domestic Sources of Canada's Foreign Policy," *International Journal*, Vol. 39, No. 1, Winter 1983-84, pp. 1-213, (Series of articles).

Dorscht, Axel and Legare, Gregg, "Foreign Policy Debate and Realism," *International Perspective*, November-December 1986, pp. 7-10.

Frank, C.E.S., "Canadian Parliament and Intelligence and Security Issues," *Indian Journal of Political Science*, Vol. 46, No. 1, January-March 1985, pp. 49-62.

Held, Robert, "Canadian Foreign Policy," *International Journal* Vol. 33, No. 2, Spring 1978, pp. 448-56.

Karn Berg, A. Han, *Canadian Legislative Behaviour: A Study of the 25th Parliament*, Winston, Hoff Richant, 1967.

Kirton, John, "Canadian Foreign Policy in the 1980s," *Current History*, Vol. 83, No. 493, May 1984, pp. 193-6.

Kirton, John, J., "Foreign Policy Decision Making in the Trudeau Government," *International Journal*, Vol. 33, No. 2, Spring 1978, pp. 287-311.

Martin, Paul, "The Role of the Canadian Parliament in the Formulation of Foreign Policy," *The Parliamentarian*, Vol. 50, No. 4, October 1969, pp. 259-66.

Miller, A.J., "Functional Principle in Canada's External Relations," *International Journal*, Vol. 35, No. 2, Spring 1980, pp. 308-28.

Nossal, Kim Richard, "Bureaucratic Politics and Foreign Policy in a Parliamentary System," *Canadian Public Administration*, Vol. 22, No. 4, Winter 1979, pp. 610-26.

"Opinion and Policy," *International Journal*, Vol. 33, No. 1, Winter 1977-78, pp. 1-247, (Series of Articles).

Stairs, Denis, Responsible Government and Foreign," *International Perspective*, May-June 1978, pp. 26-30.

Taras, David, "Brian Mulroney's Foreign Policy: Something for Everyone," *Round Table*, No. 293, January 1985, pp. 35-46.

Thakur, Ramesh C., "Change and Canadian Foreign Policy," *India Quarterly*, Vol. 33, No. 4, October-December 1977, pp. 401-18.

Thordarson, Bruce, "Posture and Policy: Leadership in Canada's External Affairs," *International Journal*, Vol. 31, No. 4, Autumn, 1976, pp. 666-91.

Tomlin, Brian W., Ed., *Canada's Foreign Policy: Analysis and Trends*, Toronto, Methuen, 1978.

"Trudeau and Foreign Policy," *International Journal*, col. 33, No. 2, Spring 1978, pp. 267-456, (Series of Articles).

ISRAEL

Avineri, Shlomo, "Ideology and Israel's Foreign Policy," *Jerusalem Quarterly*, No. 37, 1986, pp. 3-13.

Ben-Gurion David, "Israel in World Politics," *Jerusalem Quarterly*, No. 31, Spring 1984, pp. 51-57.

Brecher, Michael, *Decisions in Israel: Foreign Policy*, London, OUP, 1974.

Brecher, Michael, "Israel's Foreign Policy: Options and Opinions," *New Outlook*, Vol. 19, No. 5, July-August 1976, pp. 60-65, 78.

Brownstein, Lewis, "Decision Making in Israeli Foreign Policy," *Political Science Quarterly*, Vol. 92, No. 2, Summer 1977, pp. 259-79.

Shiaim, Avi and Yaniv, Avner, "Domestic Politics and Foreign Policy in Israel," *International Affairs*, Vol. 56, No. 2, April 1980, pp. 242-82.

JAPAN

Baerwald, Hans H., *Japan's Parliament*, London, Cambridge University Press, 1974.

Fukin, Haruhiro, "Foreign Policy Making by Improvisation," *International Journal*, Vol. 32, No. 4, Autumn 77, pp. 791-812.

Glaubitz, Joachim, "Japanese Foreign and Security Policy," *Aussen Politik*, Vol. 35, No. 2, 1984, pp. 173-85.

Kujauyu, J.K.L., "Prime Minister Miki and Japan's Foreign Relations," *Asia Quarterly*, No. 3, 1976, pp. 235-42.

Masuyama, Eitaro, "Nakasone's Foreign Policy," *Asia-Pacific Community*, No. 19, Winter 1983, pp. 116-28.

Minor, Michael, "Decision Models and Japanese Foreign Policy Decision Making," *Asian Survey*, Vol. 25, No. 12, December 1985, pp. 1229-41.

Murthy, P.A.N., "Formulation and Implementation of Foreign Policy in Japan," *Japan Quarterly*, Vol. 3, No. 2, April 1977 pp. 6-33.

Watanabe, Akio, "Foreign Policy Making, Japanese Style," *International Affairs*, Vol. 54, No. 1, January 1978, pp. 75-88.

Scalapino, Robert, A., Ed., *Foreign Policy of Modern Japan*, Berkeley, University of California Press, 1977.

Simon, Sheldon W., "Japan's Foreign Policy: Adjustment to a Changing Environment," *Asian Survey*, Vol. 18, No. 7, July 1978. pp. 666-86.

Yayama, Taro, "Nakasone's External Policy," *Asia Pacific Community*, No. 25, Summer 1984, pp. 28-40.

NEW ZEALAND

Parasher, S.C., "New Zealand and its Foreign Policy," *Foreign Affairs Reports*, Vol. 33, No. 7 and 8, July-August, 1984, pp. 51-72.

Jackson, Keith, "New Zealand Parliamentary Committees: Reality and Reforms," *Parliamentarian*, Vol. 59, No. 2, April 1978, pp. 94-101.

Marshall, C.R., "New Zealand Parliament and Foreign Policy," *Parliamentarian*, Vol. 57, No. 2, April 1976, pp. 75-79.

Mckinnon, M.A., "Foreign Affairs," *Pacific Viewpoint*, Vol. 20, No. 2, September 1979, pp. 164-72.

SRI LANKA

Appathurai, Edward R., *Making of Foreign Policy in Ceylon: A Case Study in Public Administration*, Ann Arbor, University Microfilms, 1968.

Kodikara, Shelton U., *Foreign Policy of Sri Lanka*, Delhi, Chanakya, 1982.

EUROPEAN PARLIAMENT

Bieber, R., *et. al. An Ever Closer Union*, Brussels, 1985.

Blondel J., *Comparative Legislatures*, Englewood Cliffs, Prentice Hall, 1973.

Butler, Sir M., *Europe: More than a Continent*, London, Heinemann 1986.

European Parliament, *European Integration and the Future of Parliaments in Europe*, Luxembourg, 1975.

European Parliament, "European Political Cooperation and the European Parliament," *Working Document*, 1-335/81.

Herman V. and Van Schendelen, R. (eds.), *The European Parliament and the National Parliaments*, Farnborough, Saxon House, 1979.

Herman V. and Lodge J., *The European Parliament and the European Community*, London, Macmillan, 1978.

Herman V., *Parliaments of the World*, London, IPU, 1975.

Loewenberg G., *Parliament in the German Political System*, New York, Cornell UP, 1967.

Lodge J. and Herman V., *Direct Elections to the European Parliament: A Community Perspective*, London, Macmillan, 1982.

Lodge J., (ed.), *Direct Elections to the European Parliament 1984*, London, Macmillan, 1986.

Lodge J., (ed.), *Institutions and Policies of the European Community*, London, Printer, 1983.

Lodge J., (ed.), *The European Community: Bibliographical Excursions*, London, Printer, 1983.

Lodge J., (ed.), *European Union: the European Community in Search of a Future*, London, Macmillan, 1986.

Lodge J., "The European Parliament after Direct Elections: Talking Shop or Putative Legislature?" *Journal of European Integration*, (JEI) Vol. 5, (1982) 259-84.

Lodge J., "Nation States versus Supranationalism: The Political Future of the European Community," *JEI*, Vol. 2, (1979) 161-81.

Lodge J., European Union and the First Elected European Parliament: The Spinelli Initiative,' *Journal of Common Market Studies* (JCMS) Vol. 22, (1984) 333-340.

Lodge J., The Single European Act: Towards a new Euro-Dynamism?" *JCMS*, Vol. 24, (1986) 203-223.

Lodge J., "The European Community: Compromise under Domestic and International Pressure,' *The World Today* (1986), 192-195.

Lodge J., "The Single European Act: A Threat to National Parliaments of Europe?' *The Parliamentarian* (1987).

Marquand D., *Parliament for Europe*, London, Cape, 1979.

Palmer M., *The European Parliament*, London, Pergamon, 1981.

Palmer M., "The Development of the European Parliament's Institutional Role within the EC 1974-83," *JEI* Vol. 6 (1983) 183-202.

Parlement Europeen, *Une Assemblee en pleine evolution*, Luxembourg, 1983.

Pinder J., *Economic and Social Powers of the European Union and the Member States: Subordinate or Coordinate Relationship?* Florence, EUI, 1985.

Pridham G. and P., *Transnational Party Cooperation and European Integration*, London, Allen & Unwin, 1981.

Robinson, A. and Webb, A. (ed.), *The European Parliament in the EC Policy Process*, London, PSI, 1985.

Spinelli A., "Die Parlamentarische Initiative zur Europaischen Union, *Europa Archiv*, Vol. 38, (1983) 739-746.

Spinelli A., *The European Adventure*, London, Knight, 1972.

Strasser D., *The Finances of Europe*, Luxembourg, 1981.

Taylor P., *The Limits of European Integration*, Farnborough, Gower, 1983.

Taylor P., "Political Cooperation among the EC Member States, Embassies in Washington," *JEI* Vol. 4, (1980), 29-42.

Usher, J., *European Community Law and National Law: The Irreversible Transfer?* London, Allen & Unwin, 1981.

Van Ypersele J., *The European Monetary System*, Brussels, 1986.

Wallace H., *Budgetary Politics: The Finances of the European Communities*, London, Allen & Unwin, 1980.

Wallace H., Wallace W. and Webb C., (eds.) *Policy making in the European Communities*, London, Wiley, 1983.

Wessels W., *Der Europaische Rat*, Bonn, Europa Union, 1980.

Wood D., *The Times Guide to the European Parliament: June 1984*, London, 1984.

Wooldridge F. and Sassella, M., "Some Recent Legal Provisions Increasing the Budgetary Powers of the European Parliament, and Establishing a European Court of Auditors," *Legal Issues of European Integration*, (1976), 14-52.

Contributors

JAMES CALLAGHAN

Member of Parliament since 1945; Parliamentary Secretary, Ministry of Transport 1947-50; Chancellor of the Exchequer 1964-67; Secretary of State for Home Department 1967-70; Chairman Labour Party 1973-74; Secretary of State for Foreign and Commonwealth Affairs 1974-76; Prime Minister 1976-79; Leader of the Labour Party 1976-80; Father of the House from 1983; Overseas Governor of the Rajaji International Institute of Public Affairs and Administration; President of the Royal Institute of International Affairs.

JOE CLARK

Foreign Minister; Lecturer in Political Science, University of Alberta 1965-67; Journalist for CBC Radio and TV, *Calgary Herald* and Edmonton Journal 1964-66; Member of Parliament (Progressive Conservative) for Rocky Mountain, Alberta since 1972; Leader of Progressive Conservative Party of Canada 1976-83; Prime Minister of Canada 1979-80; Leader of the Opposition in the House of Commons.

BRUCE GEORGE

Member of Parliament since 1974; a Member of the House of Commons Select Committee on Defence; Chairman of the Political Committee on the North Atlantic Assembly; author of numerous articles on defence and foreign policy.

HEMDA GOLAN

Received her M. Jur. degree from the Hebrew University in Jerusalem in 1962 and since that time has been on the staff of the Israel Ministary for Foreign Affairs, where she is currently director of the Treaty Division in the Office of the Legal Advisor. She has represented Israel at several International legal conferences and has been a visiting Professor of International Law at the University of Florida (USA) University de Montreal (Canada) and Indiana University (USA) and a visiting Research Fellow at Georgetown University (USA). She has also served as Foreign Associate in the law firm of Arnold and Porter (Washington D.C.). During the trial of Adolph Eichmann in 1961 she acted as personal law clerk to Attorney General Gideon Hausner.

CLIFF GRANTHAM

Political Researcher with government relations consultancy, Westminster Strategy Ltd; has undertaken various academic research projects and published on the work of the House of Lords. A member of the British Politics Group in the USA.

SHELTON U. KODIKARA

Professor of International Relations University of Colombo Sri Lanka; B.A. in History from the University of Ceylon 1956 Masters in International Relations at University of Denver USA in 1958 and Ph.D. in International relations from London School of Economics 1962; Research Fellow at the Institute of Commonwealth Studies in London University 1961-62 and Visiting Fellow at the Strategic and Defence Studies Centre, Department of International Relations, Research School of Pacific Studies, Australian National University, Canberra; Deputy High Commissioner for Sri Lanka in Madras 1975-1977; Publications: *Indo-Ceylon Relations since Independence*; *Strategic Factors in Inter-state relations in South Asia*; *Foreign Policy of Sri Lanka—a Third World Perspective*.

JULIET LODGE

Lecturer in Politics at the University of Hull, formerly a Lecturer in Political Studies at the University of Auckland, New Zealand; Visiting Fellow in the Centre for International Studies at The London School of Economics and Political Science and a Leverhulme Research Fellow; Author of *The European Policy of the SPD* (1976) and *The European Community and New Zealand* (1982); co-author of *The New Zealand General Election of 1975* (1976); *The European Parliament and the European Community* (1978) and *Direct Elections to the European Parliament: A Community Perspective* (1982); and editor of *Terrorism: A Challenge to the State* (1981) and *Institutions and Policies of the European Community* (1983). Author of numerous articles on EC politics and institutions published in journals of international affairs and politics in Europe, North-America and Australasia; also *Direct Elections to the European Parliament 1984* (The Macmillan Press) and *The Threat of Terrorism — Combating Political Violence in Europe* (edited).

NATANEL LORCH

Educated from the Hebrew University of Jerusalem; a prolific writer, has published several articles on parliamentary affairs in English; author of several books in Hebrew including *Israel's War of Independence* first published in 1958 and still considered the standard work on the subject; career has spanned government, where he represented his country as ambassador to Peru and Bolivia and worked as Director of the Information and Latin-American Divisions; parliament, where he worked as Secretary General of the Knesset and on which he has authored several articles, and academia, having lectured and researched as Fellow of the Truman Centre and Davis Institute for International Relations; maintains continuing association with the Hebrew University of Jerusalem, and at present is Member of the Committee for Administrative Control.

SABURO OKITA

Former Foreign Minister of Japan; President of the International University of Japan since 1982; Chariman of the Institute for Domestic and International Policy Studies since 1981 and President of the Asian Affairs Research Council since 1986; Adviser to The Minister of Foreign Affairs, the Economic Planning Agency, the Science Technology Agency, the Environment Agency, the Japan Economic Research Centre and the International Research Centre of Japan. Has held many important positions relating to economic and international affairs in the Japanese Government, and has also been involved in various international activites, including membership of several UN World Bank and OEC committees and commissions; at present member of the World Commission on Environment and Development, and Chairman of the Governing Board of the U.N. University World Institute for Development Economic Research in Helsinki; has been awarded several honorary degrees and also the Ramon Magsaysay award for International understanding (1971) and Companion of the Order of Australia (1985); author of many aritcles in English and also of a dozen books in Japanese. His latest books in English are *Developing Economies and Japan—Lessons in Growth* and *Japan's Challenging Years—Reflection on my Lifetime.*

SRIKANT PARANJPE

Reader in the Department of Defence & Strategic Studies, University of Poona, Pune; M.A. and Ph.D. from the University of Poona and M. Phil. from the School of International Studies, Jawaharlal Nehru University, New Delhi; Fulbright Fellow at the George Washington University, Washington D.C. during 1984-85; author of *India and South Asia since 1971* (New Delhi: Radiant 1985); has published several articles in national and international journals.

MANOHAR L. SONDHI

Professor of International Relations and Chairman, Centre

for International Politics, Organisation and Disarmament, Jawaharlal Nehru University, New Delhi; Educated: Punjab University and Balliol College, Oxford; Rhodes Scholar Elect; Member of Parliament (Lok Sabha) 1967-71; Member Indian Foreign Service 1957-1961; Member, Consultative Committee to the Ministry of External Affairs 1967-71; Publications; *Non-Appeasement, a New Direction for Indian Foreign Policy*; articles on foreign policy.

RAMESH THAKUR

Senior Lecturer in Political Studies at the University of Otago. Received his academic training at the University of Calcutta and Queen's University in Canada; taught at the University of the South Pacific before joining Otago University, where he has been since 1980; author of *Peacekeeping in Vietnam: Canada, India, Poland and the International Commission* (University of Alberta Press, 1984); *In Defence of New Zealand: Foreign Policy Choices in the Nuclear Age* (NZIIA, 1984; Westview Press, 1986); and *International Peacekeeping in Lebanon: Multinational Force and United Nations Authority* (Westview Press, 1987); has written some 40 articles for various journals around the world, and also writes occasionally for newspapers in New Zealand.

AKIO WATANABE

Ph. D., Professor of International Relations at the University of Tokyo, born in 1932 at Chiba, Japan; Graduated from the University of Tokyo in 1958; Master of Arts (History), University of Tokyo in 1960; Ph. D. (International Relations), Australian National University in 1967; lecturer in History at the University of Hong Kong, 1966-1971; lecturer and then assistant professor in Political Science at the Meiji University in Tokyo, 1971-1975; assistant professor and then professor in International Relations at the University of Tokyo, 1975-present. Other positions held include: member of the Board, Japan Association of International Relations; visiting Fellow of International Affairs in London (April to July, 1977). Major publications in English are: *The Okinawa Problem: A Chapter in Japan-US Relations* (Melbourne University Press, 1970);

"Japanese Public Opinion and Foreign Affairs: 1964-73", in Robert A. Scalapino (ed.), *The Foreign Policy of Modern Japan* (University of California Press, 1977); "Foreign Policy Making, Japanese Style", *International Affairs*, vol. 54, no. 1 (January 1978); "From Bitter Enmity to Cold Partnership: Japanese Views of the United Kingdom, 1945-1952", in Ian Nish (ed.), *Anglo-Japanese Alienation, 1917-1952* (Cambridge University Press, 1983).

ANTONY WOOD

Associate Professor in the Department of Political Studies of the University of Otago: Studied at Victoria University of Wellington and University of Otago; was a post-doctoral fellow at the University of Auckland, before returning to the University of Otago in 1974; publications include *The Upper House in Colonial New Zealand* (by A.H. McLintock and G.A. Wood; in press); *W.P. Morrell: A Tribute. Essays in Modern and Early Modern History* (co-ed. with P.S. O'Connor, 1973); *A Guide for Students of New Zealand History* (1973); *The Governor and His Northern House* (1975); various essays and articles on New Zealand politics and history.

Index

ACP State, 122
AEC, 191
Africa, vii, 13, 29, 181
Afghanistan, 24, 26, Soviet intervention in, 173-175, 179; Indian policy on, 173-175
African National Congress, 30
Agenda setting, 120-121
AIPO States, 122, 124
Algeria, 124
All-party groups, 17
Allied military authorities, 34
America, 138, 141, 176
American aid package, to Pakistan, 180
American blacks, civic rights of, 183
American Indians, civic rights of, 183
American Security Planners, 180
Americas, 124
Amnesty International, 156
ANDEAN Parliament, 122
Andhra Pradesh, 165
Antarctic Treaty System, 138
Antarctica, 136
Anti-Communism, 100-101
Anti-Indianism, 108
Anti-nuclear discourse (India's), 167
Anti-nuclear legislation, 153-155
ANZUS, end of, 154
ANZUS alliance, 142, 145, 159
ANZUS/nuclear ships issue, 142
ANZUS Treaty, vii, 138, 159
Apartheid, 141, 183
Approach to self government, 111
Aquino, *President*, 29
Arab-Israel Wars, 69
Arabia, 140

Argentina, 168
Armaments, competitive expenditures on, 183
Armed conflict, 43
Arms Control Committee, 149
Asahi Shimbum, 54
Asia, vii, 100, 104, 124, 175, 181
Asian-African Solidarity, 106
Asian Collective Security, 172
Asian-Pacific Region, 158, 194
Asian peace and security, 175
Asian Recorder, 111n, 199
Assembly of Western European Union, 131
Association of South-East Asian Nations, 122
Atomic energy, peaceful uses of, 39, 59, 191-192; civil uses of, 39, 41
Atomic weapons, 192
Attler, 2
Anekland harbour, 142
Australasia, 124
Australia, 122, 138, 140-141, 146, 156
Austria, 124
Azad, Maulana, 163

Backbench influence, on foreign policy, 153
Bagehot, Walter, 3, 9
Bandaranaike (Mrs), 96-97, 104-107
Bandaranaike, S.W.R.D., 97, 102-105
Bandung Conference, 101
Bangladesh, 171
Barbados, 201
Barber, James, 12
Bargaining (constructive), 164
"Basic Law: The Government", 83

"Basic Law: The Knesset", 81
"Basic Law: The President of the State", 87
"Basic Law: The State Economy", 81
"Basic Laws", 75
Begin, M., 60, 64, 66, 69, 72-73, 79
Beijing, 105
Belgrano, 25, 28, 31
Beloff, Max, 95, 110n
Bilateral relationships, 183
Bill of Rights, 76
Bipartisanship and Division, 137-142
Bofors Scandal, 165
Bogdenovsky, 82
Botswana, 16
Brazil, 122
Brecher, Michael, 86, 111n
Britain, vi, 1, 6, 31, 98, 101, 103, 123, 138, 141, 206
British Broadcasting Corporation, 23
British Labour Group, 129
British Parliament on foreign policy influence of the, 8-11
British parliamentary system, 164
Brussels, 129
Burma, 102

Caborn, Richard, 20
Callaghan, James, vi
Camp David Accord, 66, 90-91
Canada, vii, 31, 122, 140, 152, 189-190, 193, 195, 201, 207
Canadian-financed irrigation, dependence on, 201
Canadian foreign policy, 206-207
Carribean, 26
Carrington, *Lord*, 18, 31, 132
Carter, 69, 180, 192
Castro, 107
Central America, 26
Central Asia, 182
Ceylon, 102-104
Ceylon and India, 111
Ceylon Workers' Congress, 102
Chamberlain, Neville, 4

Charan Singh, 164
Chernobyl, 16
China, 105-106, 122, 152, 158, 176, 189, 191
China report, 152
China Sea, 200
China today, 112
Chmykhalov, 201
Christian aid and the Catholic Fund for Overseas Development, 30
CIDA, 201
Clark, Helen, 135, 152
Clark, Joe, vii
Cohen, H., 86
Collective security, 172
Committee of EFTA Parliamentarians, 124
Committee restructuring, *1985*, 150-153
Committee system, 150
Common agricultural policy, 132
Common Law, 86
Common Market, 140
Commonwealth, ix, 99, 103, 200-201; on South Africa, 207
Commonwealth Gleneagles Agreement, 140
Commonwealth Parliamentary Association, 141
Communism, 99, 179
Communist colonialism, 101; Party, 49, 54, 102
Comparative foreign policy, vii
Conclusion de traites internationaux en Israel, 88
Conflict Resolution, 167
Congress Party, 107, 163-164, 187; structural problems, 164
Consensus, 54, 106, 130
Constitutional law of the State of Israel, 86
Consultative Committee, character of, 182; role of the, 197
Contadora, 207
Continental shelf, 39
Cook Islands, 140, decolonisation of, 148

Index

Co-operative co-existence, 36
Council of Europe, 68
Court of Justice, 119
Crown prerogative, 11, 134
Cultural property, protection of, 40
Cyprus, 124, 200
Czechoslovakia, 173, Soviet intervention in, 168-170

Decision-making process, 66
Defence, 57; agreement, 100-101, 104; and External Affairs Sub-Committee, 20-21; and Foreign Affairs Committee, 93, 152; Select Committee, 149; Service (Consolidated Law), 1959, Sect. 26(b), 80
Democracy in America, 95
Democratic Party, 154
Deng, 202
Desai, H.M., 111
Desai, Morarji, 164, 177, 189, 195-196; statements of July *1978*, 190
Developing countries, 189, 207
Development cooperation, 166; policy, 132
Dien Bien Phu, battle of, 101
Diet, vi, role in the case of multilateral treaties, 39; system, 36
Directory of official information, 1983, 134
Directive Principles of the Constitution, 180
Disarmament, 53, 149; and Arms Control Committee, 150, 152
Divre Haknesset, 66, 78, 83, 88-90

Eastern Europe, vii, 124, 183
Eban, Abba, 70
Economic assistance, 46
EEC, vii, 73; Treaty, 121
Eelam, separate state of, 108
Egypt, 56, 66, 69, 73, 90
Eichmann, Adolf, 68
Eitan, Rafael, 70
El Salvador, 200
Elite, 162, 164, 181

Emergency, 162, 165, 179
Entebbe operation, 72
Environmental pollution, 203
EP Socialist Group, 129
EPC, 117, 126
Estimates Committee, 20, 26
Estonia, 200
Ethiopia, 29, 200
Ethnic crisis, 107-108
Europe, 123, 176
European Common Market, 140
European Communities Foreign Affairs Council, 16
European Communities Select Committee, 18
European Community, 1, 6, 90, 113, 120, 133
European Council, 127
European Parliament, viii, 68, 73, 113
European Parliament and foreign policy, 113-116
European Parliament's formal powers, 118-120
European Parliament's role, increase in the, 116-118
European Parliament's Secretariat, 130-131
European People's Party, 120
European Union, 117
'Europeanisation', 116
Expenditure, 132
Export Trade Control Order, 49
External Affairs, Ministry of, 183
External economic policy, formulation of, vi

FAC, 27, 29-31
Falklands, 5, 26, 28, 108, 128
"Famine in Africa", 30
FAO, 30
FCO, 14, 23, 26-27, 30
Federal Republic of Germany, 67, 115-116
Financial Scrutiny, 20-21
Finland, 123
First Republican Constitution, 96
First World War, 149

Flegmann, Vilma, 20
Foreign Affairs, 11-14
Foreign Affairs Committee, vi, 22-23, 42-43, 45, 49-50, 52, 151
Foreign and Commonwealth Office, 19
Foreign and Defence Policy, implementation of, 74
Foreign Affairs Select Committee, 156
Foreign assistance, 53
Foreign Exchange and Foreign Trade Control Law, 48
Foreign lobbying, 183
Foreign policy, legislative roles in, v
Foreign policy, parliamentary role in, ix, 196; role of the Diet, 41; decisions, 72; issues, 92; decision-making in, 95
Foreign policy and the Democratic process, 110n
Foreign policy and its planning, 111n
Foreign policy debate in Canada, 200-207
Foreign policy issues, 158
Foreign policy-making, vii
Foreign policy of India, 197
Foreign policy of Sri Lanka, 110n
Foreign policy planning in India, 199
Foreign policy process, 179
Foreign policy process in Britain, 13
"Foreign Policy School", 159
Foreign policy system of Israel, 86
Foreign Relations, legislative-executive relations, in the field of, 75; conduct of, 139
France, 140, 158, 178, 189, 206
Frankel, Joseph, 110n
French nuclear testing, 123
Fukuyama, Francis, 179
Fukuyama proposals, 180

Gachal, 72
Gandhi, Indira, 104, 107-109, 164-165, 169, 173; her assassination, 164; statement on May implosion, 189

Gandhi, Rajiv, 108, 110, 164-165, 181-182
Gandhian ideas, 163
General Assembly, 68, 103
General Belgrano, 4
General Council, 117
General foreign policy, 91
Genocide Convention, 88
George, Bruce, vi, 31
German reparations, 67
Germanys, 200
Glasnost and perestroika, era of, 181
Gleneagles agreement, 158
Golan, Hemda, vi
Gorbachev, Mikhail, 181, 202
Government, general powers of, 84-86
Grantham, Cliff, vi
Great Britain, 39, 75, 103, 138-139
Greece, 121
Green paper, 202-203, 205
Greenpeace, 123
Grenada, 27, 108
Gulf, 179

The Hague, 40
Hameed, A.C.S., 98, 109
Hansard, 143-144, 147, 154
Harare Resolution, 75
Hatch of Lusby, *Lord*, 20
Havana, 107
Hayden, Bill, 145
Hanoi, 175
Heath, Edward, 21
Heseltine, Michael, 29
'High politics', 114
The Hindu, 111
Ho Chi Minh, 175
Hokkaido, 47
Home-spun political style, 164
House of Commons, vi, 26
House of Common's Library, 18
House of Lords, 31
House of Representative debates, 111
Human rights, 183
Hurd, Douglas, 10, 15

IAEA, 177, 189

Index

Iceland, 123
Immigration policy, 158
"Implied and resultant powers", 85
Independence (Soulbury) Constitution, 96
India, vii, 48, 102, 104, 107-111, 179; economic transformation of, 163; role in world affairs, 163; Afghanistan policy, 174; stand on PNE, 190
India-China border dispute, 105
India-China War (1962), 105
India Quarterly, 111
India-Sri Lanka agreement, vi
Indian democratic system, resilience of the, 181
Indian foreign policy, viii, 175; in action, *1954-56*, 111; towards the super powers, 165; implementation of, 187
Indian nuclear test in a global perspective, 199
Indian Ocean, 193
Indian Peace-Keeping Force, vi
Indian political culture, 181
Indian political elite, 162, 164, 181
Indian politics, influence of money on, 165
India's freedom of movement, 184
India's nuclear implosion, *1974*, 188
India's nuclear policy, 187-188
India's peace policy, 194
Indo-Canadian nuclear co-operation, 193
Indo-Ceylon relations since independence, 112
Indo-Soviet relations, development of, 172; Treaty of Friendship, 109, 168, 170-173
Indo-Sri Lanka relations, 103, 109-110
Indo-US agreement, *1963*, 177
'Informal Consultative Committees', 186
Institute of International Affairs, 156
Intelligence Establishment, control of the, 71

Inter-groups, formation of, 117
Inter-parliamentary delegations, 121-126
Inter-parliamentary Union, 73, 123; studies, vii
Interest, concept of, v; groups, 155-157
International affairs, management of, 204; agreements, signing and ratifying of, 74; Communism, 104; economic agreements, 90; Law, 86
International relations, use of force in, 170
Investigative select committees, 21
Iran, 19, 140
Islamabad, 174, 180
Israel, vi, 75, 108; foreign relations, 56; -Arab issues, 68, Wars, 69
Israel's foreign relations, selected documents, 79, 90, 94

Janata Government, advent of, 107, 191
Janata Party, 164
Japan, vi-vii, 38-40, 42, 47-48, 98, 122, 140, 158, 189, 200
Japan Socialist Party, 35
Japanese Diet and foreign policy, 34-55; external economic policy, 55; fishery industry, 54; foreign policy, 49, 51, formulation of, 52; political system, 34
Jayewardene, J.R., 97, 99, 105, 107, 109, 112
Jennings, Ivor, 111
Jerusalem, 73
Jerusalem Post, 71
John-Stevas, Norman St., 22
Johnson, 175
Joseph, D., 60, 88
Judgements of the District Court, 85

Kadar, 202
Kamiar, 85
Karnataka, 165

Katunayake, 101, 104
Kerala, 165
Kershaw, Anthony, 23
Khao-I-Dang Camp hospitals, 201
Khartoum, 30
Kirk, Norman, 139
Klinghoffer, I.H., 89
Knesset, powers of, 75-84; and general foreign policy, 91-94; and Israel's foreign relations, 56-57; as foreign policy instrument, 73-74; building, inauguration of, 73
Kodikara, Shelton, vi
Korea, 101; UN action in, 138
Koreas, 200
Kotelwala, 100-101, 111n
Kremlin, 154
Kushnir, 89
Kuwait, 68

Labour Government, 151, 158
Labour Party, 139, 141-142, 152, 156
Lapidoth, R., 88
Latin America, vii, 140, 181; Parliament, 122, 124
Latvia, 200
Laws of the State of Israel, 76, 84
LDP, vi, 44-45, 50-51, 54-55
Lebanon, 73, 90, 200
Legislative activism, vii; scrutiny, 19-20
Legitimised dynastic rule, in India, 164
Liberal-democratic order, 163; Party, 35
Libya, 13, 125
Lippmann, Walter, 96
Lithuania, 200
Little John, Charles, 159
Lodge, Juliet, vi
Lok Sabha debates, 111, 199
Lome Convention, 122; countries/parliaments, 120
Lorch, Netanel, vi
'Low politics', 114

'Luns-Westerpterp', 118

McPhail, Don, 202
Maghreb countries, 124
Making of foreign policy, 110n
Malayan emergency, 138
Mali, 29
"Managerial" solutions to problems, 181
Maoris, 139
Maritime Agreement, 106
Martens, 127
Marxist-Leninism, 200
Mashrek countries, 124
Mesire, Quelt, 202
Mediterranean enlargements, 116
Mehta, Asoka, 170
Meiji Constitution, 34
Menachem Begin, 58
MEPs, 117, 120, 133
Meridov, E., 89
Mexico, 122, 200
Mid-East, 203
Middle East, 13, 73, 90, 115, 124; oil, 140
Miki, Takeo, 48
Military aid, 178; cooperation, 159
Misra, K.P., 111, 197, 199
Monroe Doctrine, 102
Montreal Olympic games, African boycott of the, 140
Morgenthau, Hans J., v
Morocco, 124
Moroz, Valentyn, 201
Moscow, 173, 180-181
MTN, 207
Muldoon, Robert, 153
Multilateral treaties, 39, 41
Mutara, 201
Myers, 135

National Labour policy, 129; Party, 154
Natural conservation, 53
Near East, 124
Nehru, 102-104, 163-164, 168, 177, 186-187, 197

Index

Nehru: A political biography, 111
Nehru-style non-aligned philosophy, 97
Neutralism, 104
New Delhi, 107, 172-173, 177-178, 181-183
New York, 191
New Zealand, vii, ix, 122-123, 158
New Zealand Foreign Affairs Review, 145, 148
New Zealand Institute of International Affairs, 141
New Zealand Parliament and foreign policy, 134-137
Nicaragua, embargo of, 207
Nicosia, 202
Nihon Keizai Shinbun, 40
Nioki, 201
Non-aligned Afro-Asian Conference, 105; diplomacy, 105; movement, 98, 105-107
Non-alignment, policy of, 104; as a guiding principle of foreign policy, 107; of Nehru days, 168
Non-Communist opposition, 164
NORAD, 205
Nord, Hans, 73
Nordic Council, 123
North Africa, 124; Atlantic Treaty Organisation, 99, 115-116; Vietnam, 176; Warning system, 205
Northern Ireland, 39
Norton, Philip, 8, 14
Norway, 123
"Notice question", 81
Nolt, John, 29, 31
November accords, 31
Nuclear arms, 142; development, Nehru's doctrine of, 177; disarmament, 149; energy, for peaceful uses, 190; Free New Zealand Bill, 153; Free Zone, disarmament and Arms Control Bill, 154, for South Asia and the Indian Ocean, 193, 195, proposal, 194; implosion, 185-197; issues, 158; material, sale of, to India, 191; Non-Proliferation Act, *1978*, 177, 192; non-proliferation, 176-178, Treaty, 168, 176, 188, 192; Powers, 177; Regulatory Commission (US), 177; ship visits, ban on, 159; technology, peaceful uses of, 189; Test, *1974*, vii, ban, 48

OCT, 121
Ohiro, 38, 42
Okita, Saburo, vi, 37
Olympic games, *1980*, 24
Opposition parties, 54
Otago Daily Times, 154
Ottawa, 136
Overseas assistance, 44; Development Administration, 15, 23; Economic Cooperation Fund, 46; Trade, 149

Pacific Basin, 29; Islands, status of, 158
Pakistan, 108; US arms to, 168, 178-180, 191; framework of a united, 171; recognition of, as a frontline state, 174; talk of blackmail made by, 190; French aid to, 194; reaction to Indian PNE, 193
Palestine, 84; mandate of, 75
Palestinian Question, 69
Panikkar, K.M., 101, 111
Paranjpe, Srikant, vii
Parliament and foreign affairs, 12
Parliament and foreign policy, linkages, 185-186, in Britain, 1-7
Parliamentary Assembly (Council of Europe), 68, 73, 131
Parliamentary debates, 112
Parliamentary democracy, vii, 56
Parliamentary government, 34, 41
Parliamentary leadership, 164
Parliamentary opposition, 98, 142-147
Parliamentary politics, 163
Parliamentary principles, 180-184

Parliamentary sanction, need for, 187
Parliamentary Select Committees, 147-150
Party democracy, 164
Party groups and European Parliament policy, 126-131
Patel, Sardar, 163
Patton tanks, 179
Peace and War, 72-73; and security, 175
Peace-keeping, 53
Peace Treaty (between Israel and Egypt), 66, 73, 90-91
Peaceful Nuclear Explosions, 177, 188-190; and related issues, 191
Pentagon, 206
People Act, 9
People's Republic of China, 140-160, 124, 138, 140
Perera, N.M., 103
Peres, 73
Permit-licence raj, 163
Persian Gulf States, 124
Peru, 201
Philippines, 202
Pokhran Test, 167, 177
Policy Affairs Research Council, 35
Political Affairs [Committee, 119 126
Political cooperation, 121
Political culture, 181
Political debates, 67-69
Political dynamics, 162-165
Ponsonby Rule, 57
Portugal, 68
Power, concept of, v; blocs, 104
Pravda, 171
Prebble, Richard, 153
Premadasa, R., 109
Pro-Israel policy, 140
Professional Military Establishment, controlling India's, 167
Programme for the fight against hunger, 132
Protectionism, 203

Public Accounts Committee, 20
Public Expenditure Select Committee, 149
Public philosophy, 110
Punjab, 200

Rabin, 72, 93
Racial discrimination, 40
'Rainbow Warrior' affair, 123, 142
Rajagopalachari, C., 163
Rajan, M.S., 111
Rajasthan plant, 190
Rajendra Prasad, 163
Rajya Sabha, 179
Rand Corporation, 179
Reagan, 123, 180
Red Cross, 30
Reform Act, *1867*, 8
Refugees, status of, 40
Republic of Korea, 39; South Africa, 48
Reshumat, 80
Review process, 205
Richards, Peter, 12
Richardson, Ruth, 155
Rifton, J., 58, 64-65, 88
Rifton, M.K., 60, 89
Rimalt, 72
"ripple" effect, 32
Rome Treaty, 118
Ross dependency, 136
Rubinstein, A., 86, 91
Rupee, devaluation of, 175
Russia, 158, 200
Rwanda, 201
Ryukyus, 47, reversion, 49, 51

SAARC, viii
Sadat, 66, 68, 123
Salvador, 200
San Francisco Peace Treaty, *1951*, 43
Sato, 41, 48
Scrutiny and influence, traditional methods of, 14-19
SEA, vii, 117, 133
Second World War, 148, 202

Index

Security Committee, 92; interests, 166; Treaty, 38
Select and Standing Committees, 23
Select Committee on Foreign Affairs, 32; and Defence, 157
Self-government, approach to, 111
Senanayake, D.S., 97, 99, 105-106
Senanayake, R.G., 111
Senegal, 29, 201
'Separation of powers' model, 186
Seventh Non-aligned Summit, 107, *New Delhi: Statement*, 112
Sexual equality, 40
Shahal, M., 79
Sharabi, Yeshayahu, 65
Shastri, Lal Bahadur, 164, 188, 196
Sinai, 90, 200
Single European Act, vii, 117, 133
Sino-Indian War, 187-188
Sino-Soviet rift, 176
Six Day War, 93
Sixth Non-aligned Summit, 97, 107
SLFP, vi
Social Credit Party, 143; Democratic Party, 143
Socialist bloc, 172; group, 120
Solemn declaration on European Union, 117
Sondhi, M.L., vii, 162
South Africa, 13, 25, 29-30, 68, 139, 142, 146, 149, 156, 158, 183
South Asia, 194; East Asia, 206, Treaty Organisation, 100, 138; East Asian countries, 140; India, 109; Pacific, decolonisation in the, 140, Island, 141; Vietnam, 176
Southern Africa, 158
"Soviet Communism", 163; global strategy, 169; Union, 47, 104, 106, 167, 180-184, 189, 193
Sri Lanka, vi, 96, 102, 200; Chairpersonship of the non-aligned movement, 107; Freedom Party, 102, 104, 107-109; Parliament and foreign policy, 95-110; Tamils, 108-109

Sri Lankan crisis, 100
Standing Committee on the Budget, 38, 49
State Department, 128
Strasbourg, viii, 73, 129
Subrahmanyam, K., 199
Sudan, 29
Suez Canal, 12
Sukarno, 163
Suntheralingam, C., 100
Super power pressures, legislative responses to, 168-169
Super powers, 165-166, 181; rapprochement between, 167-168; diplomatic relations between the, 180; conflict of the, 182; dependence on, 184
Supervision, 69-72
Sweden, 123
Switzerland, 86, 124
Symington amendment, 180
Syria, 66
System analysis of political life, 111

Tabakouta, 201
Taiwan Relations Act, 47
Taking of Hostages, Convention against, 40
Tambo, Oliver, 30
Tamil Federal Party, 102; refugees, 108
Tamilnadu, 108-110
Tamir, S., 79
Tarapur Atomic Plant, 190; problems, US reaction to, 192
Tasman Sea, 156
Thailand, 201
Thakur, Ramesh, vii
Thatcher, Margaret, 22, 127
Third Windon proposal, 202
Third World, 106, 163, 165-166, 180
Thomson, David, 153
Three non-nuclear principles, 49
Thirty-three Judgements of the Supreme Court, 82
Tibet, 182
The Times, 111
Times of Ceylon, 112

Tocqueville, Alexis de, 95
Tolerance, non-aggression and mutual respect, 112
Trade Expansion Act, 47
Transition Law, 64, 87-88
Treasury, 128
Treasury and Civil Service Select Committee, 24
Treaties, 39, conclusion and ratification of, 86-91
Treaty, 37; on the non-proliferation of nuclear weapons, 40; of Mutual Security and Cooperation between Japan and the U.S.A., 43, 52
Treaty-making power, 57-66
Trincomalee (Port of), 101-102, 104, 106, 109
Trotskyite Lanka Sama Samaja Party, 102
Tunisia, 124
Turkey, 121, 179
Turks and Caicos Islands, 27
Twenty-three Judgements of the Supreme Court, 76

Uganda, 200
UK-Soviet relations, 24-25, 30
UNESCO, 5, 25, 207
United Asia, 111
United Kingdom, 34, 39, 100, 116, 140
United Nations, 48, 116, 141, 173-174, 201; on nuclear tests, 191; peace keeping, 201
UN High Commissioner for Refugees, 30
United Nations Convention for the elimination of all forms of discrimination against women, 156
United Nations Legislative Series, Laws and practices concerning the conclusion of treaties, 87
United States, 34, 38-39, 42, 51, 57-58, 98-99, 105, 114, 116, 123, 128-129, 136, 140, 142, 157, 159, 167, 180-181, 183-184, 189, 192, 200, 203, 205-206; peace initiative, 93; War in Indochina, 139; Vietnam policy, Indian support for, 175; security policies, 178-179; Pakistan military alliance, 178; Congress, 32, 54, 123
University of Otago, 159
UNP, vi, 99-100, 102-103, 105-108
Uranium, supply of, 192
USS *Buchanan*, 156-157
USSR, 16, 99

Vashchenko, 201
Vietnam, 200; US intervention in, 168, 175-176
Vietnam War, 138-139, 141, 158
Vins, Georgi, 201
Vredeling proposals on industrial co-determination, 125

Walfish, Asher, 71
Wallace, William, 13
War and peace, 72-73
Warhaftig, M.K., 88
Washington, 178, 180
Webb, Sidney and Beatrice, 163
West Asia, vii
West Bengal, 165
Western alliance, 203
Western Europe, 56, 113
Western Samoa, 140, 149
Western-type parliamentary institutions, 99
Westminster, viii, 9, 68, 70, 134, 157, 163
White House, 128
Who makes British foreign policy, 12
"Who needs Canada", 201, 207
Wilkinson, P.I., 152
Wiston House International Conference Centre, 25
Wood, Antony, vii
Woodward, Michael, 31
World Food Programme, 30

Yaounde, 200; Arusha and Lome agreements, 115
Yom Kippur War, 85
Yugoslavia, 124, 171

Zaire, 201
Zambia, 16
Zimbabwe, 16, 200-201